Winning in the New Job Game

The purpose of this book is to introduce you to a new way of looking at your worklife and to provide you with practical tools for achieving an exciting new way of working. Through proven tactical exercises—our guerrilla tactics—we will show you just how unique an individual you are and how you can make the most of this uniqueness in the dramatically changing workworld of the 1990s.

Our book will be grounded on what we believe to be the fundamental opportunity of any job: to produce value for others and increased aliveness, satisfaction, and success for yourself.

You are invited to be a player in the New Job Game. This book is a player's manual for working in the 1990s and beyond. It comes out of over 20 years of direct, on-line experience with tens of thousands of individuals it has been our privilege to support in their search for personal career fulfillment . . . and a great paycheck.

D0391893

Books by Tom Jackson

Not Just Another Job

The Perfect Job Search

Perfect Resume Strategies

The Perfect Resume

Guerrilla Tactics
IN THE New
Job Market

Tom Jackson

BANTAM BOOKS

New York • Toronto • London • Sydney • Auckland

GUERRILLA TACTICS FOR THE NEW JOB MARKET

A Bantam Nonfiction Book

PUBLISHING HISTORY

First Bantam paperback edition published August 1978
Bantam revised trade paperback edition / March 1991
Second Bantam paperback edition / January 1993

BANTAM NONFICTION *and the portrayal of a boxed ''b'' are*
trademarks of Bantam Books, a division of
Bantam Doubleday Dell Publishing Group, Inc.

ISBN 0-553-56099-9

Published simultaneously in the United States and Canada

Bantam Books are published by Bantam Books, a division of Bantam
Doubleday Dell Publishing Group, Inc. Its trademark, consisting of the
words ''Bantam Books'' and the portrayal of a rooster, is Registered in U.S.
Patent and Trademark Office and in other countries. Marca Registrada.
Bantam Books, 1540 Broadway, New York, New York 10036.

PRINTED IN THE UNITED STATES OF AMERICA

RAD   0 9 8 7 6 5 4 3 2

Acknowledgments

There are people in my life who make a difference. They have created this book with me, and through me. Heidi Sparkes is a warrior who won't ever take the easy way out—always through. Lynn Stiles is articulate and clear where I am dumb. Ron Bynum has gifted me with his outrageousness and compassion. Louise Jones keeps my life in order and stands behind me. Patti Fox, Bill Williams, and Lynn Krown are workers who create their own jobs daily out of love and support. And Ellen, of course, is the music to my words.

More acknowledgments:

The extensive revision and refocusing of the current edition of GTJM calls for additional heartfelt thanks. These go to: Marie Kerpan and Steve Lowy for great idea forging and research, Jerry Lee for ruthless word production, Jeff Herman for patience, and Bantam for waiting.

This book is from all of us.

Have It Your Way

CONTENTS

Foreword

Gentle Reader:

This book is designed to awaken in you a new sense of how to get what you want from the part of your life that you see as your worklife. It is written with the understanding that most people pretty much take for granted the enormous amount of time that they spend either on a job, or trying to get a job, or wishing that they had the right kind of work. It comes out of the recognition that most of us rarely get the opportunity to experience our own power in identifying and locating work opportunities that feed us in a deeper way than with a paycheck.

The information and observations of how the workworld is structured come from the author's direct experience over the past two decades with thousands of job seekers, employer representatives, career consultants, philosophers, authors, and other authorities engaged indirectly or directly with our relation to the workworld. We have tried to examine and digest everything valuable in this area, and to incorporate whatever could make a contribution.

Besides observations and principles related to the work experience, we have provided the reader with a set of action-based tactics that can be used to actually produce specific results in the search for increased work satisfaction or a better job. These tactics arise out of the pragmatic experience of work with real individuals confronting the real world of the job search. They have been proven to be effective in actual case by case experience. By following the tactics, readers will be able to obtain for themselves the kinds of results and benefits promised in the text. The tactics frequently require a confrontation and a lot of work and participation. There is no easier way to get what you want.

This book deals with the contexts of the work experience— the underlying principles that are rarely discussed or revealed. It is by understanding and experiencing this foundation and applying the tactics that readers will be able to generate their own experiences and successes in their worklife, and to free themselves forever from the idea that there is a scarcity of opportunity and personal aliveness in the work experience.

Much of the underlying space or context from which this book has been generated is the result of the author's experience with Werner Erhard, the source of *est* training and The Forum, to whom the book is dedicated.

Tom Jackson
New York City
November 1990

1

Life Working

Hello

The purpose of this book is to introduce you to a new way of looking at your worklife and to provide you with practical tools for achieving an exciting new way of working. Through proven tactical exercises—our guerrilla tactics—we will show you just how unique an individual you are and how you can make the most of this uniqueness in the dramatically changing workworld of the 1990s.

Our book will be grounded on what we believe to be the fundamental opportunity of any job: to produce value for others and increased aliveness, satisfaction, and success for yourself.

It is a great tragedy that many of us feel trapped in our jobs. We know how burdensome the nine-to-five grind can be—it is too easy to save our real living for after five and on weekends. And yet, given the dynamics of the evolving global, technical, and people-focused decade of the 1990s, and the transition to a more liberating and positive working world, it is now possible to match the true human qualities that are our personal prerogative with the competitive market forces of change. We are working with you to meet this challenge.

You are invited to be a player in the New Job Game. And here's part of the game plan as articulated by James Carse in *Finite and Infinite Games:* "A finite game is played to win but an infinite game is played to keep on playing.'' We encourage you to keep moving the boundaries of your life, and not get stuck in an unchanging field of play. We are here to help you experience this new expansion. While reading and following the exercises on the following pages your task is to simply relax and let the ideas flow.

Waves of Change

Not many realize the unprecedented scope of the current worklife revolution. The 1990s and beyond mark the transition not only to new tasks and job titles, but to entirely new forms of work: community work centers, independent work teams, networks of tele-work families, and a still greater surge of independent consultants and temporary employees. Greater competition for good people has demanded that corporations provide multiple work options: alternative career paths, extended leaves, flexible scheduling, job sharing, and tele-commuting.

Already we witness the growing number of us engaged in providing services that were not available (or needed) ten years ago. For instance, as computers and robots are being used more and more to replace mindless assembly work, whole industries are being created to produce and maintain the new technology.

These job market changes require a totally different attitude in the way you approach your career. Complacency will keep you boxed in. To create your own future you will need to know how to navigate the terrain.

Playing the New Game

Work is a game. It is the game of this particular era of humankind. The stakes are high, the traps and faults hazardous, and the strategies needed to succeed complex. But it is clear now that earlier fears that people would be held in dronelike servitude to the machine have proven unfounded. Technology creates jobs, and the game continues. Every new burst of practical creativity attracts a new population of workers.

The essence of a game is to get from where you are to where you want to be. The goal is a solution to a problem, the filling of a need, the answering of a question. The only way to approach the game of work is as a vehicle for personal aliveness and joy—to use the experience in a way that fulfills you, and allows you to express yourself as you do it. You can enhance enormously the way you live your life, and the contribution you can make, by selecting opportunities that relate to your basic satisfaction and abilities.

The new job game starts with two propositions:

- Your work experience is the primary social/economic/ spiritual relationship in your life.
- The quality of your life is a function of the quality of your work experience.

In other words, *Work* and *Life* are inseparable! And as we enter a new millennium we will increasingly realize just how important our worklife is, and the planning it takes to maximize its potential.

This book is a player's manual for working in the 1990s and beyond. It comes out of over 20 years of direct, on-line experience with tens of thousands of individuals it has been our privilege to support in their search for personal career fulfillment . . . and a great paycheck.

Although you probably picked up this book for assistance in looking for an immediate job, we hope that it also gives you some long-term skills in what we call Strategic Career Managing. This is the ongoing ability to navigate your own careership through the rocks and shoals of our turbulent world economy. You will have the opportunity to learn the underlying principles of work and economy, personal excellence, managing your future, and career entrepreneurship, and how to put these principles into practice in the real world.

Strategic Career Managing includes securing new jobs, achieving promotions, changing jobs within companies, changing employers, knowing the most appropriate fields to train for, starting your own business, and making the most of your postcareer years.

We want you to see your worklife as an opportunity to

play, and in the playing to experience a lot of personal satisfaction. We ask you to be alive *and* working at the same time, riding the waves of change like an agile surfer.

Learning by Example: Case Histories

(Throughout the book we will be providing a number of real case histories of people with whom we've worked. For obvious reasons we have changed their names.)

NORM BLESSING—A "Permanent" Temporary Job

When Norm Blessing started working at a factory he thought it would only be for a few months, "until things straightened out." He took the work because it paid well, and because he didn't know in what direction he wanted his life to go. In his words:

> This job really is for "yo-yos." But, hell, it's a good place for the money and the work isn't all that hard. I'll hang in there for a little while and then I'll see. Maybe I'll get involved in business after I save a little. . . . Who knows?

Well, Norm kept saying that for 12 years. In the meantime, he married and had a child, and Norm's "Who knows?" became "What now?" Here's what his wife, Maggie, has to say:

> Norm is a dreamer and that's probably why I married him. He stays optimistic and positive. But he did get stuck in his work. He knows it, too, and isn't happy about it. Sure, he tried to get out, but he never really went about it in the right way. He had a new work idea every other month. But then he'd get scared and wouldn't give up the factory work. Then when Laurie was born he was even more reluctant to think about changing.
>
> The real shame is that he really could do so many other things. He's a good carpenter and can fix almost

anything. And he just lights up when he works around the house building things. I still wish that something would come along for him. But how . . .

Norm's story is not all that unusual. Millions of people endure jobs they don't like because of the security of a predictable paycheck at the end of each week.

Norm has worked 3,000 days of work at a job he can't stand. He has 7,000 workdays left in his life. He might spend the rest of his days at the factory. Or he could learn that there are ways of working and earning a living that go beyond the paycheck, and include personal satisfaction and freedom as well.

How many workdays do you have left?

We didn't tell you Norm's story or ask this question to scare you. We only want you to look at the number of days a person can work and the ways in which people realize their worklife. Here's another story, which again is not that unusual but will demonstrate that people do have choices.

TRISH DAVID—From Hobby to Career

Trish David had just finished high school and was eagerly looking forward to university. She talked about nothing else for months. Unfortunately, her parents couldn't afford the college she chose. However, she remained insistent. Luckily Uncle Bill stepped in just at the right moment and offered a loan if she would promise to pay it back by working summers. She eagerly accepted.

One of Trish's hobbies was fashion designing. She would sit for hours with magazines teaching herself. She experimented and made clothes for herself and her sister. She even designed costumes for a local theater company one summer.

For her first two college summers she worked as an assistant designer at a custom dress shop near her home. She was very pleased with just how easy things were coming her way.

But then at the beginning of her third year at college, Uncle Bill had some financial difficulties and could no longer support her education. It was a major shock for her to learn that she could not return to school. For two months she was depressed and took several more months to come out of it.

Not knowing what to do, she took a job at her sister's travel agency and though the work did not excite her she thought it would be fine for a while.

But then "a while" turned into five years and she was still doing the same thing. In the meantime, she had married Barney, a real estate agent who could "take care of her." So now she had a choice of either continuing to work for her sister or becoming a housewife.

So she decided, Trish says:

Here I was 28 years old and I felt like I was ready for retirement. The thought of becoming a housewife just felt unnatural for me. It's all right for some, but I wanted to do something else first. So I wasn't about to go that direction.

At the same time, I realized that working at the travel agency had become too easy and it wasn't work that I was all that interested in. I hadn't really been satisfied. I found myself asking, "Where had those five years gone?"

I took a long, hard look at myself and also asked where did that ambitious fashion designer go. It was then and there that I decided to get back to it. Everyone around me tried to discourage me. However, I knew this was what I wanted to do. I started to feel the old fire return. And quite frankly, once I made that decision everything else fell into place.

Trish proceeded to mount an intelligent job search campaign that was equivalent to a top drawer marketing plan. She clearly defined her needs and wants (personal and fiscal), researched for months, and then discovered three different career targets—for each of which she plotted, and followed, tactics to achieve. Each became a true choice for Trish and, turning finally to her instincts, she formed a partnership with a popular retailer in her area. With the flexibility she built in, Trish found that perfect balance between work she loved to do and the family she soon started with Barney.

Trish learned that the key ingredient in a successful work-life is having work that lets you do for pay what you would choose for play.

The High Cost of Earning a Living

As stated, the average worklife is ten thousand days long. People devote more time to their work than any other activity in their lives. Work time uses up the prime years of our lives (after schooling and before retirement). The message from parents, teachers, coaches, psychiatrists, counselors, gurus, and others concerned with your state of well-being should be quite clear:

> The degree of satisfaction you experience in your work directly affects the health and vitality you experience in the rest of your life.

If you settle for work that costs hours of boredom and dissatisfaction just to pay the bills, you will find that you are paying for your job in human terms at a cost that far exceeds the worth of your paycheck. An office with a window view, a carpet on the floor, and a title is no insurance against feelings of futility about work that does not represent your true aspirations and potential. More money and a fancier title can never compensate for true satisfaction.

Unfortunately, "making it" is among the least assailable things in life. It is approved by church, state, schools, parents, friends, and the society at large. It is a natural step in the familiar "child-school-work-marriage-children-more-work-retirement-death" scenario. "Get a job" is the battle cry of both contented capitalists and comrade communists.

THEM: Get a job!
YOU: Where?
THEM: It doesn't matter; stay close to home.
YOU: But doing what?
THEM: Whatever you've been trained to do.
YOU: I don't think there are any jobs in that field.
THEM: Well, don't worry about that. Just get something. Start at the bottom.
YOU: Why start there?
THEM: To get to the top!
YOU: But I want to find something I *like* doing.

THEM: Like? Who said you had to like your job? Having a job is all that counts.

As we fast approach the 21st century, we must realize that the stress found within the workplace is one of the greatest contributors to disease. Being "on the street" or working at a job you don't like is harmful to both your health and sanity.

We get very lonely when our friends are at work while we sit home trying to figure out what to do next. We start to question what went wrong: "Is it me, or them?" After a few weeks with no direction and no guidance we feel more and more like a loser and will gladly take the next acceptable job offer that comes along.

"Hi, Helen. How's the new job?"
"Oh, it's not so bad. It could be worse. It's a job."

Short-term gain, lifetime loss.

Tactics

But now it is time to move more directly into the practical management of your own career search. Shortly, we will provide you with a number of specific exercises developed from thousands of actual training experiences. These exercises and techniques represent the "action" component of managing your career. The key principle to follow as you come up against each of the numbered tactics is: Action Works! Without moving ideas to action, nothing happens.

You may want to follow these exercises as you proceed the first time through the book, or you may want to read the book quickly and then begin again completing all the tactics. We have selected the most powerful 25 tactics and listed them again at the end of this book. We call these the Fast Track Tactics.

Our personal recommendation is to go through the book chapter by chapter with a small notebook. Along the way make note of any material that interests you, or any ideas that occur to you. When you have concluded each chapter, if a specific tactic is urgent to your job campaign now, do it right away.

Otherwise, go through the book as a reader only and do the Fast Track system at the end.

The Opportunity Revolution

Believe it or not, you are in the middle of an opportunity revolution!

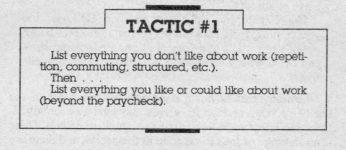

TACTIC #1

List everything you don't like about work (repetition, commuting, structured, etc.).
Then . . .
List everything you like or could like about work (beyond the paycheck).

At the time this book was written, there were two to three million *brand-new* jobs being added to the marketplace each year. In other words, 40,000 brand-new jobs were created each week. Even though the actual figure changes year to year, there is no question that the job market is expanding.

No, we're not ignoring the national unemployment rate, which seems constant at 5% to 7%. Even if this rate goes to 10%, what then would be the *employment* rate? The answer: 90%!! How many situations are there that will give you 9 to 1 odds every day?

Permit us a short digression.

Fear and Scarcity

The fear that takes hold with the rising unemployment rate is similar to what happens in a falling stock market. Panic spreads and people create self-fulfilling prophecies.

For instance, when the newspapers announce another rise in the unemployment rate:

Manufacturer Bud Colleger, on his way to work, makes a mental note that things are going downhill and holds back producing 100,000 solar barbecue units until "things turn around."

Lynn Cohen gets concerned when she reads the story and decides not to hire two new production assistants. "There may very well be some layoffs!"

Jean and Harry Altshuler have a family meeting. Perhaps this is not the best time to ask for a two-month leave of absence. "Let's hold off!"

Dan Christopher looks very satisfied. He knew this was coming. Now he's got the perfect excuse for being out of work. "It's hopeless. Millions are looking. How can I find what I want when the market is so competitive?"

Unemployment is not a condition that rises out of the cranberry bogs and wafts across the land like pollution. Unemployment is a reflection of a society in transition. There is no shortage of jobs to be done in this world, and there are enough jobs to fill several lifetimes for each of us.

Unemployment is simply the measure of the imbalance between what tasks need to be done in society, and the time it takes to recognize and mobilize the resources that are needed.

The Myth of Scarcity

The prevailing economic myth about employment is that there are only a limited number of jobs that are created "up there" by industry and government, so some must do without. *Don't fall for this myth!* Don't write off the unskilled. The route to full employment isn't a matter of creating more slots into which more people can be plugged. In the emerging workworld, the unemployed must be trained in two life systems: the self-directed process of personal ability identification, job targeting in problem areas, and communication of potential value and benefit; and the skill-edge (skills backed by knowledge) related to a job target area with relevant applications.

The tools to accomplish these goals are available. All that

is needed is for the realization of the correct work context to take root:

A job is an opportunity to solve a problem.

There are an unlimited number of problems in the world today, therefore: there are an unlimited number of jobs to be performed.

Here's a classic example from the past:

In 1973, the oil shortage that everyone had been predicting for decades finally becomes a reality. Within six months, Detroit discovered what the Japanese and Europeans had known—and been building—for years: the compact, fuel-efficient car. Naturally, the first thing that happened was that America's big car plants were closed down and thousands of workers laid off. Workers in related fields were also laid off. Many stayed out of work while the manufacturers discussed ways to unload the "gas guzzlers" and start producing the smaller cars.

Three years after plans and budgets were made, the Big Three finally started to hire again and employment in the car industry headed back up—leaving a small army of the older and most senior workers untrained for the 1980s, and beached.

There is not a piece of legislation, technology, or major weather pattern change that does not affect the job market. Unemployment is simply the measure of imbalance between what tasks need to be done in a society and the time it takes to recognize them and mobilize the workforce.

It is also a measure of an individual's inability to get in touch with necessary skills and to translate them effectively into new opportunities. Yes, the individual creates unemployment to the degree that he or she doesn't know how to best use his or her own abilities.

End of digression.

. . . The Opportunity Revolution, Continued . . .

The working world of the 1990s generates an abundance of newly created jobs—the gains are both qualitative and quantitative. Technology breeds newer technologies and these find more applications which in turn create more job possibilities. The demand for knowledgeable and resourceful workers provides astounding opportunities for those who take advantage of these growth conditions.

Those who write about our changing world (John Naisbitt, Buckminster Fuller, Alvin Toffler, and others) all point to the hyperacceleration of population growth and technological advances. We are clearly moving into a new age of global industrialization—third-world centered—and saturation levels of information and the means to manage and manipulate it—prime–(Old and New) world centered. As the political climate undergoes upheaval in nation after nation, uncertainty adds even further chaos. We are experiencing a degree of lifestyle and workstyle change that was not even possible a generation ago. Alvin Toffler has said, "We are creating a new society. Not an extended, larger-than-life version of our present society, but a new society."

The 1990s offer a diversity of jobs five times greater than those offered in the 1970s. About one-half of today's twelve-year-olds will hold jobs for which names have not yet been invented. Virtually every field, from agriculture to zoology, has been affected by the changing times. And even experts have a hard time explaining what is going on in their fields.

And this of course is good news. Never before have we had so much personal opportunity to creatively address problems in our community on the local, national, and global levels. With all our rapid progress there are more than ever challenges to meet: environmental degradation, war and disarmament, nutritional and health crises, social unrest. Out of this chaos arise the opportunities to create whole new worlds of work.

The work revolution means a great deal to you. You can now design your own career to meet your needs, and your aspirations. Start with the understanding that each of us is responsible for the quality of our worklives. Then learn the necessary principles and tactics to realize this. Then act!

A System to Beat the System

How much does it cost to educate us?
  (The following figures reflect the average projected cost of

education in 1990, including government subsidies, private foundation support, tuition costs, grants, etc.)

IF YOU STOPPED AT . . .	YOUR EDUCATION COST
2 years of high school	$ 25,000
4 years of high school	$ 30,000
2 years of college	$ 50,000
4 years of private college	$ 90,000
4 years of college	$ 75,000
Master's Degree	$100,000
Ph.D. or Lawyer	$125,000
Doctor	$175,000

TACTIC #2

In your newly started notebook, list six problems (large or small) that currently exist in your home community. List real-life problems that are calling out for solution today.

Training and education are two of the planet's biggest costs.

We have learned how to read and write, to run multibillion-dollar corporate machines, to read stars millions of dark years away, to transplant hearts, speak to dolphins, and make music. We've forgotten one important skill:

> How to create work we all can participate in,
> nurture, and enjoy.

Education for many is like building a very fine spaceship and then leaving out the navigating system.

In visits to several hundred college campuses, we discovered that perhaps one out of every four students has a specific job target and that one out of every ten has a clear understanding of the relationship between work and personal satisfaction! Very few have the ability to articulate their value to a potential employer. Even fewer have a comprehensive job search plan. Those who do are the leaders of the new job game.

In most cases you will find those who get the best jobs are not necessarily those who are most qualified, but those who are most skilled in job finding. Once you have learned the basics of strategic career managing (personal appraisal, targeting, identifying opportunity, communicating value, job finding, coping with change), you will be in an excellent position to locate jobs that can work for you; jobs that provide ongoing pleasure and satisfaction, and rely on no favors or good fortune for their existence.

This book was written to put you in touch with a system to beat the system.

Success

DRAKE VAUGHAN—Money Isn't Everything

When I got out of the Navy, I took a job in Seattle as an assistant dispatcher in a trucking firm. I started at $19,000 per year, which in the late 1970s was pretty good. The money was more money than I had ever made. I set up a pretty nice life then and was able to save enough to get a car a year later. It was a new Pontiac Firebird.

I was happy. I thought I had it made. Except, of course, the job was boring as all hell; but I wasn't in it for the job, just for the money. Every year they kept giving me raises. After my fifth year I was making $24,000 a year.

It was in the sixth year of what I was then calling "the grind" that I met Judy and we were married. Getting by on $24,000 for one person is a snap; for two it's not so easy. And when we had our son a year later, getting by on $24,000 was downright difficult.

I wasn't going to let Judy work, though she offered to start just after six months of having Jeremy. Then when we had Brent a year later, the idea of Judy going back to work was definitely out of the question. By now though,

I was making much more money at the firm. I had moved up into management and was bringing home $35,000 a year before taxes. And still it was difficult: the house payments, food costs, clothing for four, furniture, car payments, medical expenses, and all those other day-to-day expenses that just eat away at the paycheck.

We were able to save about $50 a month, which was about as much as I was able to save ten years earlier!

I felt very trapped into the whole rat race. I was constantly busy with work pressures and couldn't enjoy the family. I also couldn't give up my job (which I still hated) because I had a family to feed.

The heart attack ended it all. I had been stretched just too far. But you know, in a way, that scare brought my life back together. I was put on medical disability for about a year. And in that time I thought about what I was doing, and why. I figured there had to be a better way, and there was.

My uncle Ralph owned an antique furniture store in a small town in Ohio. He was aging and was looking for someone younger to help out. He invited me to give it a try. He offered me $19,000 a year (half of what I was then making at the truck place) and the use of a small house he owned on the outskirts of town. There was a school there for the kids.

Well, Judy and I must have taken a whole 15 minutes to decide that we would accept my uncle's offer.

Things worked out perfectly. Had I known what I know now about work and life, I would have gotten out of the grind years ago. Money is definitely not everything.

What is success? Cash in the bank? A secure job? Status? All of these? None of these?

Watch out: danger ahead. Success contains a trap that has kept many good players out of the game. The trap is stated simply: There is never enough of the right stuff. When you are making $25,000, it will look like $30,000 is the minimum. When you are making $50,000, it will look like the people who are making $75,000 are even more successful. For most, success is something to chase. It's the carrot on the stick. It's always around the next corner. The plain truth is that success will always leave you hungry, wanting more, and can rarely, if ever, be fully possessed. Success is a finite game.

We are not trying to discourage you from succeeding. We just don't want you to sell out your personal worth for a lifestyle that could eventually defeat you. MONEY DOESN'T BUY HAPPINESS. You've heard it before and it is worth hearing again, especially if you don't believe it.

Our definition of success would be somewhat different: Real success is having a job that works for you! When you engage in work that is something you enjoy doing, that reflects who you are, and allows you to be who you want to be, then you will live each day with total success. Work will become child's play—a huge playground waiting for you to explore.

ED WATERS—Doing What Has Always Come Naturally

I'm a flyer. That's what I do and I love it. I'd fly at the drop of a hat anywhere and at any time. Mom used to say I was born with wings.

If you haven't been behind the stick of a Cessna 184, flying at 15,000 feet on a clear day over Wisconsin, with a flock of Canadian geese on the horizon, you can't possibly understand that flying for me is a religious experience.

I'd probably steal planes if I didn't own two of my own. Well, maybe I wouldn't. I started without anything, you know. I got a job flying with an air courier service. The money was decent and the flying was great. I lived it so much they kept giving me overtime. Next thing I know it is ten years later and I've saved enough to put a down payment on my own twin-engine craft.

I started my own company and now I have two planes. Next fall I'm planning to add a third plane to the fleet. But I don't want to get too big. You know what happens if that happens: too much paperwork! I'm a flyer, not a paper pusher.

Mister, your question, "Do I like my work?" I'd
have to answer, "Work? What's work?"

TACTIC #3

Success Is Having a Job That
Lets You Play

List a half-dozen work-related activities that you
really enjoy.
Then describe five possible jobs that feature two or
more of these activities. Try to imagine yourself
doing these jobs. Stretch your imagination and enjoy yourself.

Working Papers—The
College Degree

According to a College Placement Council study, only about
half of college graduates end up working in the occupations
they had expected to enter six years previously.

For some areas of study (such as history, philosophy, and
the fine arts) there are few *directly* relevant positions outside
of teaching others. On the other hand, for many new work
opportunities there are virtually no directly relevant courses;
the slowness with which the education establishment expands to meet the changing needs of society is an example of
one of the more highly entrenched bureaucracies keeping
itself going.

The debate is long-standing: "Education should remain
pure—untouched by the needs of the marketplace" on the
one hand, and "We need to prepare students for careers" on
the other. We suggest that the future calls for both positions
to come together. Students definitely should be schooled in
the rich tapestry of the humanities and the arts; everyone
should have the opportunity to expand his or her vision
beyond purely commercial needs. Quality thinking is at the

root of all important new concepts, and, according to Dr. Frances D. Fergusson, Vassar's president since 1986, liberal arts qualities are essential if there is to be any creativity or innovation in the marketplace. "A liberal education emphasizes historical awareness and a passion to build for the future," she said at *The New York Times* Presidents Forum in 1988.

More companies now realize this. On the other hand, it is grossly unsound to put an individual through an incredibly expensive, lengthy education and not ground her in ways she can *use* her learning in the workaday world, not only to expand her own development in practical terms, but also contribute to addressing the tangible needs of the planet.

The employment manager of one of the nation's largest recruiters of college talent says this: "We have an earnest and real desire to bring people from a wide range of disciplines into our management training programs; it adds to our depth. But sometimes it's hopeless. So many history and philosophy majors know virtually nothing about business. Sometimes we just look across the desk at each other and shrug our shoulders. Kids should be given more insight into what jobs are, where they are, how to present themselves—what the workworld is all about."

Some employers look for education; then they squander it. A low-level administrative post requires a four-year degree. Secretarial positions require at least two years of college. Part of this is a kind of snobbism: "We use only the best raw materials." Another reason is the fact that by successfully completing school, you proved something about yourself. It simplifies the hiring process. Of course, it also discriminates heavily against people who didn't make it in, couldn't get the small legacy together, or have been branded with a lousy high-school record. Unfair? Yes, but that's the way it is. If you can get together a college degree—two years are okay, four are preferred—do so, even if you are many years behind. You will be paid back lavishly in higher earning potential, increased mobility, and more interesting jobs. It is a kind of passport.

Education is important both in and out of school. "Lifelong learning is the key to lifelong earning," according to

Bob Poczik, director of continuing education for New York State.

"Sorry, this job requires a college education."

This statement more than any other has discouraged people from looking creatively for future work that leaps the bounds of the mundane.

Yes, of course if you want to design shuttle engines and you don't have an engineering degree you won't get to first base. However, there are a number of jobs that will either allow you to work toward a degree or will consider other kinds of experience as your degree. Those with military experience, homecare experience, travel experience, or just simple mature life experience all have education of another sort that can be appealing to a potential employer.

Later you will learn about techniques for communicating value to another person. For now, just realize that no job is unattainable if you have a sincere desire and are willing to commit to the work that is involved in securing it.

In Chapter 5 you will learn more about education and training, and many ways to return to education if you have a mind to do so.

One Worklife—Four Careers

Work has a bad name. People often confuse it with something boring, tedious, and monotonous.

When *we* write about work we are defining it in another way: the basic relationship of human life in our society. As Sigmund Freud suggests, when you come down to it, the two primary human relationships in life are love and work. And just as you can have different loves in your life, you can also have several different kinds of careers as well.

People used to think that entering into a career was marriage and that once you were in it you were stuck for life. Well, that isn't necessarily true.

It used to be that if you worked in a banking establishment at the middle management level it was virtually impossible to get a job at another bank. This was back in the era of employee loyalty and employer responsibility. The cages have been rattled, and after the third wave of middle manager layoffs, employee loyalty left town. The professional protocols for career changing went from traditional and "stay put" to contemporary and bottom-line.

Today Career Entrepreneurship is the main game. The average job duration is five to six years, and in some cases two to three years depending upon the level of responsibility. A kind of technical/managerial interchanging has allowed people to move from job to job carrying their expertise and experience with them—for a price.

As new technologies become available, employers seek new expertise to implement them. The information explosion keeps fueling an ever-increasing demand for new personnel to keep up with it all.

Today the game of "musical chairs" is getting worse in the corporate world of computers, telecommunications, finance, import and export, and other extremely competitive industries. An official at Western Union states that 80% of their current job titles did not exist a dozen years ago. Eighty percent!

The good news is that this creates an abundance of opportunities; the bad news is that you may not be any happier with this new position than you were with the last one. That is why career planning becomes all the more important in the 1990s and beyond.

As you learn to adapt to a faster-moving world, you can plan ahead of time the ways in which you would like to move. This is so much more preferable than escaping from one boring job to another. Instead you become the navigator.

From construction worker to landscape gardener
From word processing to programming
From graphic artist to fashion designer
From secretary to legal secretary
From legal secretary to lawyer

There is no one right way to move; there is only your way to move. You can move from fast pace to slow pace and back again. You can stay put for 20 years or you can move around from year to year. Take your pick. When great technical and social changes are happening as quickly as they have been, you have as much chance as the next person to use them. The climate of the 1990s is perfect for total career satisfaction.

Our Position About the Position

There is no one position that is intrinsically better or more satisfying than another. Some jobs may appear that way to you; however, don't be fooled by appearances. The only measure of real work ability is what works for you. The secret of finding the best kind of work is a process of coming to know yourself better. Then you can pick and choose in an informed manner.

In the pages ahead we will explore some of the proven techniques for getting you the best job to suit your personal needs.

Reminders and References

REMINDERS

- You can make a difference in the quality of your work-life.
- You are in the middle of an opportunity revolution with millions of exciting jobs being added every year.
- It is not the most qualified person who gets the best job; it is the person who is most skilled in job finding.
- Real success is having a job that works for you.

REFERENCES

Career Maps for the 1990s. Tom Jackson. Random House, New York.

What Color Is Your Parachute? Richard N. Bolles. Ten Speed Press, Berkeley, CA, revised annually.

A Whack on the Side of the Head. Roger Van Oech, Ph.D. Creative Think, Los Altos, CA, 1983.

The Courage to Create. Rollo May. Bantam, New York, 1984.

2

Who Are You, and What Are You Going to Do About It?

Here's a good example of someone who moved herself out of a rut.

ELSA FROM—Creating It

I wasn't always a hairdresser. I used to be a nurse. Really. My mom had been a nurse before she married Dad and quit. She always wanted me to do it. She bought me nurse caps and little hospital stuff, and I had sick baby dolls and a stethoscope. And if I was ever sick, forget it. She would darn near put on a uniform. She would take my temperature, write it down on a card, and bring me pills in a little cup while *General Hospital* played on the TV. It's a wonder I didn't grow up wanting to be a permanent patient!

But, like mother like daughter! I did really well on my regents exams, and I was able to go to Monroe County Community College for Nursing. It was a two-year program, and very difficult. I got out of school in 1987 and got a job not far from home in Rockland County Hospital. I hated it. The hours were terrible, and the work was very hard. We were always on the move, taking this patient down to the recovery room, holding that one's hands, handling a hundred different prescriptions, making beds. There wasn't a moment to just sit down and have a chat. Of course, Mom loved it—she would not let me gripe about it at all. It wasn't all bad, of course. I was helping people and using my education, which is something. But frankly, it wasn't for me.

After a couple of years at the hospital, I had it out with my mother. We had a big fight. I told her that I didn't like nursing, that I wasn't going to do it anymore, that it wasn't me. I felt terrible about quitting. It was like throwing away something you've saved up, but I knew that if I stayed there I would just get more resentful. Mother came out of it all right finally. It was our first really big argument, and it got her to see that I wasn't her little child anymore. And I realized that, too. From then on the decisions were mine, sink or swim.

After I quit, I had the blues for a couple of months. I took some time off and went up to Woodstock with some friends, and just hung out for a while. That was nice, but I couldn't help thinking that they would all go back to work at the end, and what I would go back to was more vacation. Weird feeling.

When I got back home I sat around for a few weeks still feeling sorry for myself, wondering what kind of job I could do or wanted to do. It was hard to focus on it. Jobs all seemed alike. I didn't have a clue about them.

My friend Bob, from the Woodstock trip, invited me to New York City for a week and I went. I had to get away to clear my mind. While I was there Bob set me up with this friend of his who is a career counselor, and I had a couple of great sessions with her. One of the things she had me do was go through this five-page thing she had, an exercise I guess you call it, or a process. Very interesting. I had to make lists of things about myself, what did I like to do, what didn't I like, what were my skills, my interests, where did I want to live. I got to find out a lot of things about myself. Stuff I already knew, but better organized. Fascinating. I don't understand why we never did this in school. You know most of us never really look at ourselves, we just do what someone else tells us. Someone's mother wants them to be a nurse so they are, or a kid gets an erector set and his dad praises him for something he builds, and twenty years later he's a civil engineer.

Anyway, this woman and I went over these lists of things about me, boiled them down, and came up with a half-dozen things to look for in a job. I don't remember the list now but working with my hands was one thing, direct contact with people was another. Something about sales. Several other things.

Anyhow, I came up with a long list of jobs that fit in with things I liked to do, boiled it down to some job targets, and started to look.

Hairstyling wasn't on the list. But there were a few things like it, and so I was primed when my friend Sue told me about this hairstyling salon that she and her brother were starting. I got very interested and asked her if I could be involved. It sounded great and actually hit a lot of the things that I had found out about myself.

I had to go back to school for six months, going full-time during the day, but it was fun. Now I can't wait to go to work each morning. I really do a great job, make close to $600 per week, meet lots of people, can take off time when I need to, and more than that I feel that it's my job. I created it.

TACTIC #4

If you have worked, list your past two jobs—each on the top of a sheet of your workbook—and then under each job title, list every main duty or task included in that job.

When you have listed each work duty, select the two that you enjoyed *most*— and the two that you enjoyed the *least*. Then write a paragraph for each describing why you enjoyed it or didn't like it.

The Starting Line

The job search starts with a journey inward. You may have been ready for us to hand you your ticket, pat you on the back, and tell you about a good job down the road. Sorry. You aren't ready for that. You already know what you want? Good, just put it aside for a few days, and let's check it out together.

Probably the single biggest oversight in the job search is self-exploration and job targeting, or life/work planning as it's sometimes called. People resist looking very long and hard at themselves. They are afraid to challenge their self-image, to penetrate the protective veil of attitudes, opinions, and rules with which they have become familiar.

And yet invariably, when one pierces the resistance and takes a look, the result is personal expansion and growth, more consciousness, and the potential for more satisfaction. The payoff can be immense. An early change in direction can transform a person's experience of themselves and their work, give them new directions and new games to play.

Most people will automatically seek out a particular job title that fits their picture of themselves (their role) rather than risk another work area that could be more satisfying and enriching to them. This is one of the problems of people leaving school to enter the workworld. They have inherited a catalog of roles from their family, or childhood heroes, or media images. They have a fully developed slate of who the "good guys" are. But they haven't directly experienced these roles themselves, and are often not even consciously aware that they are beginning to act them out automatically. In many cases, they have very little sense of the reality of a given role, what values it holds for them, and what its costs are. Many of us can recall this in our own history. We left high school and took the kind of work that's been in our family for generations. Or we left high school, went to college, and chose a major that was popular at the time. This accounts for a lot of the confusion and masked fear that stalks schools around graduation time.

TACTIC #5

Think of four people whose jobs you would like to have, even if you don't know them personally. List the names of these people and their jobs, and then write a short paragraph for each describing what it is you like about his or her job.

Our Roles

What most often happens is that people succeed in establishing themselves in a role, and then, one day when they are well into it, they wake up and ask themselves, *"What on earth am I doing here?"* Then a little voice in the back of their head says, "Too bad, Charlie, this is it. You can't turn back now, it's too late, you've got the bills to pay, the mortgage, the kids. . . . Charlie, stop thinking and get back to work!"

You are not now, nor will you ever be, your job title.

Underneath the roles that you play is a very healthy, feeling, thinking, sensitive being who is all right just the way you are, and who doesn't need a role to guide your behavior. You are able to identify what you do and don't like, what skills you do and don't have (at least not yet), and how you can make a contribution in the workworld.

The purpose of this chapter is to take a look at this essential self and start to get in touch with your real capacities, abilities, and interests. The goal is work aliveness and satisfaction, not role playing.

TACTIC #6

Start a fresh page in your workbook, and list at least 25 things you like to do whether at work or not. List anything that occurs to you, even if you consider it very basic, such as driving, cooking, writing reports, or just listening to music! List everything.

Pleasure Profile

It's useful here to get some basic understanding of how we cut out pleasure from our very *concept* of work:

Q: What's the difference between work and play ?
A: Well, work is difficult and physically demanding.
Q: Just like mountain climbing?
A: Well, that's not work, that's play.
Q: Again, what's the difference between work and play?
A: Work is something that you have to do.
Q: Like sleeping and eating?
A: No, but work has elements of labor, and a schedule.
Q: How about research, or programs, no heavy labor there?
A: You're right.
Q: What's the difference between work and play?
A: Work is boring.
Q: Who makes it boring?
A: It doesn't matter. It just is.
Q: Like camping out for a week?
A: No, dummy, like stacking paper clips.
Q: What's the difference between work and play?
A: Work is a *drag,* they make you wear a coat and tie, get there on time.
Q: Like a dance or a wedding?
A: This is getting nowhere.
Q: You're right.
A: Say, what *is* the difference between work and play?
Q: I don't know, I've been trying to find out. I don't think there is any.

The difference between work and play is what you call it. It is really that simple. There are a few other elements that we'll look at, but the point is that many of the same activities will shift from work to play and back depending on your position about them. If you have to fly cross-country for *work* you are likely to be preoccupied, not liking it, not having much fun. But if someone gave you your own private Boeing 767 and crew, and you had them fly you around, the same flight would be a peak experience.

A major element is the question of choice. If someone *makes* you do something, it's a chore. The same task created by you for your own purposes is pure play. Changing work into play is as simple as deciding what you want to do, and choosing a job that will allow you to do it.

Choice comes in two flavors: You can decide what you want to do, and then go out and find it, or you can take a good look at what you are already doing, and choose that with renewed appreciation and vigor.

In this book we're dealing with the first category of choice, although we support both positions and know that each can be satisfying.

Translating your top pleasures into work can be done easily. It is done all the time by flight attendants, actors, food critics, accountants, musicians, ski instructors, yacht captains, financial planners, craft makers, artists, and others.

TACTIC #7

With what criteria would you evaluate a particular job opportunity? List five or more specific criteria (e.g., advancement, location, salary, interacting with people) that would be personal measures of satisfaction.

You Are Not Your Job Title

You are probably starting to get the picture that a job title isn't what it seems; yet many people see the job as the title. They are determined to achieve the title at all costs. A writer friend went through this recently. She decided that writing was "it." She wouldn't accept any other permanent job— good, bad, or indifferent. As a matter of fact, she would take the least attractive temporary jobs so that no one would think for a moment that she had stopped being the suffering writer. She was obviously acting out a very strong role.

After much confrontation with an expert job counselor,

she began to analyze the job target and see that it was made up of its own components: working alone, using her imagination, becoming famous, meeting interesting people, having a steady royalty income, etc.

When she was finally willing to look beneath the surface, she saw that there were half a dozen other jobs that could meet most of the criteria she had set up.

By going beyond the job title to its building blocks of skills and interests, we break its structure apart and open the way for creating new structures, new job targets, all of which contain the pleasure of . . .

IDEAL JOBS

They really exist.

- Close your eyes for a minute and get a picture of yourself in an *ideal* work situation. Go ahead—do it.
- Close your eyes for another minute and picture another *ideal* job for yourself.
- Now do it again, and this time see if you can pick up the following details:

What does the workspace look like?
How are you dressed?
What tools or equipment are you using?
What other people are around?
What problems are you solving?

Relax—close your eyes, fantasize.

A dream job is one that seems so outrageous that your first instinct is to say: "Why bother? I could never get *that* job." But the job that fits your fantasy pictures does have a place in the real world. An important thing to understand about dream jobs is that what's ideal for one person may be a drag for someone else.

According to New Age author and workshop leader Shakti Gawain, "Most people do have some sense, at least deep down inside, of what they would love to be doing. This feeling is often so repressed, however, that it is experienced only in the form of some wildly impractical fantasy, something you could never do. . . . Even if it seems impossible, there is at least a grain of truth in the image. It is telling you something about who you really are and what it is you really want to be doing.'' That ''wildly impractical fantasy'' is your dream job.

Here are some dream jobs that people in a recent workshop came up with:

- To work for a travel guide and go all over the world.
- To be an entertainment manager with Club Med.
- To be a trial lawyer.
- To be in a secluded cabin, writing and getting paid for it.
- To be a costume designer on Broadway.
- To buy and sell foreign currencies.
- To work for David Letterman.
- To be a PC home troubleshooter.

How do we know that you will actually get your dream job? We don't. What we do know is that someone will get it, and that all you need to do is to be willing to accomplish the steps between where you are now and your ideal. What this requires first is a sense of purpose. A purpose is a *direction*, not a specific goal. *If you are organized, and have a clear sense of your work purpose, you can use everything that happens, even obstacles, as a way of contributing to the achievement of your purpose.*

For example, every time you find that there is a requirement or connection or needed skill that you don't have, this clearly helps your purpose, since now you know the next thing you need to handle. Keep going, one step at a time.

Warning: Don't make the mistake of thinking that when you get the dream job you will have suddenly arrived in job heaven. It doesn't work that way. When most people finally

TACTIC #8

List three dream jobs—positions that would give you maximum pleasure, but that are so far out that you instinctively feel you would not be able to get them.

"make it," their first reaction is inevitably "This is it?" and a big depression sets in. Dream jobs or ideal jobs are only valuable in terms of the sense of direction they provide.

Problem Solving

A job is a formal opportunity to solve problems.

It is not just a list of duties, or a title, or a place to go. It is, at its most basic, a problem-solving situation. Most job titles don't tell you much about what is done, what the results are, what the purpose of the job is, or what the problems are.

To fully understand the meaning of a job at any level— potential employer, manager, interviewer, or worker—you need to go beyond the description to the purpose of the position. When you start to do this, you open up a greatly expanded understanding of what's involved, and how you fit into it. For example, what do the following job titles mean?

Account executive
Administrative assistant
Technical adviser
Media planner
Project engineer
Production coordinator
First-line manager
Management trainee

What do they tell you about the daily nine-to-five routine, the communications required, the resources, the stress? Virtually nothing. Of course, if you have worked as an administrative assistant you will have an idea that it's just like your old job—and this could be very wrong.

Frequently the job title indicates that a manager has already decided how a particular problem should be solved. By listing all the skills he is looking for, he is laying out his already chosen way of solving that particular problem. Even if you don't have the necessary skills, once you find out what the underlying problems are, you may see how your own particular combination of skills could solve the problems.

We will never run out of problems in our lifetime. That's a

promise. (It's a safe bet when you realize that just about every solution creates at least two more problems.)

In work terms you are a problem solver—a person who can produce specific results, given specific situations. The problems don't have to be complex, or the solutions intricate and brainy. Problem-solving skills include driving a car, hemming a dress, programming a computer, composing a form, organizing a new business, motivating others, editing, running a tractor, raising money, and selling.

You can handle even the most complicated high-level jobs with very simple problem-solving skills. Keep looking into the task for the next simplest level of activity, then pull apart that activity and see what skills are called for. For example, an advertising media planner has a number of tasks, one of which is *presenting cost per thousand (CPM) figures on advertising plans*.

Breaking this down, we see that in order to accomplish this the planner needs:

- To consult the client's overall budget sheet.
- To consult *Standard Rate & Data* or space/time sales people for media costs.
- To consult Nielsen and Arbitron reports for listener strength of various scheduled spots.
- To divide media cost by readers/listeners to determine CPM—cost per thousand.

Breaking this down even further, we see that familiarity with ratings reports could be acquired by someone with a reasonably analytical mind in about six hours of coaching. We could go even further to show the type of personality most likely to be able to perform this job accurately and professionally.

Even in fairly technical jobs, we see after task analysis that about 70% of the job can be accomplished by using nothing more than basic skills such as:

Communicating clearly
Obtaining feedback
Applying correction
Negotiation
Targeting

Budgeting
Managing time

Beneath their fancy titles, most jobs stem from the same problem-solving roots.

Objection: **"I knew it would come to this. Before you even ask, I've got to tell you that I know how to do very few things. I've only finished school, and it wasn't one of the best. And even though I had decent grades, I've forgotten everything I learned."**

Communication received. And it's okay. You can bail out now if you want to. Pass the book along. If you're panicked because you don't feel that your skills are worth anything, you're in good company. Roughly the same reaction was registered recently by a large group of MIT alumni, some of them out of their honored school for over 15 years and drawing down salaries in the six figures. One of the recurrent themes was the fear of having very few marketable skills.

We weren't that surprised. Particularly at the highest levels, people have resistance to listing their skills. Everyone feels it might be discovered that they aren't as qualified as people think. *When you come right down to it, most jobs, even the more demanding ones, can be expressed in rather basic skill terms.*

Stay in the game.

TACTIC #9

Now, list 25 things that you can do, problems that you can solve, results that you can produce. Don't stop short. Keep pushing until you get 25. Don't be surprised if you get some that are also on the list you created of things you like to do. That's the way it should be.

More Success

Success is a promise that is never kept. It is always *out there*. The only way that many people can deal with their own pain or disappointment at the place (or state) they are in now is to justify it in terms of possible future success or achievement.

BOB ROBINSON—Law Firm Associate

This job has been a drag for the past few years. I'm waiting until I complete my first underwriting. When I have that, I think I'll be invited to become a partner, and then I'll get to handle the kinds of cases that are really worthwhile. Then I won't have to put up with all the hassle around here.

JEANNINE CARRIS—Law Firm Junior Partner

I thought that when I made partner, things would automatically get better. Very naive. As a new partner, I do virtually the same things as when I was an associate. Oh, I get to go to a few meetings. I've got a better office. I make a little more money; not as much more as I thought. The people who really have it made are those who have been around longer. The senior partners. They get to travel all over the world, work on the really good cases, and they pull down really big dollars. You've got to stick it out. You can't quit when you are a partner. You've got too much invested.

KEN RILES—Law Firm Senior Partner

I wonder what my partners would say if they knew I was behind in my taxes. You would think that $250,000 a year would be enough. There is never enough in this damn game. I guess I sound a little bitter. I've been at this for 20 years now, and I'm bored. How many SEC registrations can you do in your life without going blind? And how many business lunches can you put away? I've got to lose 20 pounds or else, the doctor says. They bring these young kids in right out of the best law schools. They work really hard for five years or so, and become partners at some point. Those that don't are practically finished, back to the minor leagues with

them. When they make partner, it's another five years or
so until they get any responsibility. After 15 years
they're really part of the firm, but that doesn't mean
they'll like it. No guarantees.

I don't really mind the work that much. The money's
good but most of us spend everything we make anyway.
It's just that the repetition gets to me. I have this idea that
some big company will come along and put me in as an
executive VP or president, or I'll get a post in Washington. It happens, you know. That's where the action is.

Satisfaction

As we said: *Success is the promise that is never kept. Satisfaction happens only in the present time: Now. Now. Now.
Now.* Moment by moment. You can't satisfy appetites with
future bread. You can't experience future joy.

By now it's obvious that work satisfaction is not only
about money.

Work satisfaction is having a job that works for you. Now. A
job that allows you to be. *Now.* A job that supports your own
inventory of interests and skills. *Now.* A job in which you can
play. This doesn't mean that you can't have a future purpose
(we encourage you to). It does mean you must make sure that
the path you are on has room in it for your own day-to-day
personal, deep-felt sense of satisfaction and aliveness.

TACTIC #10

Now go back to your "I like" list from Tactic #6.
Select the five items on the list that you now identify
as your top interests or likes. Write them in your
notebook. Next, select the top five things you can
do to produce results from the list prepared in response to Tactic #9. Write these on the same sheet.

The Career Entrepreneur

There is a new spirit of entrepreneurism afoot in the world, and it goes beyond the brave soul who quits his job with a blue chip company to launch a new computer technology from his garage, or the dedicated venture capitalist who takes risks on new service opportunities. The career entrepreneur is the one who realizes that his own unique capabilities and qualities are a product, and that the job market is an open market, not a closed system. Career entrepreneurs are a new breed of employee. They do not look for businesses to start, they look for bigger and better jobs to do.

Most career entrepreneurs get on track early. In starting with a firm they may turn down job offers that pay more, but offer less personal challenge and growth. They know what's going on in their field; and they know how to ask questions and take some risk in their day-to-day work, establishing personal networks in the company and beyond. They aren't afraid to shop around internally for the best match for them and the firm. As with business entrepreneurs, career entrepreneurs innovate, and have a nose for new possibilities.

The career entrepreneur is the one who recognizes that every job is a risk, with the potential for delicious rewards, or for interim disappointment. The career entrepreneur pays attention to enhancing the "product" knowing how to package it in the resume and sell it in the interview. The career entrepreneur keeps an eye on the way the wind is blowing— what changes are in the wings, what new skills need to be mastered, what new career strategies are called for.

The old wisdom is simple: You go to school, you find a job—if you're lucky, a good one—you stay in that job until things get so bad you quit in desperation, or they fire you in anger. You find another job, and repeat the cycle a few times. If you have any really bad problems, perhaps you see a counselor or a psychiatrist to straighten them out. By trial and error you finally make a decent living, and then retire to talk about the good old days.

To embark on a self-directed entrepreneurial search for rewarding and satisfying work is still a relatively rare occurrence. Your parents never did it, most of your classmates haven't done it, and even if a coworker has started the process, she's not talking about it. This book asks you to address a new reality. You are asked to look at the workworld in a new way. The tactics and self-discovery exercises may be difficult, and you may feel reluctant to complete some of them. Change isn't easy, and most of us would rather stay put than tinker around with our destiny.

The main thesis of this book is that it's important to periodically—annually, at least—take a fresh look at your job, update your credentials, check how you are doing against a career plan, analyze the direction and values of your employer, stay in touch with colleagues in other firms, and keep your thinking fresh. To identify where you are boxed in by old assumptions, roles, and habits. We consider that you, too, are on the leading edge of this fundamental change in the way people perceive themselves in the workworld. We see you as an innovator, a trailblazer, a revolutionary—actual or potential. The fact that you picked up a book to get some perspective on the job search puts you way out front—among the selective few who are willing to learn the know-how of creating your own future.

Be encouraged; more and more schools are conducting classes in life/work planning. Dozens of books about the job search and several hundred about the quest of personal fulfillment are available. The Sunday newspapers in major cities around the country have dozens of ads for high-priced guidance and counseling sessions. Midlife change, career planning, and other career-related topics are becoming part of the management training curriculum.

Your willingness to look at the possibilities, do the exercises, and target what you want will carry you far in this life probe. We know you can use some reassurance: *The self-directed work search technique works.*

After one series of workshops we conducted, the State of California tracked the job experiences of the 500 participants. They found that of this group, most of whom had been unemployed for over six months, some 40% had located new and satisfying jobs—most within 60 days after the last workshop.

Knowing what you want and going out to get it is not that difficult. You may find that you feel reluctance, resistance, and discomfort associated with the material in this book. Often you may consider the steps useless or irrelevant. A job target that you have come up with will suddenly feel impossible: no one would hire you to do *that*. You will want to put down the book and race to an employment agency instead, where only 20% of the actual available jobs are listed. You will get bored. You may decide to take the next job that comes along, and reserve the approaches in this book for later in your life when you have more time.

Everybody looks for excuses. We'd all like to blame someone or something else for our worklife. Here are a few of the most frequently used excuses:

I'm too young . . . or too old.
I don't have the right experience.
There are no jobs.
My field is not hiring.
I don't know what I want to do.
I have no real skills.
I've had too many jobs.
They're not hiring blacks.
They're not hiring women.
I'm overqualified.
The unemployment rate is 7%.
This is a hard-hit area.

Survival

Most of what we do in life is in response to the big number-one fear/need: survival. Somehow we don't think we're going to make it. We can get three degrees with honors from a top-ten school, and we wake up in the morning knowing it won't work out. We can get a great well-paying job, and know that it's not enough. We're still in jeopardy, so we try harder. We've been taught that the key to survival is hard work. Make yourself indispensable, build security. Pensions, retirement, social security. Money, and more money.

If you're reading this book now, you have handled survival. There is little question about your being able to make it to the end of the game. All of your effort, discomfort, sacrifice, hard work, putting up with, making do, skimping, saving, cheating, hustling, hoping, plotting, and planning will probably not add one day to your life. You have survived, and like most of us, you refuse to believe it.

What's the survival payoff? Just take a look around:

- A civilian Pentagon worker has put in 25 years in the Defense Communication Agency, hates her work, but wants to play out the last five years to retirement. Her stooped body reflects uncommunicated anger and resentment.
- A widowed schoolteacher is in constant fear of being laid off and is afraid to take chances or to be innovative in her job. "I can't afford many mistakes," she says.
- An executive is in what he sees as "the danger zone," but he has worked so long for the same company that he doubts his own abilities in the outside world. He goes to work each day scared.
- A plumber works six days a week and complains about having worked all his life to build a good business. Now that he has, he doesn't know what to do with it.
- A garment manufacturer has made a fortune. He has a house in the country, an apartment in the city, and two months a year off. He's bored to tears.

They've all survived.

We have nothing against you handling your survival needs. We have nothing against you making lots of money. This book will help you do both.

But we want to create the possibility for you to *live* at the same time you survive. You can use your worklife to continually express yourself in a way that brings you a direct day-by-day experience of satisfaction *and* a good paycheck. At the same time, you can contribute value to others.

Life/Work Planning

As we've said before, there is no job title that describes who you are. You are not definable in role terms.

You have an ever-changing inventory of skills, interests, aptitudes, ideas, needs, values, connections, and resources.

You live in a world that is exploding with potential and change. Every solution carries the seeds of new opportunities.

You will have a direct relationship with the workworld for 70% of your life, and the way you handle this worklife will have a direct payoff in the only coin worth having: satisfaction, growth, contribution, and self-discovery. The way you handle work will also determine the amount of money you make, the people you know, and where and how you live.

It is a big game that requires some long-term strategies to score well.

KENNY ADA—Drifting on the Tide

I was a glorified bellhop when I went to college. Not that glorified, actually. I worked at the Bellevue Stratford in Philadelphia before they closed it. When I was in the army, I told them that I had hotel experience, and they put me in the food services area. I got to work in menu planning, budgeting, mess-hall operations, and so forth.

When I got out, it seemed easy to stay in the food service area, so without much looking around I took a job with a local fast-food chain that had stores from Atlanta through Durham. I did this for four years without a spectacular rise in fame and fortune. It was really just a replay of my army experience, except the hours were better.

Then I met this fast-talking cookie from California who was sales director for a new string of franchised party equipment rental places. It looked like a good way to fatten up the old bank account, so I took it. Fast food, fast money. What's the difference, right?

This chance of a lifetime lasted for about two years, not counting the three months that I never got paid for when the company collapsed.

My next job was taken out of panic. Assistant Manager at the Redwood Club. I felt it was my way to jump back on the bandwagon in food, but when I reported I found that the entire food and bar had been contracted out and my connection with it was mostly in terms

TACTIC #11

This is the synthesis of your top five "I likes" and "I cans" as uncovered in Tactic #10. List them in the form of a grid—with five skills down the left-hand side and your five interests across the top. Then draw horizontal and vertical intersecting lines. This will create 25 intersections of a skill and interest. Select 10 of these intersections, and for each, invent or recall two or three possible jobs utilizing the intersecting skill and interest. The result is a list of 20 to 30 job titles created from your own skills and interests. Important to do this one.

INTERESTS

SKILLS

- _____
- _____
- _____
- _____
- _____

of booking banquets and supervising our staff. The salary was embarrassing.

Now I'm doing better financially, but I've had to start over. There's nothing wrong with insurance, it's an immense field, but I feel as though I've just drifted in on the tide. No plan. I'm earning what kids right out of school are earning, and it's embarrassing. I've got to sit down with someone soon to start planning my career. Better late than never.

CECILIA RABET—Planning Her Career

You would not believe how on your toes you have to be in this business. It's incredible. I mean, publishing used to be about books and authors. Today, it's about packages. When I got into it from college, I knew that this was my field.

My first job was as an assistant copy editor for three months in the summer, or rather as an assistant copy editor/typist/messenger. I had planned to go back to school for my master's, but in August I canceled out. That was ten years ago, and I'm still going strong with this love affair with publishing.

I have done it all, from copy to production to sales. I spent a year out in the field calling on retail outlets.

I've had six jobs with two publishers, and my new job as a literary agent is the most exciting so far. And it is according to plan. I want to keep on top of every new development, look it over carefully, and keep aligning my own personal strengths with what's happening in the industry. Every July or August I sit down, generally on my vacation, and take a look at my job. I list the stuff I like, what I don't like, what things I want to accomplish, what I want to find out more about. When things start to get stale, I put in some changes in direction. I feel that I will be an executive with a major firm within five years. Which one? Ask me this time next year, and I'll tell you.

A life plan is not a blueprint of your career carefully worked out and exactly followed. Rather, it is a battle plan, constantly revised and updated. It *is* a plan, however, and once established or revised, it is to be followed. It starts with your personal objectives (what continues to bring you satisfaction and reward), it includes an ongoing appraisal of what works and doesn't work, what new skills you would like to acquire, what your salary targets are, and when you realistically plan to achieve them.

If you are willing to go through the amount of effort required to put your life plan in writing, to revise it once a year (keep all old versions), and stick with it between revisions, you will see your direction and intention appearing. The power to be master of the job game comes from knowing and living this direction and intention.

Warning: Do not try to overplan the future. Specific job targets for more than five years ahead are too far removed from present experience for most of us.

A five-year work goal is good, and can be reasonably specific (for example, assistant publisher for one of the top ten firms). A ten-year goal must be more general (top executive). Your life purpose and direction can be clear regardless of where you stand currently on the career ladder. (For example, purpose: to influence the quality of people's lives through publishing books that create tangible value for the individual and society. Goal: to keep my earnings at least 25% ahead of my expenses.)

TACTIC #12

Look over the results of previous tactics, particularly the list of possible jobs uncovered in Tactic #11. Select one of these or another ideal job target that you would be happy to see yourself in five years from now. Write it down. Under this, list a job you would need to be in three years from now, to be on target for your five-year ideal target. Under this, list the entry point for you to start the ball rolling toward your three-year goal.

The Specialist and Obsolescence

The more specialized a particular job is, the easier it is to locate it precisely, to define how you can produce value in it, and to communicate about it. It is also easier for you to become obsolete when a new process or technology, or political change, or whatever, eliminates what you've been doing. Some engineers have been having this problem for a long time. They spend four years polishing an up-to-the-minute space defense technology, work at it for three or four years, become an expert on "explosive decompression escape-hatch release mechanisms," then one day discover that the space race has been canceled or de-emphasized, and along with it the need for experts on hatch releases. The job market is moving from the specialist who is soon obsolete to the generalist who can adapt.

There is a dilemma here that traps many: *You need to have a specialty to get a good job, but if you're a specialist you run the risk of obsolescence.*

The way out of the dilemma is to continually upgrade your speciality. Keep your eye on what's happening in your field, where the growth and change are, what the most obvious areas for realignment and breakthrough are. Become a member of the professional society that relates most clearly to your field. Keep your reading of trade journals and relevant books up-to-date. Keep expanding the game. If you have selected a work field that represents you, your energy in this field will continue to propel you forward beyond obsolescence.

At the same time, keep refining your general skills—organizing, managing, communicating, etc. These skills have become increasingly valuable in today's job market. A 1986 *Wall Street Journal* survey of accounting firms found that one third were dissatisfied with the communication skills of their entry-level accountants. As part of their effort to have accountants who speak and write as well as they handle numbers, many firms now look at applicants' verbal scores on college entrance exams.

By the way, all of the complaints you list on the next page may be true. Life is not fair. The world rarely works the way we want it to. There are plenty of barriers around. You will find a lot of people who will agree with you about the barriers—misery loves company.

Having gotten this far in the self-directed work search, you have the opportunity to be either a trailblazer or a bystander.

We look forward to having you stay in the trail.

TACTIC #13

List at least five barriers or excuses that you feel could get in the way of your own entrepreneurial job search.

These can be internal barriers, or what you see as external barriers—list anything that you feel could stop you, or slow you down in your quest for an expanded, satisfying worklife.

When you complete the list, go back and, alongside each item, write down an action you can take to move through or eliminate the barrier.

Reminders and References

REMINDERS

- The job search starts with a journey inward.
- Close your eyes and picture yourself in an ideal work situation. Are you willing to organize your approach to make this real? Answer yes or no.
- You are not now, nor will you ever be, your job title.
- Success is something outside yourself; satisfaction is *always* right now.
- Real success is having a job that lets you play.

REFERENCES

Career Anchors: Discovering Your Real Values. Edgar Schein. University Associates, San Diego, 1985.

Taking Charge of Your Career Direction. Robert D. Lock. Brooks/Cole Publishing, Pacific Grove, CA, 1988.

If You Knew Who You Were You Could Be Who You Are. Gerald M. Sturman, Ph. D. Bierman House, New York, 1989.

Strong-Campbell Interest Inventory. Available at many counseling and testing centers.

Myers-Briggs Type Indication (MBTI). A valuable tool for self-discovery available through counseling and testing centers.

The Three Boxes of Life and How to Get Out of Them. Richard N. Bolles. Ten Speed Press, Berkeley, CA, 1978.

Suggestion: **Feeling stuck? If so, go back and do Tactic #13 over again.**

3

On to the Future

You are riding in an imaginary horse-drawn coach leaving Boston in 1776, moving very slowly in a primarily agricultural, preindustrial world. The population of the entire earth is less than 750 million, with four million people in the newly formed United States. An average workweek is 60 to 70 hours, and there is very little choice of the kinds of work you can do. Although there are probably 20–30 different kinds of jobs or careers recognized, outside of the ruling gentry, the work performed is essentially physical labor: farming, seafaring, and fighting wars with aboriginal Americans, the British, and the French.

By 1850 you have just reached New York State by steam railroad, heading to the Midwest. You are now moving faster; there are more people around. The US population has soared to 24 million in the rapidly expanding states, and immigration is at flood-tide levels. The work situation has changed markedly. Northeastern factory and mining towns produce coal, iron, and textiles, as well as aching backs and damaged children. Workers are appendages of the machines and the bosses that drive them. The Protestant work ethic, abetted by "rugged individualism" and social Darwinism (survival of the fittest as a justification for greed and power), has relegated increasing numbers of workers to demeaning, demanding, low-paying jobs.

With few exceptions, the work you are expected to do is largely an accident of birth. If you are born among the lower classes, or of an unfavored racial or ethnic background, your working life is a prison sentence for a crime you didn't commit. In the growing middle and upper classes, work is hard, respectable, and necessarily unending. Six days a week, 350 days per year.

As we speed through the 1890s and into the 20th century, we see accelerated industrial growth. The decades after the Civil War show an almost complete transformation of the economy from agricultural to industrial, from rural to urban, from a young and struggling upstart conglomeration of states to a major world power. Machine-driven processes combined with staggering population growth and seemingly unlimited land are engendering a new world in more than geography. You now see telegraph, railroads, trolleys, oil, coal, electricity, mass production, and the mass-produced automobile.

The world-class hero of these early decades of the 1900s is the American business inventor—the entrepreneur. Yankee ingenuity is the New World's rare metal from which is being fashioned a new US work ethic: inspiration, perspiration, persistence, and hard knuckles. Rags to riches through hard work is driven to tycoon proportions by Carnegie, Rockefeller, Ford, and other ground-breaking commercial leaders and philanthropists. A "build your own" work legacy is planted that continues to have important offshoots to the present day.

By 1925 your Pullman parlor car has reached Chicago. It's been a rough ride. One million of our young men have returned from the killing mud fields of Europe and are going about forgetting it in a big way with a dynamic burst of optimism. Factories that had been producing armaments for World War I are now turning out cars and home appliances. The concept of the good life—a new American Age, including the Jazz Age and the Roaring Twenties—brings strivings for the trappings of prosperity to the middle classes for the first time in world history. The idea of "career growth" is born. However, there is a looming darker side: as white-collar work increases, large numbers of the blue-collared are overworked and underpaid, or unemployed and homeless. Farmers face bankruptcy.

At the end of the day, we go too far. By 1929 the system is so overheated that optimism has turned to fantasy. The stock market crashes, teaching cruel lessons of risk and the economic cycle. Career fear is born in the insecurity of unemployment and poverty. A job—any job—is the prevailing principle for success. Roosevelt's New Deal and ten years of brutally hard work brings reconstruction and renewal, and then leads into the dark tunnel of World War II and its sobering and maturing realities.

In 1955 you are in the Vista Dome car on the Santa Fe Transcontinental Express. You are about to arrive at Union Station in Denver. World population is now 2.8 billion. Despite the staggering cost of World War II, the American economy is in bliss. The New Deal, plus wartime mobilization of industry, has reformed and revitalized the economy from the depression years. Germany and Japan are surely rebuilding their futures. Standard of Living is the new religion. Second- and third-generation Americans are breaking into college educations as fast as the GI bill will pay. A career with a future comes with the degree. New technical fields warm up. The hot places to work are the old-line blue chips of American industry: GE, Ford, GM, AT&T, Zenith.

In the 1950s and 1960s working conditions have rarely been better. Union strength and a liberal government are providing a new range of benefits to the average employee: health care, social security, overtime, unemployment compensation. However, unrest is still high among many workers. Violent strikes are not uncommon. The price of living the "good life" has pushed wage demands to high levels for the times. The "baby boom" is underway, and the new parents—with their expanded sense of the opportunities of life—create the first true consumer society: homes, schools, cars, highways, shopping centers, and recreation are now on the basics list for a growing part of the population. Sloan Wilson's best-selling novel, *The Man in the Gray Flannel Suit,* characterizes the irony of the new, upwardly mobile managerial class (white male): the more successfully you play the business game, the more alienated you become from personal values and rewards. Conformity in the corporate setting is expected from all.

It is 215 years after your trip began. The tires of your jumbo jet, screeching to a touchdown at the futuristic LA International Airport, awaken you from your Rip van

Winkle sleep. Outside, you enjoy the welcome warmth. You decide to do some checking before launching your next career search. You need some time to catch your breath, however, because the last generation of national and global development has produced levels of change that are hard to comprehend:

The charismatic Kennedy New Frontier with its court of youthful, vigorous whiz kids strengthened the American image worldwide to a postwar high. The space race was launched. The accent on social progress and civil rights reached historic proportions. The Johnson Administration's Great Society carried the Kennedy vision further, added jobs and training and then got bogged down in Vietnam. The women's movement was launched with a spirit of activism. The economy and jobs are up and away. Defense and aerospace are big employers.

By the late 1980s a kind of erosion is showing up. The space race has come and gone, and the hippies have had their twentieth Woodstock reunion. After galvanizing action on the women's movement, Equal Employment Opportunity, welfare, and (now) reform of welfare, radical liberal politics and activism have faded and the nation is at war with the frightening forces of AIDS, crack, and homelessness. After two decades of prodding from the intelligentsia and New Agers, fixing a sick environment is now a real national priority.

In a global perspective, Europe is launching its common market unification, the Soviet Union and Eastern Europe are trying to turn back years of social and economic stagnation and totalitarianism.

High technology, spawned in the Edisonian age, accelerated by World War II, and kicked into orbit by billion-dollar NASA and Defense Department R&D budgets, has favored the return of the entrepreneur. New ways of working that empower the workforce rather than subjugating it are characteristic of the best-run companies. Multinational competition is frantic, as are financial takeovers, reorganizations, and foreign leverage in the management of US companies. We are in the Competitive Age, and the deficit and trade balances are the national scorecard—showing a losing balance.

Although millions of jobs have been lost to Pacific Rim

manufacturing, domestic profit margins trimmed, and wages constrained, you can see the enormous opportunity expansion through all of this with your longer historical perspective: Four out of five jobs are now in the service sector. Fifty percent of all jobs are information jobs. The technology of telecommunications and computers has, and is, revolutionizing the forms of work. The fastest-growing segment of the labor pool is married women. Recruitment of retired people is gaining.

In addition, the degree of variety and flexibility in new work offerings is mind boggling, and the acceptability of "doing your own thing" is solid: consultancies, free-lance, part-time, and temp work. A shortage of skilled young workers keeps wages up for many. For the untrained worker there is trouble.

All of this impacts your worklife and work choices of today.

Q: Is this history lesson really necessary?

A: Yes, I believe it is.

Q: Give me one good reason, please.

A: Can you now feel how dynamic the American work heritage has been?

Q: Yes, it's interesting in terms of the general population. But, what can I *do* about it? I want a good job, not a history course.

A: If the future is anything like the past, what could you project for your own career?

Q: Beats me. The whole thing seems to have moved so fast that nothing is predictable.

A: That's right. In less than two lifetimes we have seen a number of major transformations in type, location, and quality of worklife. The kinds of change that used to take centuries now take decades. What used to take a decade to change now takes a few years.

Q: So, what does this mean for me? The situation is out of my hands, right?

A: Well, yes and no. You can't fully predict the job openings, or probably even the specific skills which are hot. But you can predict that there will be major waves of change, and that these will have an impact on you.

Q: So, to ride the "waves" of change, I've got to take swimming lessons?

A: That's the old way. Try surfing. Rather than fight the waves, join them. Ride the directions of change moment by moment, always keeping alert for the next wave.

Q: Maybe you'd better draw me a picture.

A: Okay.

A Picture of the Future

Another workday begins. You wake up to find yourself in the future. You reach for the remote console on your nightstand and touch a green button that instructs MultiMaid to run the bathwater at 105° F, brew the coffee, warm a bran muffin, and display the morning's weather forecast. A mere 20 minutes later you're eating breakfast and going through your E-mail on the private channel Videotext.

Today, most of us take for granted a level of technology that was barely imagined ten years ago. As we close in on the year 2000, this dizzying pace of change will accelerate, and ever-new products, services, ideas, information access, communications connections, bioengineered materials, and worldwide markets will revamp the way we live and work. Even our ordinary concepts about how time works—and what time is—will be expanded.

Workers in virtually every sector of the economy will have to adapt to new tasks and expectations over the next five years, as nearly half of the nation's companies introduce new technologies. These developments will change the way we think about our work and do our jobs. The how, when, where, and even the why of careers will be challenged.

You push the refill button (the coffee maker automatically switches to decaf for the second cup) and scan the preselected business headline briefs that have been digested to your customized needs from 50 major global news sources. You review topics of particular interest, pausing every few minutes to request more detailed information. As a human resources professional you're interested in reviewing the latest report on the condition of the US job market. You read:

Skilled Entry-Level Jobs
Abound In Services Sector

In this you learn that the most powerful engine of job growth is the entrepreneurial small-business sector, now generating 30% of all new jobs in the nation. As expected, many of these are in new types of personal service.

In addition, labor shortages in the 16–24 age bracket are providing a bountiful number of skilled entry-level opportunities, while competition for a reduced base of middle-management jobs is becoming increasingly fierce. Wage scales richly reward broad combinations of technical knowledge.

Middle Management Ranks Suffer
More Reductions

Yet another article talks about troubles in the middle management ranks. A dilemma is surfacing. On the one hand, employers are simply short of talented people. On the other, employees who stay too long in the same position, don't exercise their learning options, or grapple with new ways of working end up costing too much. More of the old-style control-based managing is gone now, and computer-based systems are handling more and more of the routine tasks. Early buyouts are still prevalent as a cost-cutting technique, although many forward-looking firms are revising their employment agreements to make the relationship more flexible from the start.

The reason for competition in middle management ranks is also demographic. A majority of employees are now in their middle years. Fresh good talent is scarce.

Education opportunities and relatively low wages (escalating however) are an attraction of the young entry-level employee. Meanwhile, promotion to the executive ranks is increasingly rare. New ways to manage career mobility to include lateral change are growing. Merger mania is still taking its toll, and insecurity is still rampant.

You're absorbed in your reading until an on-screen message alerts you that you're due to meet a friend at a nearby health club in 30 minutes for a game of slow-moa, a gymnastic variation on handball played in a weightlessness room. You take another, more wistful look at the statistics on middle management jobs. Will you be stuck at Colossal Life forever? Perhaps you can cash in on the early buyout feature of your cooperatively funded employment security plan, and go to work for a smaller, less bureaucratic firm—perhaps take a pay cut and a new direction now to avoid future surprises.

With the large surplus of middle management candidates, those who land the top jobs won't necessarily be the most qualified. It is increasingly difficult to know exactly which skills to look for and how to measure them. The employees making it to the top ranks will have self-managed their career development. If you don't stay abreast of fast-changing organizational needs, and how to market yourself in an intelligent and imaginative way, you could miss the best opportunities of the increasingly hidden job market. And some of these opportunities might be outside the mainstream corporation.

The screen automatically dims on your way out.

You grab your gym kit and walk over to the community health club. Stopping at a magna-guard that controls entry to the weightlessness rooms, you slide the slim medi-disk off your watchband, clasp and place it in the illuminated circle. The disk contains your medical records in case of emergency, but today it serves a different function. Your pulse rate appears instantly on the screen and a green light flashes, indicating that the equipment has been calibrated for your exercise program. You marvel at the appearance of this new, high-tech service, and recall the two entrepreneurs who started it on a capital grant just three years ago. They must be millionaires by now.

As you change clothes, you notice you are still pondering your career prospects. You're doing well as a personnel manager at Colossal Life, but the tasks have become tedious and repetitive, and you don't see much more room for growth. A lot of personnel functions are automated now, and you don't know how long the company can justify live employees in the function. You muse to yourself: "Will I be replaced by a robot in less than ten years?" Perhaps this is the time to make the move—to strike out on your own. You've been thinking about buying a franchise for a new service that provides a range of temporary workers to handle everything from car pooling to vacation planning.

Entrepreneurial Opportunities

There is good news if you feel entrepreneurial urges:

As money markets become increasingly competitive, capital is getting more accessible. People with good ideas and the right marketing skills will find it easier to get their ideas underwritten and off the drawing board. Relatively inexpensive technology tools for the small user give a power previously reserved for larger businesses.

Many of the new entrepreneurships offer support services to organizations that maintain a policy of limited in-house head count. In this decade, small start-up service companies will create over three million new full-time and part-time jobs: trainers and consultants of every stripe, systems analysts programmers; accountants and auditors; writers and editors.

By the time you're ready to leave the club it's 10:30 A.M. You're in no particular hurry because your flextime arrangement allows you to work any six hours in an 18-hour period, except two days per week when you meet for four hours with colleagues and employee candidates. You slide your pay-out card into the cashier slot to settle your bill, walk to the transit tube, and head for Colossal North, your company's local satellite workspace.

Six minutes later you're at work. You check the monitor near the entrance for an available workstation, slip into the stressless chair, and log onto the Colossal Life system. You pick up a brochure promoting new workspaces at the Independent Work Center near your apartment. . . . "Just in case," you say to yourself.

Working At Home Now Popular

The tele-information revolution frees many people who have spent decades commuting to offices an hour or more from home. You are much more likely to work off-site, possibly at a satellite work center, or in a modularized office system in or near your own home.

The US Office of Technology estimates that over 15 million computer-related jobs can be moved to homes and other out-of-office sites. As new generations of office technology take hold there are ever-newer and more humanely engineered approaches. These new systems will keep you in constant contact with coworkers and clients, both visually and intellectually.

Home working arrangements are particularly important for those workers whose ranks are growing fastest: parents with small children. Home work environments will bring others into the job market as well, including retirees, workers with disabilities, students, and those who live in locations remote from the most popular work centers.

Late in the afternoon your desk monitor informs you that Janet Saunders has arrived. Janet dropped out of high school eight years ago, at age 15, when she became pregnant. Recently she finished a high-school equivalency course and became involved in a novel job program sponsored by Colossal Life to help young people qualify for entry-level positions. As her mentor, you are working with Janet five hours per week—on company time—to use your new disk-based learning stimulator to help her improve her math skills and to move toward workspace and computer literacy.

Private Sector Report

A renewed commitment to social service and a healthy dose of self-interest spurs the private sector to offer a range of training and support services to young people. Some corporations have introduced personal mentoring programs to train capable entry-level workers. Others have developed a pay-for-knowledge policy, training young workers in a range of skills and paying them according to the skills they master. Most companies provide vocational testing and career transition counseling for all employees.

Another workday ends. In a couple of hours you're meeting a friend for dinner uptown at one of the new Uzbek restaurants, but first you have an appointment with Axel Lot, your own career coach, for your monthly session. You're anxious to show him the results of the "career of the future" simulation you went through last week on your Mac LX. Then you want to get right into strategic thinking. Ideas about your new business have been popping into your head all day.

Instead, you follow his suggestion, starting with warm-up exercises in visualization and stress reduction. Although life here in the future is more convenient, it isn't less challenging. It takes all your resources and skills to cope with an unprecedented rate of change as you prepare today for tomorrow's career.

The Ever-Presence of the Future

Assuming we held your attention for the above whirlwind tour of the US world of work from past to future, it is worth reviewing the ground we have covered to see what we can discover about the vision itself. We are agreed, certainly, on the experience of dramatic and rapid change.

We see change of technology followed by change of values, followed by overproducing and swamping, a leveling off of sorts—short-lived now—and then the speeding toward yet one more set of technological breakthroughs.

In the same historical time frame we can observe a loss of the manifest destiny, pioneering spirit in which our globe was simply background for immediate consumption, and a turning to today's recognition of Planet Earth as an essential home ground with limits and damage to be repaired—or else! We also see the emerging of a global politic clearly based on wide world cooperative entrepreneurship.

The Age of Information has already had the same pervasive impact as the worldwide industrialization of the last century in terms of lifestyle, communities, global survival, evolution, and spirit. Information is the new world's capital.

Lesson for You

We think that you should pay very close attention to this issue of an accelerating change in the background of work. Even if it isn't clear what to do about it in any given moment, consider all important changes as opportunities for personal involvement. We think that you must pry yourself open, if necessary, to the inevitability of the constant change required. Get your fingers on the latest tools and make your mistakes early. Explore the possibilities offered by each shift in the ways of getting the job done. Don't be the last one on your block to learn how to operate the videocomp.

Watch your company or department at work, and don't let an old-fashioned manager neglect the obvious developments of the next leaders in your industry. Coach for innovation and freshness, and hold on to the human values that can be strengthened with the shifts in workstyle. Prepare your own self-defined career trajectories, and help others who get stuck.

Masters of Invention

The world of invention leads to the world of business which leads to the world of work. Most of what most of us are doing now and will be doing in future careers is directed by the on-going, fast-spiraling inventions, ideas, and applications of technology—mitigated in the global circuit by the dynamics of social economics, third world development, and political forces. The result of this powerful interplay is more than simply a good prime-time TV special.

The rise and fall of whole industries and economies will occur not only before our very eyes, but in our take-home pay. Abrupt job displacement, truncated careers, crash retraining, and employment insecurity will be the norm, not the exception. Although career change has been an integral part of the 20th century, the accelerating rate of change is an increasingly disruptive and stressful phenomenon that takes the kind of preparation you are engaged with in this book.

A classic example: The nation's preeminent rail station— Grand Central Terminal—opened in 1913. It looked like a monument to stability. Fifty years later rail travel was outdated and stations, rolling stock, and careers discarded. Today—25 years after that—a rebirth is underway in recognition of the need for mass rail transit to combat pollution and high transportation cost.

A contemporary example: Atari put video gameware in the home in the early 1980s. Big hit. The company expanded exponentially. Recruitment of new talent soared with the company's stock. Then, within four years, the whole enterprise crashed. Tens of thousands of jobs lost. Six years later— patiently upgrading the technology and game quality—comes Nintendo to storm the marketplace with better techniques and a significantly higher quality product, and Nintendo is now attempting to capture the home computer market. By the time you are reading this . . . who knows? Poignant question: How many fast-track video game designers changed fields when Atari went down, and are now kicking themselves for not hanging in?

Listed below are some selected inventions and events so far this century that have dramatically changed, and are still changing, the fabric of today's working world. As you review the list, get a sense of the job-related impact each has had, and the influence that the most recent listings, and events you can think of but are not listed, could have in the job markets for your future:

1903 – The Wright brothers launch the first airplane flight.
1907 – The radio is introduced.
1913 – Henry Ford introduces the assembly line.
1921 – The concept of robots is created by Karl Capek.
1923 – First photoelectric cell.
1932 – Lawrence develops the atom-smasher.
1942 – Antibiotics discovered.
1943 – Continuous casting of steel invented.
1944 – The first digital computer is completed.
1945 – First atomic bomb is exploded.
1946 – First photocopier is designed.
1947 – Supersonic flight achieved.
1948 – Transistor invented by Shockley at AT&T.
1950 – First commercial color TV is broadcast.
1955 – Optical fibers are first produced.
1958 – First integrated circuit made.
1960 – First laser fired.
1961 – First human orbits the planet.
1964 – Green revolution starts with high-yield rice.
1969 – First moon landing.
1969 – First artificial heart implanted.
1970 – Floppy disk invented.
1970 – First synthetic gene produced.
1974 – First pocket calculator.
1976 – First successful home computer introduced—
       Apple.
1977 – Voyager I and II interstellar vehicles launched.
1977 – First VCRs commercially available.
1979 – First useful software for microcomputers—
       Visicalc.
1980 – Compact disks introduced.
1981 – Space shuttle debuts.
1982 – Soft landings on Venus.
1984 – First cloning of a gene from an extinct species.
1985 – Lasers used to unclog arteries for first time.
1986 – Chernobyl nuclear disaster.
1988 – AZT—AIDS restraining drug introduced.
1989 – Voyager II photographs unknown storms on Nep-
       tune.
1990 – Communism falls.

What's Hot, What's Not?

That is a trap question. The "Hot Careers" articles in the weekly Sunday supplements, or turn-of-the-new-century futurists' and labor economists' essays, are always good for interesting predictions about the fields of growth for American careerists. They can produce several thousand words of copy at the drop of a writer's fee. You have read them: "the ten fastest growing . . ."; "dead-end jobs . . ." Like annual stock predictions, the assessments go on. Students at career lectures and classes, mesmerized by the possibility of insider tips, line up for the job-of-the-week fortune cookies. Bad news: the prediction of the week comes too late for the job of the lifetime. These lists, in addition to simply skimming the surface of the mass market, are usually rather straight-line projections from the last period surveyed, with the newest recognizable trends thrown in.

There are a couple of inherent shortcomings for the practical applications of these hot career lists. One of them is the survey statistical base. It *might* interest you that the largest numerical growth predicted for the period 1990 to 1995 is in cashiers, registered nurses, and janitors; or that the highest percentage growth, over 1,000%, will be in an esoteric field such as high-static particle precipitation engineering (from 50 to 500 persons worldwide). On the other hand, it might not faze you at all if you are a general business or marketing major looking for a fertile field to build on your interest in consumer electronics. It shouldn't even surprise you to know that the predictions of a slowdown in this field may be blown sky-high ten months after the next home entertainment miracle is created.

On a day-to-day and individual basis the specifics of the predictions are usually irrelevant. When the call went out a few years ago for thousands more financial types with MBAs in arbitrage, or leveraging debt, or tele-finance, and the rumors of first-year salaries approaching six figures flooded the campuses and news columns, the schools and headhunters responded. People got serious about what they needed to learn and whom they ought to befriend and interview. Then, just as the new wave of recruits got their resumes polished, the market crashed, the good and faithful got their pink slips, and the new crop were back to the help-wanteds. Space engineers were grounded, just when they were supposed to be riding a crest; military guidance systems engineers were shot down in a bulletproof career; and programmers could be automated out of the game. Next?

The moral of the story for us is that, regardless of the predictions, there are great opportunities in almost any field at any time—if you keep your eyes open and your imagination going. Manufacturing is folding up and yet the top innovators are overworked helping to automate and reorganize. GM is losing out to the Pacific Rim at the same time as its industrial engineers are plotting its comeback.

We don't say keep your head in the sand and ignore the articles or journals. We do say to keep looking at the forces before they become statistics or job openings, and keep open the idea that each job can be customized to fit. The big mistake is not ignoring the predictions, but avoiding the general news. Don't sit back and believe that since your job never needed a computer before you needn't learn how to operate one now. Don't stay boxed in to your oldest management styles or your distrust of new products or practices. Keep your mind open to new ways of working on your present job, in new technologies. Most of all, keep on learning.

When it is time to review future predictions there are many sources of information available as close as the local library. It would be foolish to recap what they are espousing here in the early 1990s, since by the time you read this, there will already be some major changes no one anticipated.

Sources of Future Career Information

The biggest *unofficial* source of information to aid you in plotting your future is probably either *Business Week* or *The Wall Street Journal*. *Not* their help-wanted section, but the main news. New products, consumer trends, technology companies going public, or facing a crisis. All of this is grist for your information mill. Also keep up your reading in the trade and technical publications of fields you are studying or are interested in. Go to conventions, learn about allied fields.

Most *official* career information is derived from the US Department of Labor's Bureau of Labor Statistics, and particularly from their premier publication on jobs, *The Occupational Outlook Handbook*. This telephone directory-sized publication describes hundreds of occupations, giving facts about job titles, duties, employment level predictions, educational and training requirements, and earnings. It also indicates valuable sources of additional information and training in the fields described. Copies are available in most libraries and career information centers, or from the government. In addition to the annual edition there are quarterly updates and local analyses.

Trends from Our Crystal Ball

Although selection of your own particular career vision should be based more on your natural capabilities and desires than on the most popular growth fields, it is important, and interesting, to stay on top of the social/economic considerations and concerns that are molding the business multinationals and social policy. Catalogued below are trends and personal observations; we hope they can stimulate your thinking about what to watch for. Like other predictions, by the time you read them, they may be out-of-date or irrelevant. Even as they are being written they are not very conclusive.

• **The Learning Factor.** The most senior issue of the workforce today is the issue of job training and capability development of our workers: too many people lack the skills and qualities that employers think they need to fill their more demanding job descriptions. Literacy rates have actually dropped over past decades, and fluency in written and spoken English is lessened further as more Hispanics, Asians, and other immigrants fill our labor pools. By staying in the learning process you will continually enhance your marketability. Communications skills—reading, writing, presenting, editing, describing, reporting—will keep you in demand.

Above all, the willingness to be open to a new way of working, to challenge the old and threadbare assumptions while exploring the new concepts, is your best guarantee of a rewarding worklife.

New jobs will develop at all levels of traditional teaching, special ed, workshop leading, computer-based education, video learning, New Age disciplines, personal growth, health coaching, and more.

• **On-job Technology.** Job growth will be extreme in those fields using person-directed technologies such as workstations, videos, keyboards, simulators, instrumentation, and robotics. The personal computer and telecommunications technology will open doors to home workstations and a large variety of new workstyles from which you can choose. Every executive will need to be computer-familiar even to conduct day-to-day communications.

• **Information Engineering** with telecommunications and videotext-ware is only one way to attempt to define the revolution in the exchange of information from point to point, country to country, person to person. Rapid information exchange is the most dynamic underlying social and workstyle necessity. Buying, selling, corresponding, reserving, meeting, deciding, negotiating, interviewing, are all impacted by the information and communications networks.

The medium is the big message here. You could invent ten jobs right now as you are reading this section that we couldn't think of as we are writing this section.

• **Health** will continue to be a big consumer item, even as it becomes more socialized: health care, wellness, eldercare, AIDS, and nutrition—not to mention the exotics of laser operating, genetics, and psychobiotics. Watch for new technologies to revolutionize old practices in all fields of medicine, dentistry, cosmetics, geriatrics, therapies, and life extension. Room for all kinds of jobs from orderlies, nurses, professionals, paraprofessionals, community health activists, social workers, technicians, consultants, counselors, HMO staff, diet coaches, sports medics.

- **Entertainment Services.** The consumption of information as fantasy and adventure expands to interactive video, dial-a-movie, game videos, ultra high definition TV, room-sized viewing chambers, computer graphics, live global multiplayer strategy games, keyboard conversation, and love mail. More room for liberal arts: writers, composers, artists, choreographers, jazz and space sound creators, directors, actors, animators, fashion designers, newspeople, teachers with humor and charisma.

- **Financial Services.** Look for new investment opportunities in which you change your positions daily with your on-line computer while you consider the offerings of global exchanges. More play with savings and equities. Your charitable-giving networks put you in communication with the actual world-game daily by computer terminal. Jobs to find are in product design, service, specialty research. Sales and marketing will be further expanded in the new investor marketplaces.

- **Food Services.** Pick the world-class restaurant, get the menu by fax, order and receive the dinner later that day or later that hour depending on the delivery routes. Home banquets with your visiting chef and shopper. Aquaculture, herbiculture, bioagronomy. Another feeding revolution. New freezing/microwave technology compete and win against the old gas range for home cooking favor, it not flavor. High quality international cuisine is a regular feature of dining out. Jobs as food technologists, reconstitutors, menu designers, marketing, transport, catering. And restaurant design and managing.

- **Direct Marketing.** Purchase by phone, mail, fax, terminal, subscription, TV, or, if you actually have to, by going out mall crawling. Everything from collectibles to consumables is at your fingertips 24 hours a day, and in your hands less than a day later. Look for innovations in worldwide products, uniqueness of services, better media communications, computer shopping, customized product search services. Job growth in marketing, advertising, service management, sophisticated buying and purchasing reps, transportation, packaging, and imaginative copywriters.

• **Engineering and Science** are big sellers and active traders in the knowledge revolution. How to imagine, design, build, produce, refine, adapt, translate, and maintain the multidisciplined scientific materialism in which we live. Can you immerse yourself in the guts of supercomputing and make it purr? Can you write the logic of AI (artificial intelligence) or do the equations for electronic funds transfer? Can you keep the competitive edge as the technologies are constantly upgraded? Pure science or applications, the jobs are solid. Especially valuable are the technologists who can skillfully interact with the political and commercial systems that fund them.

• **Environmentality.** Cleaning up the air, water, and earth will be an important concern for all. Governments, foundations, universities, and the media will have expanding roles. There will be high demand for environmental engineers, lobbyists, recyclers, community activists, chemists, biologists, maritime types. And attorneys!

• **Human Resourcefulness.** The new wave in managing is the art of organizing, motivating, and upgrading the resourcefulness of the workforce. This new emphasis on the art of building people is here to stay. Work in hiring, training, designing new work systems, coaching performance, building capability, and loyalty will increase in demand at both private and public organizations.

• **Legal and Corrections.** Drugs and their spinoffs in terms of policing, incarcerating, counseling, rehabilitating, community rebuilding, sociological understanding, and all the painful rest will provide career opportunities for both the good guys and, unfortunately, the bad guys as well. Enormous costs and social pressure will demand more jobs in this area.

And there are more:

- **Teaching and training**

    An aching need for those who can get the job done in creating work-ready employees

- **Personnel services**

    Job exchanges, counseling by computer, part-time and flex

- **New materials**

    Biodegradable plastic engines, space ceramics, fiber optics, chips, memories, sensors

    Fuel cells

    Power from the sun and the elements

- **Insurance**

    Protect us from everything, manage our wealth, watch over our retirement.

- **Travel and leisure**

    Include relationships, learning, earning in one trip

- **Senior citizen services**

    The newly discovered "third half" of life

- **Child care**

    At the office or at home, or community based

- **Fiber optical systems**

    All the world connected by one thread

- **Real estate**

    New work/play communities

- **New agriculture**

    Fish farming, nontoxic, genetic

. . . and even more as you open your eyes to the changes in manufacturing, appliances, packaged goods, and the rest.
As we said, it's all right there in the daily papers.

Another Way of Looking At It

As we suggested earlier, and as Alvin Toffler, Peter Drucker, John Gardner, and others who examine new ideas have pointed out indirectly, there is another, entirely different way to look at jobs: to see them in terms of the problems that need to be solved rather than as "fields" or industries or occupational clusters. When you look at the job world from the context of problems and solutions, exciting new channels of potential open up and worklife no longer looks so stuffy. Here are some examples of day-to-day problems, large and small, that need solutions:

* How to get people around conveniently with less energy, time, and at a lower cost.
* How to create a delicious soft drink that is highly nutritious.
* How to get people to release the pent-up tension in their lives, relax, have more fun.
* How to monitor potential heart attacks.
* How to organize an office so that everyone works together, gets the job done, and likes it.
* How to write commercials that really communicate.
* How to make it easier for mothers and fathers of young children to have both careers and the joys of family building.
* How to reduce drastically the cost of housing.
* How to combine entertainment or adventure with true education.
* How to reduce traffic deaths.
* How to provide psychic substitutes for drugs.
* How to empower the "disadvantaged" in enduring ways.

There are varieties of jobs approaching in the '90s that the Bureau of Labor Statistics never heard of. They will be created by people with the ability to produce direct value with their skills, and they will be created by economic, social, and environmental problems that demand solutions.

This book shows you how to put together what you've got and what you like in a way that produces value for others and satisfaction and aliveness for yourself.

TACTIC #14

Invent a job that will fulfill your personal aspirations. Don't let what you have just read sway your preferences. The sole purpose of this information is to provide you background.

Then list five observations comparing your job to the job futures we outlined above. Does your job fit into one of these categories? If it doesn't, is it close in terms of activity to any of them? Is it something other people currently do? Is there a move away or toward that kind of work? What are some of the issues you must face in realizing your job target?

Relocation

Just as surely as technology moves forward through time, people are increasingly moving onward and outward in location. Today, the average family picks up and changes location once every four to five years until midcareer. Given the regional, pan-national, global emphasis of the organizations we work with, these moves are often essential to career growth. The wise strategist plans the geography to include overseas assignments, and has learned French or Italian and is working on Russian or an oriental language. Euro-business is expanding, and world markets—especially in the developing nations—are hungrily sought after.

SUSAN DIAMOND—A New Way of Working

Susan Diamond is a gourmet cook who occasionally catered dinner parties from her home in a Detroit suburb. She developed a loyal and appreciative clientele and kept in touch with them the usual way by telephone and a Christmas card. One Christmas her 12-year-old son, Peter, received an Apple Macintosh computer and after he learned how to use it, which took him about a week, his mother took time out one day to let him show her the basics. She was mildly interested in using the machine for, perhaps, bookkeeping for her home business. Something about the screen and the way it lit up with her words both intrigued and inspired her. She went so far as to read the user's manual and to find out what a modem is. Late one evening, as she was composing a letter on the machine after Peter had gone to bed, Susan boldly decided she would buy a modem for her own use and allow Peter to use it if he didn't call long distance.

After the initial exploration of the possibilities opened up by the modem, Susan found an electronic bulletin board and wrote a small ad offering her catering skills and leaving a telephone number. She was amazed to get a call the next day from a Chrysler engineer who asked for her pork loin recipe. He was going to entertain guests that weekend and the idea sounded delicious to him. He suggested she use her computer to create an updated electronic cookbook with heavy emphasis on menu creation and seasonal dishes.

Because Susan shopped several times a week at the local farmers' markets and the wholesale markets for her parties, she was aware of best buys in fruits and vegetables and even special bargains available at meat-, fowl-, and fishmongers around the city and suburbs. She took notes daily and committed much of this information to her computer. As a public service she left a copy of her notes on several local bulletin boards.

Not long thereafter one of the partners in the largest wholesale meat market in the city—who also owned a Mac—called her and suggested that she make her menu, recipe, and buying guide available in independent grocery and meat markets, and his wholesale business would pay for the printing, distribution, and promotion of "Susan's List." Since the entire publishing operation could be done via her computer and his computer, a laser printer on his end, and his copying machines, Susan agreed. He offered to pay her $50 a week for the use of her material, and she would get a certain amount of publicity for her catering business in the bargain.

"I was shocked," she said. "I was also pleased and said okay right away, although I had reservations about being committed to doing my list regularly."

Over a year "Susan's List" began to engage the attention of savvy shoppers and she received notes, telephone calls, and computer communications from an increasing number of

them. Her catering business grew as fast as she
and "Susan's List" was mentioned several times in the
columns of the *News* and the *Free Press*. Her publisher
offered her an extra $50 weekly for her material and a small
local publishing company approached her with an offer to
produce a "Susan's List" book of her favorite recipes and
menu tips.

"With the extra income from the 'List' and a small advance for the book," Susan said, "I was able to buy my own
laser printer for better quality letters, I bought Peter several
games for his birthday, and I've established a useful mailing
list I'm using to sell a barbeque sauce I make in the summer."

The tentative way Susan entered into the world of modern
communications is the rule rather than the exception for
women in the early 1990s. But the profitable results of her
explorations and the possibilities opened up for the future
were not lost on her. "It was as if I had added another brain to
my business," she remarked. "I speeded up and branched
out with ideas that would have made me shake my head no,
no, no before. I realized that I could communicate with an
ease and a sureness I'd always thought was beyond me
before, and I could provide useful information for an audience that is amazingly hungry for tips, facts, new ideas, and
clues. Any businesswoman who intends to grow in the 1990s
must, I feel, become 'computer literate,' and the sooner they
get over the fear of computers the better."

Without question, we are now engaging so many changes
in our values, composition of the labor force, demands for
intelligent and skilled workers, need for collaboration and
cooperation, technology and lifestyle changes, that we can be
said to be in the midst of a worklife revolution of enormous
proportions. We are rapidly evolving new ways of viewing
the role and relationship of employee and employer. The
birth of a new way of working is at hand.

As the work of the economy entwines itself with the
fast-moving realms of information systems and communications technology at all levels, the demands for employees
who can understand and ride these waves of change, while
maintaining focus and commitment, is very high. In many
instances the opportunities and problems come so fast that
there isn't time to work out each transaction in advance up the

line, and new jobs must be created by the workers themselves right on the spot.

This new working style requires confidence, collaboration, and a certain surefootedness and self-trust on your behalf. Developing and maintaining your marketability requires strategic career managing practices that are sound and practiced. New thinking by employers about the resourcefulness and validity of people, and the need for putting long-espoused human values into practice in real ways puts a premium on new organizational cultures and styles. High touch emerges with the same importance as high tech.

For you, the worker, the new workstyle will include shorter-term employment, with positions lasting an average of three to four years. Movable pension rights, supplemental unemployment insurance benefits, and strengthened career development and educational opportunities will ease the transition from job to job and career to career. Temporary and part-time work will be increasingly popular and professionally acceptable.

The demand for specialized skills will accelerate. Automation, information processing, and robotics will render much drudge work obsolete. Hierarchies are being leveled and solutions sought in a more participatory way. In the best possible way, people can reorient themselves in relation to the workworld. Many will see themselves as independent contractors, providing solutions to the highest bidder.

"Experience," the chronological measure of exposure to a particular work area, is becoming obsolete as the primary measure of qualification for a job. Versatility and adaptability are key. That you have done Task A for 12 years is no longer a measure of your ability to do Task B, or even to continue to work creatively on Task A, since the nature of problems shifts rapidly and new tools are constantly available. If you haven't kept up with the latest techniques, you may find that a college graduate without experience is more up-to-date on current approaches and is competing for the job you have held for years. In a competitive, solution-oriented world the one with the freshest answers gets first prize.

Career Entrepreneurship

To maintain growth and success, you will need to look at your career as a kind of small business, with you as the main product. Entrepreneurial thinking works well in career development scenarios. Our experience in more than one project shows conclusively that with the right coaching and career training, employees themselves will create the new job definitions or redesigns that are most appropriate for a company's emerging needs. Considering the entrepreneurial mode, an important factor is that climbing someone else's career ladder is not the only way to go; a sense of active and changing self-direction pays intrinsic rewards that are often more motivating and energizing than simply following a traditional career path. Career development begins and ends with a fundamental principle: human resourcefulness is both the end and means of the corporate enterprise. Meaningful work is the natural activity of mankind. By nature, you are inherently versatile and innovative, changing and growing. This is the true entrepreneurship; this is what turns deserts into oases, rocks and mud into cities, and organizations into effective contributors to society. The challenge of the new way of working is to facilitate this versatility and resourcefulness and to bring together your performance and satisfaction in a way that strengthens your ability to create and manage your own worklife.

Demographics

The short story on demographics is this: the "baby bust" is upon us and the number of people in the 18–34 year age group has dropped by 15% or more. The greatest volume of entrants to the workforce comes from nonwhites and previously unemployed women. There is a smaller entry labor pool, and more competition for the qualified, with a shocking number of poorly educated job candidates. Baby boomers are aging happily together and the number of 35–45-year-olds will increase by more than 50% by the year 2000. This aging of the workforce produces a surplus of the older, more experienced employee—those who in times past filled middle management ranks.

Given the flattening of organizational structures, and the demands for new talent, we can foresee a period of vast leveling of opportunity for those who haven't kept their career bargaining power high. As a result, more people will be buying out their old "employment contracts"—in the enlightened firms who honor the concept of an implied long-term career relationship—and taking early departure. A major workforce segment becomes the newly retired. These people, living what Mobil Oil's former Human Resources Manager Jack Ballard has called the "third half of life"—the postcareer years from 55 to 75—are defining a whole new concept of retirement: free-lancing, entrepreneuring, working part-time for the old firm, consulting, telecommuting, and so on. And high on the list, of course, is the lifelong learning that helps insure personal growth.

Doing Your Own Thing

The passion to "do your own thing" has reemerged in full bloom. Scores of books, talk shows, lectures, courses at important schools, and corporate slogans espouse the idea. By recognizing this phenomenon and placing it in the context of your worklife development, it is possible to expand significantly the range of opportunity and career adventure available to you.

Small businesses, consultancies, and spin-offs will probably generate the most jobs over the next ten years, as people put their entrepreneurial urges on the line. Networks of these small businesses will often be united in a single ownership structure, whereas the core organization—primarily financial-based—will feed power and marketing into the smaller firms, each of which is responsible for its own success, survival, prosperity, and above all, management.

The development of personal entrepreneurship and small businesses—many of them based at home or in new communities focusing on this new telecommuting phenomenon—is one of the more exciting possibilities of contemporary times. Even with the great global conglomerates continuing to expand their power, we believe that the most exciting growth sector of the new work economy will be largely self-generated. The spirit of the innovative, service-driven entrepreneur is more available to you now than ever before.

Risk and Reward

Career entrepreneurs are willing to take risks: to risk changing fields, learning a new skill, changing location or lifestyle. Some of the most important risk-taking is the willingness to stand outside of your familiar point of view or attitude and to challenge old assumptions and opinions you hold about yourself and your own capabilities.

In considering your own level of risk-taking, it's important to remember that people are inherently versatile; and that we have a natural problem-solving capability. Dare to risk—to stretch yourself—and you will experience more of who you really are, and what you are capable of.

The rewards for working on your own, though not guaranteed, can be enormous: the ability to combine environmental and locational advantage, eliminate commuting, adjust hours to family schedules, dress comfortably, reduce the costs associated with the usual work formalities, earn in accordance with your productivity and creativity, bypass restrictive corporate salary schedules, and often, that greatest gift—to work with those you like and love, with less corporate politics.

Worktime

Besides the many ways of organizing and timing your day-to-day work, in the new world of work, you will find an expanding number of leading-edge organizations who will increase their own flexibility to attract and suit the needs of their human resources. By the way, working a more flexible or even shorter work year might not be at a reduced wage. The savvy organizations now know they can pay a full paycheck for many jobs performed off premises, or at off-shift hours. This they can do with less generous benefits, less management or administrative cost, and get improved cost-effectiveness. Pick your own best workstyle below, and if none of these satisfy you, try inventing your own:

1. An agreement to work on a year-to-year "renewable by both" contract, with a termination payout equal to 10% of the salary paid to date (funded equally by employee and employer during the employed period).

2. Work two to three days per week, with those days negotiated to meet the needs of both the employer and the needs of the worker.

3. Work a six-month "season" during which you put in ten hours per day, six days per week. Pay = 75% of regular annual, with full benefits.

4. Work at a 10% reduction of salary to fund a three-month sabbatical at regular pay every three years. (Use off time for relaxing, schooling, community work.)

5. Contract for a minimum number of hours of work per year to be scheduled monthly a couple of weeks in advance. No requirement to go over the minimum, get paid for full minimum period.

6. Work four days per week, ten hours per day. Every Monday or Friday off. Full pay and benefits.

7. Work regular hours at a slight reduction of regular pay, and have an employment security agreement that allows you extended compensation benefits (say 70 percent pay for two years) if you lose your job for any reason.

8. Design your own creative employment agreement and try it. Be sure to show how both you and the employer will benefit.

These alternatives are especially attractive to those who are seriously attracted to activities outside regular work structures, and don't want to jump into the pure entrepreneurial risk-rich roles. These outside diversities can range from travel, writing and painting, community and ecological volunteer or part-pay work, formal or informal learning; and, of course, committed family time, child rearing, and romance.

Back From Retirement

More of us are in our "postcareer years" now. Retired? Not exactly. Although only 60% of those of us between 55 and 65 are still in the normal workforce, and only 15% over the age of 65 work full-time, this hasn't created major growth in the rocking chair set. Given the great improvements in health care, medicine and, most importantly, individual habits of diet, nonsmoking, exercise, meditative and stress reduction practices, the potential fullness of our lives approaches our longevity. As one commentator said, "Today, people 'bop' till they drop." People are less likely to lower participation levels in their postcareer years. Travel, sports, and working the new ways are the most popular activities. Part-time work, consulting, operating new businesses, community action, coaching, and teaching are some of the popular new work formulas that allow people to get back to work without returning to the rat race. With the shortages in fresh younger talent, this new working style has captured employer interest in almost all but the most physical work areas.

It is not at all uncommon for people to go back to their former employers on temporary part-time assignments. By stressing their knowledge base plus motivation and willingness to learn new things, the older generation is demonstrating a new way of working that combines lifestyle interests with interesting, income-producing work situations, and still maintains a well-earned sense of independence.

New Time

In the late 1970s an imaginative and dedicated woman, Ina Tortin, recognizing her personal need for a more flexible work schedule, invented a company called NewTime, Inc. The purpose of this firm was to expand beyond the traditional temporary help agency, provide employees to organizations on a regular but still less than a full nine-to-five basis. The foundation of this sound concept is that a large number of tasks can be handled in 15 to 20 hours per week, and that organizations are unnecessarily saddling themselves with a number of full-time, full-salaried personnel out of an unconscious adherence to traditional work arrangements.

This new employment service (and those like it) attracted a cornucopia of jobs and employers needing everything from baseline clerical to top-line managers on regular part-time assignments:

Clerk to catch up on filing two days a week
Restaurant shift manager
Editor for company in-plant publications
Researcher for PR firm
Telemarketeer
Weekly computer trainer/maintainer
Once-a-week bookkeeper
Interviewer for business school
Traveling recruiter for expanding electronics firm
Tutor
Personal shopper
Communications consultant
Fund-raiser
Drug counselor

This phenomenon has spread and has been expanded by new corporate needs to keep costs down, and by the needs and values of multicareer families with children, retirees who want to keep some worklife going, creative types who need the time for studio work, and many others whose workstyle calls for both regularity and diversity.

Traditional temporary and part-time work remains one of the fastest growing categories of occupation. Temporary help services provide staff to employers who need a replacement for a person on vacation, workers to handle new product introductions, to fill in at workload peaks, or to supplement their regular staff for any reason.

According to Mitchel S. Fromstein, former president of the largest and oldest of the temporary service firms, Manpower, Inc.: "We have some people who find this to be the only possible workstyle: housewives and mothers, students and people with seasonal professions such as teachers. Others find this to be the workstyle that gives them the kind of freedom and flexibility they want. An assignment can last from a few days to many weeks and can range from file clerk to engineer/designer."

As more and more industries experience changes in direction and require more flexibility in manpower planning, the temporary service agencies continue to expand.

When you work through a temporary service firm, you are on their payroll and are paid weekly on the basis of the number of hours you work. There is no direct fee to you for the service: the employer pays a marked-up hourly rate. Working for a temporary service is an ideal way to gain experience and improve your skills as you earn a basic salary. Most temporary services offer free testing and skills improvement programs.

Once reserved for mostly clerical and lower level jobs, the growth in more professional level temporary service is great. John Thompson, chairman of the newly formed Interim Management Corporation in New York City, talks about the task-team approach: "We will help analyze the needs of a company moving in new directions through restructuring, new products, relocation or emergency, and provide them with a team of from three to a dozen managers, engineers, marketing experts—or a combination. Our people will operate in the day-to-day work of the firm anywhere from a month to a year, and then come back to us for reassignment. Our clients get what they need, and only that; and our professional workers get to pick the work which best conforms to their personal objectives."

There is no need to be signed on to a full-time job unless you want one. Permanent work on a part-time basis is something you can use to develop new skills, to fulfill your family obligations, or to limit your participation with the material realm. You can use the services of the various temporary and part-time agencies—which you can find by calling your local Chamber of Commerce, or find on your own through the research and targeting techniques described later in this book.

The School We Never Graduate From

With the assistance of researched statistics, we have provided you with a picture of how the current job market is growing and in what directions. All of this will help you to orient yourself as you proceed to set a career search agenda.

As you research your specific career targets and areas, you

will at the same time be receiving an education into the steps you must take to achieve your goal. This may lead you to short-term or long-term formal education at a college or university, or it may start you on a path of self-learning and discovery that will (hopefully) last the rest of your life.

But you may ask, "Is this really important? Why must I spend needless hours dredging up material that has no obvious connection to my current situation?"

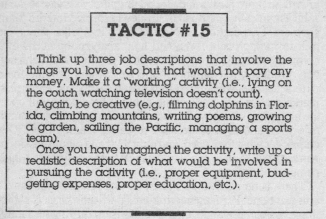

TACTIC #15

Think up three job descriptions that involve the things you love to do but that would not pay any money. Make it a "working" activity (i.e., lying on the couch watching television doesn't count).

Again, be creative (e.g., filming dolphins in Florida, climbing mountains, writing poems, growing a garden, sailing the Pacific, managing a sports team).

Once you have imagined the activity, write up a realistic description of what would be involved in pursuing the activity (i.e., proper equipment, budgeting expenses, proper education, etc.).

The answer is quite simple: The more informed you are, the more informed your decision, insuring that what you are doing is correct and that you're not wasting your time.

We tend to think that our education stops with a formal education in an institution. After 12 years of public school (elementary and secondary) and possibly some postsecondary study at college or university, most of us would rather not hear about education. We had such a bad time jumping through the hoops of boring, disinterested teachers we can only associate learning as something that has to be done and gotten over with as soon as possible. Well, we are here to tell you that this is just not so!

Finding the Facts

At this point, you might want sources of further information on some of the things we've talked about in this chapter. The following are resource materials that will lead you to other materials as well as some overview as to what is currently happening. We have also included a short list of books that you can use as a reference library.

BOOKS

Megatrends 2000. John Naisbitt and Patricia Aburdene. William Morrow, New York, 1990.

The New Realities: In Government and Politics/In Economics and Business/In Society and World View. Peter F. Drucker. Harper & Row, New York, 1989.

The Occupational Outlook Handbook. US Government Printing Office, Washington, DC 20402.

High Technology Careers. Texe W. Marrs. Dow Jones, Homewood, IL, 1986.

Emerging Careers: New Occupations for the Year 2000 and Beyond. S. N. Feingold and Norma Reno Miller. Garrett Park Press, Garrett Park, MD, 1983.

Futurework: Where to Find Tomorrow's High Tech Jobs Today. Diane Butler. Holt, Rinehart and Winston, New York, 1984.

Looking for Work in the New Economy. Wegmann, Chapman, Johnson. Olympus Publishing Company, 1986.

AGENCIES

International Association of Counseling Services (IACS). 5999 Stevenson Avenue, 3rd Floor, Alexandria, VA 22304.

This agency will provide you with the listing of accredited counseling services in your area. They also publish *The Directory of Counseling Services,* which may be available in your library or school career counseling center.

US Department of Labor, Bureau of Labor Statistics, 200 Constitution Avenue, NW, Washington, DC 20210. Phone: (202) 523-6631.

The Department publishes *The Occupational Outlook Handbook* and *The Occupational Outlook Quarterly*. Both these publications you will find at your local library.

National Audiovisual Center. 8700 Edgeworth Drive, Capitol Heights, MD 20743. Phone: (301) 763-1896.

The Center rents and sells material on jobs and careers produced by the US government. Catalog of materials is available upon request at no charge.

State Occupational Information Coordinating Committees. Addresses and telephone numbers for SOICC are listed on page 442 of *The Occupational Outlook Handbook*.

These committees can help you locate state or area information. They can provide information directly or refer you to other sources. Note: 46 states have Career Information Delivery Systems (CIDS), which use on-line computers, microcomputers, printed material, microfiche, and toll-free hotlines to provide information on occupations, educational opportunities, student financial aid, apprenticeships, and military careers. These systems can be found in secondary schools, post-secondary institutions, libraries, job training sites, vocational rehabilitation centers, and employment service offices. Contact the SOICC for a CIDS in your area.

Association of Independent Colleges and Schools. 1 Dupont Circle, NW, Suite 350, Washington, DC 20036. Phone: (202) 659-2460.

The Association will provide you with a free copy of *The Directory of Educational Institutions*. This is an annual publication that lists accredited business schools. These schools offer programs in secretarial science, business administration, accounting, data processing, court reporting, paralegal studies, fashion merchandising, travel/tourism, culinary arts, drafting, electronics, and other subjects.

National Association of Trade and Technical Schools (NATTS), Department of OOH, P.O. Box 10429, Rockville, MD 20850.

> Write for information on private trade and technical schools. They publish a list of schools that offer trade and technical educations. They also produce a series of pamphlets, including "How to Choose a Career and a Career School."

National Home Study Council, 1601 18th Street, NW, Washington, DC 20009. Phone: (202) 234-5100.

> The Council provides information about home study programs. They also publish *The Directory of Accredited Home Study Schools*.

Bureau of Apprenticeship and Training, US Department of Labor, 200 Constitution Avenue, NW, Washington, DC 20210. Phone: (202) 535-0545.

> The Bureau can provide you with information about apprenticeship programs offered by various industries. If you are interested in apprenticeship programs for women, ask about their *Woman's Guide to Apprenticeship*.

INFORMATION FOR SPECIAL GROUPS

President's Committee on Employment of the Handicapped, 1111 20th Street, NW, Washington, DC 20036. Phone: (202) 653-5044.

National Federation for the Blind. This agency has a Job Opportunities for the Blind program. Call toll free: 1-800-638-7518.*

League of United Latin American Citizens (LULAC), National Educational Service Centers, Inc., 400 First Street, NW, Suite 716, Washington, DC 20001. Phone: (202) 347-1652.

---

*Also: *Take Charge: A Strategic Guide for Blind Job Seekers* by Rama Rabby. Available in print, braille, cassette, and computer disk from the National Braille Press, 1989.

National Association for the Advancement of Colored People (NAACP), 4805 Mount Hope Drive, Baltimore, MD 21215-3297. Phone: (202) 479-1200.

Department of Veterans Benefits, Veterans Administration Central Office, 810 Vermont Avenue, NW, Washington, DC 20420. Phone: (202) 872-1151.

Women's Bureau, US Department of Labor, 200 Constitution Avenue, NW, Washington, DC 20210. Phone: (202) 523-6652.

Catalyst (Women's Assistance Group), 250 Park Avenue South, New York, NY 10003. Phone: (212) 777-8900.

Wider Opportunities for Women, 1325 GT Street, NW, Lower Level, Washington, DC 20005. Phone: (202) 638-3143.

Most of these agencies are run by the government with your tax dollars. They may not directly provide you with a job. However, by taking advantage of some of their services, they may lead you on the right path.

4

Targeting

Your Are Not Your Job Title (Again)

Some pages back we tried to get you to realize that you are
not your job title . . . that job classifications do not describe humans any more than song titles describe the music
you will hear, or a city's name describes its climate.

You are a multifaceted creature who can put together a
rock garden one day and a financial report the next. You have
the ability to learn new languages, wield new tools, listen to
computers, and talk to God.

You are essentially restless and craving, conquering the
seven seas and coveting the planets. You are a nomad, for-
saking green New England hills for midwestern plains, giving up rugged seascapes for downhill skiing, plain home
cooking for gourmet vegetarian fare, and deserting old and
tried mill towns for untried boomtowns. You have learned a
hundred schemes and routines, and can pick up more. You
are ready, willing, and able, though it doesn't always look
that way. As a matter of fact, on any given day—to a person
who hasn't seen you perform—you may easily look stuck in
a rut. And sometimes you are.

The purpose of this section is to give you an insight into
some of the ways you can marshal your abilities and best
direct your true potential into the workworld. This procedure
is called targeting or, more specifically, job targeting.

Job targeting is a process in which you look at all of your personal purposes, goals, and capabilities, and then choose specific work areas (out of thousands) that will best satisfy them.

Once you have established particular job targets that reflect who you are and what you seek, the rest of this book will show you methods of obtaining these jobs.

You already have some insight into the relationship of your work to your life, and how to align the two. Using nothing more than your own knowledge you have invented over a dozen possible positions. In this part you will add a new dimension—the outside world. You will now play the game for real stakes. Ante up.

Intention: Young Jim

A funding grant is canceled. Young Jim is let go with dozens of others. He gets a super resume together, prints 100 copies, and buys the *Los Angeles Times* and *The Wall Street Journal*. On Sunday afternoon he selects the choice advertised jobs, mails out a dozen or so resumes, then takes his wife and kids to Disneyland.

Ten days go by, and Jim hasn't heard anything. He blames the postal service and mails out half a dozen more of his slick resumes to newly advertised jobs. Then three responses arrive in one morning's mail. Jim is shattered by the cold formality of the three turndowns: "Your resume is being retained and we will let you know if anything . . ."

The next day brings two more rejections, both on printed forms. By the end of the week he has accounted for all but four of his inquiries. All the responses have been negative. In the following weeks and months, Jim mails out hundreds of resumes, now twice revised. No more Disneyland.

For over six months Jim keeps score patiently: 225 resumes mailed out, 130 turndowns, and eight interview requests, of which he only took five. No offers, no job, no ideas. Betrayed by the very system that inspired him to get into teaching in the first place, he is now driving a cab and trying to piece together a nervous marriage. End of story.

Jim played out his role nicely in an old familiar scenario:

"There are no jobs out there—I've answered hundreds of ads."

Q: Jim, what are you looking for?

A: "At this point I'll take just about anything. I've tried everything in my field."

Q: What have you tried?

A: "I've mailed out hundreds of resumes for teaching jobs. If there's anything out there that I missed, I'll eat my hat."

Q: Did you have any particular kind of job in mind?

A: "What do you mean *particular*? A man can't be particular in today's job market. I answered every ad I could find."

Q: Did you do anything besides answer ads?

A: "Like what? I tried a half-dozen employment agencies, but they were worthless."

Q: Did you try anything outside of teaching—other types of jobs?

A: "Well, I'm sure that would have been a waste of time. If they aren't interested in my teaching skills I doubt that I could interest them in anything else, except driving this cab. It's a very tight job market around here. . . ."

"They" strike again. *They* aren't interested, *they* don't have any openings, *they* are unfair to innocent teachers. The familiar litany of the (not fully responsible) job seeker. If instead of mailing out hundreds of resumes to try to get advertised positions, Jim had developed specific job targets and then located the firms who could hire him in these areas, he would have had a satisfying job in six to eight weeks.

The Tip of the Iceberg

A job rarely gets advertised until a firm has been unable to locate the person they seek through internal channels, referrals, contacts, job posting, and anything else the employer can think of to avoid the high cost of hiring by advertising.

Eighty-five percent of the available jobs on any given day are not advertised. These jobs comprise the hidden job market, and this is an essential place to scout out the custom-tailored positions that we are talking about in this segment of the book.

Jim's big mistake was that he didn't have a specific job targets to go after. He, like thousands of others inexperienced in the dynamics of the job market, made the mistake of thinking that the more general his job target—in his case, *all* the advertised jobs for teachers—the more possibilities he would open up. The opposite is true.

By clearly specifying a job target in as many aspects as possible, you expand rather than diminish your ability to locate prospective employers.

Being without specific job targets keeps you floundering in the job stew, chasing after every carrot or potato that bobs to the surface. You lose the sense of purpose necessary for sustained energy.

Expansion

Before you can focus on specific job targets, you must expand your thinking about jobs and become more aware of opportunities in the workworld. There are a number of approaches to assist you in this, and one of the simplest is the job family process described on the next page.

STEVE LYNN—The New Old-Boy Network

At the workshop I came up with this job target of being an advance planner. Only then I didn't even know what the job was called. I knew that big companies must have smart frontline people to help them decide where to go when they are relocating a division or plant. Advance work that would get me involved in all aspects of a community, and many aspects of the corporate/political field.

I decided to follow the personal referral network technique that we had discussed. Interviewing for information rather than directly for a job.

I first called city hall and found out about the Eco-

TACTIC #16

A job family is a common interest grouping of jobs described under a single category. Each job family category includes dozens to hundreds of specific work descriptions, job titles, and opportunities for problem solving. For example, the automotive job family would include jobs in designing, selling, repairing, and transporting cars, writing safety brochures, and making safety inspections, to name a few.

Shown below are 72 job families. Go through the list three times. First, draw a line through each job family that holds no interest at all for you. Then go back and circle each family that interests you somewhat.

Then select the top four families that are most interesting and relevant to you. If you opt for a family we haven't listed, so much the better.

Accounting	Engineering	Music
Advertising	Entertainment	Oceanography
Aerospace	Family services	Office services
Agriculture	Finance	Paper
Animals	Fine arts	Performing arts
Architecture	Food	Personal services
Automotive	Geriatrics	Photography
Banking	Government	Politics
Boating	Health care	Public speaking
Bookkeeping	Human resources	Publishing
Building services	Industrial design	Real estate
Children's	Information	Religion
services	services	Repair services
Commercial art	Insurance	Retailing
Communications	Interior Design	Sciences
Computers	Journalism	Selling
Construction	Law	Sports
Consulting	Leisure	Systems design
Counseling	Management	Television &
Crafts	services	video
Criminology	Manufacturing	Textiles
Ecology	Marketing	Toys
Economics	Mathematics	Transportation
Education	Medicine	Travel
training	Mental health	Wellness
Electronics	Museum work	

TACTIC #17

List each of the four job families you selected (in Tactic #16) on a separate sheet of paper in your notebook. Under each job family list as many specific job titles, positions, opportunities, or descriptions of possible jobs as you can think of, regardless of whether they are jobs you feel you would like to do. List menial as well as senior jobs. Invent new ones. Keep at it until you have been able to list at least 20 different possibilities under each.

The object at this stage is for you to continue to expand the number of possible job situations that you are aware of in a given field. If you have difficulty in coming up with a full list, brainstorm with your family, call someone in the field, read trade journals or books about the subject, or call the relevant professional association.

TACTIC #18

You now have a list of 20 job possibilities in each of the job family areas you selected. Go over each list and cross out all those you *know* you would not find personally satisfying.

Then go back over the lists and cross out each job you feel would be highly impractical for you to identify or obtain. (Be careful here. Don't cross anything out unless you are certain there is a very real prerequisite that you don't have.)

Then list all of the remaining possibilities from all lists, in rank order or maximum satisfaction. Read down the list one by one and ask yourself the following question: "Am I willing to do what's necessary to get this job?" If the answer is yes, allow it to remain. If not, cross it out.

nomic Development Agency, the group that keeps track of corporations that are relocating out of town. They gave me the names of vice presidents of three large corporations that were planning moves within the year.

I called each of them, reaching a man at a large oil company who agreed to meet with me for 15 minutes to answer any questions. I told him I was doing some research for an article, and that I was also personally interested. I really did intend to do the article, and possibly I still will. Anyway, the oil company guy was great and gave me lots of information, such as how to get into the field without the normal real estate background.

He also gave me, at my request, the names of three other people, two at other Chicago corporations and one with a well-known consulting firm.

I started to fill a three-ring binder with notes and questions to ask, and I also did some library research. I read one very good article.

All in all I had around fifteen information-type interviews. Each one would give me expertise that I would use the next time. After one month I was an expert.

I had saved two consulting firm referrals for last. I blew one of them: the guy was either threatened by what I knew, or else he felt I was a professional spy. The other was just what I wanted. The junior partner returned my call, which was disappointing since I had wanted to meet the big guy. After our lunch, I did nothing and, sure enough, a week later I got a call at home from the senior partner.

He was warm and friendly. So was I. We met for drinks at the Princeton Club.

At the end of about an hour together he asked me if I was looking for a job. I told him that I had thought about it a couple of times, and wasn't sure I was ready yet. But what did he have in mind?

He said $30,000 to start and I said, "Hmmm." Nothing else.

To make a long story short, he finally offered $35,500, and threw in the tuition for my MBA at night at the University of Chicago.

It was great fun. I got the job I wanted, learned about a new field, and made a lot of good contacts to boot. And I never even had a resume.

You can do an abbreviated practice version of the above referral network by phone if you are willing to cold call a dozen people. Start with the Yellow Pages in virtually any subject and call the firms whose names are listed. Ask for the names of leaders in the field, trade publications, and business associations.

The new old-boy network works. You can build one in any field you like. Just keep letting people know, directly and simply, that you are looking for advice from an expert. If you have qualms about the call ask how you would go about it if you were doing an article or research for a term paper.

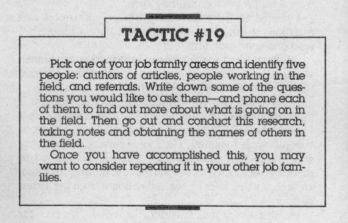

TACTIC #19

Pick one of your job family areas and identify five people: authors of articles, people working in the field, and referrals. Write down some of the questions you would like to ask them—and phone each of them to find out more about what is going on in the field. Then go out and conduct this research, taking notes and obtaining the names of others in the field.

Once you have accomplished this, you may want to consider repeating it in your other job families.

Obstacles

You will continually run into obstacles in your work search. Obstacles are as much a part of this game as cold weather is a part of Midwest football. Expect them, and don't be surprised or put off course when you find that two out of three people you call aren't in or don't want to talk. So what? If you are committed to obtaining the results, then the disappointments and snags that get in the way will become just one more sign that you are moving along the path to your objective. If it takes three attempts to reach one person, then the calculations are simple: Be prepared to try thirty calls to reach ten.

Many people have such a deep-rooted conviction that they aren't going to make it in life that they will eagerly grasp any disappointment or obstacle as a way to prove it. In the work search this self-invalidation is particularly intense. We have been conditioned to invest so much of ourselves that a problem or setback will usually bring up our worst fears of failure.

Therapists and counselors report that job failure is one of the most common recurring fears of their clients. It doesn't matter if you are entering the job market for the first time, hoping for that promotion, or coming back to work after seven years devoted to bringing up children. You are probably scared silly that at long last you will be found out, discovered to be the base imcompetent that you always knew you were.

Obstacles, missed opportunities, rejections, disappointment, self-reproach, and fear will all occur in your job search. They are an integral part of virtually every job campaign that ever produced any positive results. Of course, you ought to know that the same human failure responses are also part of every other worthwhile, expanding activity. People who resist failure rarely succeed. People whose main purpose in life is to be comfortable rarely expand.

When you know in advance that the roller coaster ride is going to be a bit scary, there is really only one approach to take: Sit back, hold on, and enjoy it.

TACTIC #20

You will find it helpful to know in advance what personal barriers or obstacles will get in the way of your job search. At this time, list all the things that you suspect might inhibit you or slow you down this time. List everything.

The View From Inside

The job search begins with a look inside. Who are you? What are your skills, interests, aptitudes, and motivations? What are your dreams? What do you consider to be your reality?

The next step is to look from this internal vantage point out to the world, and identify the work areas that would allow you to express all these components of yourself.

There is no "one" ultimately perfect job for you. There is only continued expansion and growth, and maintaining the inner direction and control that allow you to find work that you love. *Real success is having a job that works for you.*

Geographic Imperative

Where would you like to live? If you could have the job you want anywhere in the country, or in the world, where would it be?

Are you stuck in your own hometown because that's the place you are most familiar or comfortable with? Take a look outside. A full 17% of the US population changes location every year. We are an enormous traffic pattern, flowing from city to suburbs, from Northeast to Southwest. The US labor market is truly a national market. Jobs are virtually interchangeable from community to community, and in an ever-growing way from country to country.

You can probably pick almost any area you would want to live and work and, using the techniques in this book, identify viable job possibilities there.

The Global Village

It is definitely possible to relocate to an exciting and well-paying job outside the United States. Possible—but not easy.

The first thing you need to handle is language. The odds are ten to one against your locating the kind of job you want if you don't speak the local language well, unless you have very highly specialized skills that are in demand in the country of your choice. If you have aspirations without linguistics, you are in for an uphill fight.

TACTIC #21

Quick vision exercise: read this paragraph, then close your eyes for a moment—wherever you are—and take three deep breaths, exhaling slowly each time. Then let your mind wander over several places you have visited on vacation or business trips, places you liked to be. In your imagination see yourself living and working there—taking the best the location has to offer.

Enjoy the fantasy trip. Don't forget to come back.

When you open your eyes, list five cities, towns, or areas you have visited that you wouldn't mind living and working in. Next list five locations you haven't been to but would like to try.

From these ten listings, select four. Get a map and locate the four you have selected, spot each of them, and then draw or imagine a circle 25 miles in radius. Look in the areas bounded by these circles, and see if you can come up with at least five new locations in which to focus your job search.

The second thing you need to deal with is the fact that many foreign nations have policies or local protectionist laws that discourage hiring foreigners except in areas where labor is in short supply. These short-supply areas tend to be grouped at the very low end of the scale (migrant farm workers, physical laborers) or in the rarefied upper atmospheres (nuclear physicist, open-heart surgeon, counterspy), and sometimes in the high-demand bilingual secretary field where looks, skills, and *savoir faire* can almost always open a spot legally or illegally.

Let's talk about the possibilities and approaches that will produce results despite the obstacles. It is a fact, within the free enterprise world, that *if you can demonstrate an ability to accomplish a result better than anyone around, you will probably be able to create job opportunities*. For example, if you are a specialist in 16-track recording techniques, speak enough Spanish to get by, and find yourself in Madrid one Monday morning, look up the local recording studios, call the manager, and ask if you can stop by to see how *they* do it. When you see the equipment, make friends with the personnel, and feel on safe ground, ask if you could stop by and assist them at a session—free of charge, of course—and perhaps show them some little things that you've happened to pick up. After they have a clear picture of what you can do, let a few days go by and then get back in touch with the manager. Let him know that you'd be willing to help him out on a more regular basis, for a modest salary.

The idea is not to break in like gangbusters and put everyone on the defensive. Start with a clear target, something you can do to create value. Locate the people who could utilize the value, *demonstrate* the value, and only then ask to be paid for it.

Look for introductions and referrals. Who do you know who knows someone who has a contact in your target country or city? Have him or her write or call in advance.

Look for areas where your specialized American knowledge could be of particular value to an overseas employer. It might be someone marketing goods to the United States or Canada, or someone introducing a product or service internationally that has been around for a while in your country.

Another slant is to locate American-based firms with offices overseas, or the ever-expanding multinational corporations or agencies. Take inventory of your friends and relatives; see which of them work for a firm with overseas connections. Often a bank or a law firm will have contacts you can use.

Get a copy of the *International Herald Tribune* and read the classifieds, locate foreign newspapers and periodicals (most large cities will have newsstands that carry international newspapers and magazines), or skim professional journals for news about what's going on. Check with trade associations for their overseas affiliates. Call consulates or trade offices for information.

Targeting Tomorrow's Job Today

We live in a society that has changed more in our own lifetime than it has in the two previous centuries; a society that is caught up in an apparently irreversible cycle of problem followed by solution, followed by bigger problems that grow out of earlier solutions. It is a world where change is substituted for progress, and growth replaces contribution as the major life force. You are in the middle of a technological tornado that is burning up its center at an almost incomprehensible rate.

And, if you have recently entered the workforce, you will probably have four or five careers in your worklife. Start now to target them.

As far as we can see, there are only three approaches available for playing the job game:

1. You can resign yourself to whatever the workworld brings you, and attempt to gain as many material rewards as possible to numb yourself into a feeling that, somehow, you have made it.

2. You can expand the full recognition of yourself and realize that it is not the position that's important, but the way you hold it—your position about the position. Creating an enlightened context for your life does, indeed, improve your worklife.

3. You can realize that you are responsible for the worklife you end up with, and the satisfaction it holds, and identify the dynamic relationship that will allow you to feel that satisfaction as you continually express yourself in the workforce.

TACTIC #22

Visit your local library. Ask the librarian to put you in touch with some reference books or articles that discuss the development of industry and business (or other fields that appeal to you). Look through an index of articles in *Business Week, Industry Week, Fortune,* or *The Wall Street Journal.* Alternatively, call a trade association and ask what articles they recommend in your field.

With a reasonably well-thought-out program you can easily identify target areas that represent the next generation of hot jobs, those that wield economic power and prestige and are in the mainstream of the world game. All you need to do is open your eyes and see what's coming down the road, and then, by identifying the growth pattern, select or *create* the kind of job targets that will be appropriate to the directions you see. All it takes is a little confidence.

You can create a job by identifying an obvious future trend, seeing how this trend relates to what you have been doing and to your interests and skills, adding whatever education and/or training you need, and communicating this to the right person:

"Ms. Mallory, I was looking at your plans to erect that new microwave transmission network, and I wonder if you are aware of some of the new laser-beam techniques that could cut transmission costs by 40 percent."

Or:

"Mr. Paullin, I have an idea how you could bring more people into your training seminars. I think that we could establish connections with local industry, and probably bring in 25 to 30 new people per month. I could assist you in setting this up."

Job creation is simply advanced problem solving. You don't have to be a genius, and you aren't required to be able to see what's happening two decades down the line—two years is more than enough.

JAN JOHNSTON—Life Interests to Rewarding Work

After hanging around the house for years convincing myself that I was really not equipped for anything in this world other than raising kids, taking care of a house, and from time to time playing secretary, I actually went out and created a career for myself. A career that gives me what I want, feeds my ego, lets me talk to people who are more than 12 years old, and also pays me now, after six years, $49,000 per year. Here's how it happened:

In college I took some pre-law courses and some

credits in business. I had this vague idea of going to law school, but at that time there weren't as many women doing that as there are now, and my family really didn't support the idea. So instead, I got a job in a small law firm in Crescent City as a legal secretary.

It started well. I was single and got to meet people and go out a lot, so I could forget the tedium of typing legal briefs and depositions all day long. I can't believe that some women actually do that day in and day out, week after weary week, year after year. I'd rather be a house-wife. Which is exactly what I became when I married one of our clients. That, of course, was the end of my career at that law firm.

I had Jamie a year and a half later, and decided to stay home a few years, which stretched into seven before I even knew it. I broke out of my rut after I joined a women's group. I wasn't a strident feminist, but some of my friends were going, and I joined them.

One day a woman spoke to us about jobs, and the legal movement to bring women and other people into jobs that they had previously been excluded from. I was intrigued.

My friend Bev and I got very interested in the area of equal opportunity. At first we were concerned about how it applied to us, but then we began to realize that with the government pressure escalating, companies would be very interested in learning how to stay out of trouble and, since the whole equal employment opportunity thing was only a few years old, there weren't many people around who knew what was going on. It was a natural, and tied right in to my earlier interest in law.

Bev and I spent three months learning about it together. We read every article we could dig up. We contacted the National Organization for Women and got some stuff from them. We went to Washington for a solid week, visited the EEOC, read and made copies of the legislation and hearings, and got a strong sense of the direction in which things were moving.

Our most productive step was to call a woman we had read about. She was doing some consulting with AT&T,

which had already had some EEO problems. Martha met us for lunch twice, let us sit in on some meetings she was running, and gave us the names of some of the people we should contact.

Once we got over our fear of the phone, we each made up a list of 25 corporations in our area that we would be willing to work for and called them up. I would suggest to the personnel manager that we should get together and talk about what they were doing in the EEO area, and how I could possibly help them. I got to actually meet with 12 companies, and got job offers from four. I could have gotten three more if I'd pushed. I took a job with Consolidated Refineries as EEO specialist. I've changed jobs twice since then, and am now personnel manager of a retailing chain, and I love it. I know now that all it takes to find a good job is to stay in touch with what's going on in the world.

TACTIC #23

Get on the telephone and call the personnel managers of a couple of firms in the area of your job target interest. Ask them to tell you how they see their long-term openings shaping up. What kinds of people will they need in the next year or so?

What skills are the hardest for them to locate? Don't push for a specific job, just more information and experience on the phone.

Your Crystal Ball

You are living in the middle of an information complex, and probably everything you need to know about areas of future job development and growth is at your fingertips if you are willing to dig it out.

Are you willing? Or are you still stuck in the traditional point of view that the job you get, the work you do, is pretty much something that someone else—the placement counselor at school, the employment agent, your family, the newspaper classifieds—suggests to you?

It's hard to break old patterns, and this "Show me where I report" attitude about work is one of the oldest. We aren't trained to look upon work as an opportunity for creative expression. Most of us are never shown how to use the resources at hand to open up new careers for ourselves. There *are* resources that will provide you with information on what's happening. Here are three obvious ones to start with now:

Business publications like *Business Week,* Section Three of the Sunday *New York Times, The Wall Street Journal, National Business Employment Weekly, Forbes, Barron's, Fortune*

Professional societies in your target area

Trade publications in your field

Affirmations

REPEAT:

I am not my job title.

I am willing to relate to work in a way that reflects my own internal satisfaction and joy in life.

I am able and skilled, and willing to use my abilities to create value in the world in the best way I can.

I am willing to uncover specific job targets that reflect my skills and abilities, and to undertake the job search only after I have become clear about these.

Once I have selected my job targets I am willing to do what's necessary to achieve them.

Now go back over these affirmations again, and this time make them even more real for yourself. Stop at each one and see if it is true for you.

Are you really willing? If you encounter resistance along the way, will you continue to press? For how long?

It's easy to agree with the statements, but quite another thing to experience them in living terms. The traditional thinking is generally in the opposite direction:

"I am best described by my job title."

"Like it or not, you've got to work."

"I hate the work, but it pays well."

"I'm looking for a job—do you have anything?"

"The job market is tough. You're lucky to find any job."

This negativism is an integral part of our education for work. You find it reinforced at every turn, by parents, teachers, newspapers, even many career counselors and consultants.

The consciousness that work is something you *do* with your life, not something you *get,* is a recent phenomenon. But the new awareness won't have any value for you if you simply "believe" it just because we say so. You've got to look more deeply within to see if you are willing to create the truth for yourself. Are you?

Targets

A target is a statement of your intention and willingness. It is not a hope. It is not a dream. It is a reality that has yet to be formalized.

The only way to effectively approach job targets is to envision yourself at the final objective, and then identify all the apparent obstacles between you and success. See the obstacles as the steps you need to take to actualize the target for yourself. Just include them within the purpose of your objective, and notice that they actually support you in getting what you want, by pointing up the next thing to be done.

Objection from you:

It sounds like double-talk. I don't understand how the obstacles to the target actually help to support my achieving it. It's a semantic trick. Frankly, I don't know if I can accomplish my target at all, and I'm not willing to buy this theoretical positive thinking stuff. I'll do the best I can: I'll try to make my targets but I won't guarantee that I'll do it.

Response from us:

Thanks for being honest. Most people never really target anything. They pretend to really want something, then get "determined" and "try" to make it. And their point of view is essentially that they won't make it unless they are lucky. People don't achieve their targets because they allow the obstacles to become reasons for not making it. If you are not willing to take absolute responsibility for the results of a particular target, then change your target to something you *would* be willing to achieve. Don't set yourself up to be a loser in your own terms.

Your rebuttal:

You mean I should pick an easy target so I will be sure I can make it. What good is that?

Our reply:

No. Every target you set for yourself should be an expression of your willingness to be uncomfortable. If it does not require some effort or some confrontation, it isn't a valuable target. All real growth or movement is accompanied by a feeling of discomfort and challenge. Think of the first race you ran, the first big date, the first time you made a speech, acted in a play, or disagreed with a popular opinion. The other side of being uncomfortable is accomplishment.

Select job targets that you know will produce some discomfort and challenge and be willing to handle everything that comes up along the way. If you do that, you will achieve your targets.

TACTIC #24

Go back to the list of potential job targets you were left with when you completed Tactic #18. Rank them in order of interest to you. Then select the top four as your job targets—with the understanding that you are willing to do what's necessary to get one of these positions.

Write each of the top four on a separate sheet in your notebook, then list all the things you can think of that could get in the way of your achieving these targets. After you have listed all the obstacles, go back and write down the things you would have to do to overcome the obstacles.

GERALDINE NEWTON—Free Lance

The first people to get fired are in public relations. At the merest hint of the economic sniffles, out they go. I mean, why not—the client isn't all that excited about what we do when everything is rosy, so what the hell do they need us around for when they're chopping the budget? It's a fickle career. I know some fine publicity people who have probably put in more time behind the wheel of a taxi than behind a typewriter.

A few years ago things got so bad where I worked that the whole agency folded. It was a very sobering situation.

I decided that this time, whatever I did, I wasn't going to be back at the same old game. Very brave, but what to do? The idea of changing careers gave me this hot sinking feeling in my stomach. I spent this one very spacey weekend by myself. Very sad, very thoughtful, playing out my life over and over. Real thoughts of failure, frustration, and regret that I hadn't picked a different field, or had stayed married. Lots of stuff like that.

Anyway, I came through with flying colors. I came up with the idea of going into free-lance public relations.

To build up my own clients on small jobs or projects. At first, I thought it was a crazy idea. I wanted security, and here I was going out on a limb.

I knew that one of the things I had to do was to improve my ability to communicate, to let people know I could do the job. I meditated, which really calmed me. It was fabulous. I realized quickly that whatever I wanted I could get if I was willing to take a position of responsibility. That I could be responsible for my own worklife.

I contacted everyone I knew personally in the business—clients, media people, and other people in PR firms. In a short time I picked up three small accounts, which at least paid the rent. This gave me the courage to make my new career exactly the way I wanted it. I decided to represent authors who had just published books, and who felt that they weren't being actively represented by their publishers.

I had a package deal in which I charged them $2,500 for four months, plus expenses. I now have around ten clients at any one time, the product of an initial phone campaign to publishers and friends, and lots of follow-up. I love it, and I have more security, since I can go out and get a new client whenever I lose one, and I make more money than I ever made before. And I have more fun. The only security you have is inside yourself.

There are scores of work areas in which it is an accepted and established *modus operandi* to provide your services on an hourly, daily, or per project basis. And as we break our traditional attachment to the nine-to-five work routine, the number of areas that open up for free-lancing will continue to expand.

You are a free-lancer when you have clearly dedicated yourself to the full-time project of providing your skills on a part-time basis to a variety of clients, and are responsible for soliciting your own assignments and billing them directly.

At a higher-paid, more expert level, the same workstyle is called consulting. Some of the more recognized areas of free-lance work are:

Writing	Advertising	Public relations
Editing	Casting	Talent manager
Research	Gardening	Artists'
Illustrating	Bartender	representative
Decorating	Catering	Tour guide
Bookkeeping	Plant care	Translator
Accounting	Costume designing	Real estate agent
Nursing	Typist	Child care
Designing	Masseuse	Shopper
Landscaping	Music teacher	Programmer
Architecture	Photographer	Systems analyst
Specialized	Filmmaker	Stylist
engineering	Word processing	

—and about 100 more.

This is the beginning of the list. You can take it from there. The essence of free-lance work is that you are responsible for developing your own customers or clients. It can be done by small ads in local newspapers, notices on community bulletin boards, direct solicitation by phone or mail, and most importantly, by word of mouth. Satisfied clients tell others.

If you are shy or embarrassed about letting people know how good you are, or billing well for your time, then free-lance might turn into part-time starvation for you. A rule of thumb for charging for your time is to bill three times or better what you would get if you were working for a salary. This will compensate for the lack of fringe benefits, and for your downtime when you are developing new business.

As your own boss you face a major management problem: how to keep you, the employee, at work. As a beginning free-lancer, you need to set up a weekly and daily schedule of specific things to do to let the right people know what you can do for them. Even though you are booked up with work, you need to continue to develop new leads and contacts for the future.

Your Own Show

The quest for fame and fortune lures over 600,000 would-be entrepreneurs into starting their own businesses each year, according to the Small Business Administration, the federal agency responsible for policies and programs to aid and help finance small businesses. Unfortunately, as divorce frequently follows marriage, business failures provide a sobering view of the other side of the entrepreneurial dream.

According to the *Dun & Bradstreet Business Failure Record* published for 1988, the most common causes of bankruptcies are incompetence, under-capitalization, unbalanced experience, lack of experience in business, loss of market to larger firms, trouble with partners, and lack of managerial experience to handle growth.

Having your own business is an exciting and frequently rewarding and remunerative approach to your worklife, one that can motivate you for many, many years. It can also hold much pain, frustration, hard work, and low return. It is almost always an adventure. There are five essentials that must be met in starting your own profitable business:

1. A product or service that produces substantially more value for the customer than it costs and that can be produced or delivered for significantly less than it sells for.

2. A conscious, tested way to communicate this value to potential customers in a way that cost-effectively creates sales.

3. A management or manager willing to set up and observe objective criteria for measuring performance against a predetermined plan, and to let go of ideas that demonstrably aren't working.

4. An organized, clear, time-oriented, truthful business plan that sets out specific goals and timetables, and an accurate, realistic budget reviewed by an accountant.

5. Enough money to carry you through your business plan even if 50% of your goals are not met on time.

If any of these essential conditions are not met, think seriously about holding off until they are. If you have prepared yourself carefully, go to it, and play the game outrageously. Keep looking for the things that produce value for others and move in that direction. Do what works and drop what doesn't.

Be willing to try again if the first time around doesn't produce the results you are looking for. In a TV interview a few years ago, four men who had made a million dollars before they were 30 years old were interviewed. Among the four, they had collectively been involved in 75 different ventures, businesses, jobs, and other activities before they made their fortunes.

Moving on with the Targets

By this time, if you are following this book responsibly, doing the exercises, and keeping your workbook, you should be clear about four specific jobs targets that you can *own*, that is, that you can get behind and be responsible for. Using the tactics in the remaining pages, you will be able to achieve them. Really. It's that powerful.

If you have been willing to do the exercises and tactics, and to confront your resistance and excuses, terrific! Take out some time to acknowledge yourself, pat yourself on the back, have a beer. You have accomplished what many others have excused away or have not found time or space to go through.

If you are feeling guilty right now, you know you haven't done your homework. You've probably put together a few justifications like "I'll do it later," or "I already know that," or "Who has the time for that kind of stuff? I'm looking for a job, not a dedication." Or perhaps you have some other ideas that have kept you skimming rather than digging into the material in this book.

We hope that after you've scanned the book looking for quick fixes, you will return to examine some of the basic personal issues raised in these pages. We continue to support your search for a more meaningful connection to your work-life. *If you can, before moving on, go back and complete any of the exercises or tactics that you've skipped. Your plan will work better.*

If you're not up to looking back right now, just make a note of that. Move on, and please help yourself to whatever you can use.

Reminders and References

REMINDERS

- Work is not something you get; it is something you do.
- A full 85% of the jobs available on any given day are not advertised.
- You can use the phone to start collecting *information* from people in your field of interest. Find out the facts from people who are daily on the line. Make the job area *real* for yourself.

REFERENCES

Dictionary of Holland Occupational Codes. John Holland and Gary Gottfredson. Psychological Assessment Resources, Lutz, FL, 1989.

Work in the New Economy: Careers and Job Seeking into the 21st Century. Robert Wegmann, Robert Chapman, and Miriam Johnson. JIST Works, Indianapolis, 1989.

International Jobs (Revised Edition). Eric Kooher. Addison-Wesley, Reading, MA, 1984.

Insider's Guide to Franchising. Bryce Webster. Amacom, NY, 1986.

Working for Oneself. Philip Namanworth and Gene Busnar. McGraw-Hill, New York, 1985.

Question: Do you have a job target(s)? What is it?

5

Learning for Earning

New Education and Training

Listen to what futurist Alvin Toffler has to say about education:

What passes for education today, even in our "best" schools and colleges, is a hopeless anachronism. Parents look to education to fit their children for life in the future. Teachers warn that lack of an education will cripple a child's chances in the world of tomorrow.

Yet for all this rhetoric about future, many of our schools face backward toward a dying system, rather than forward to the emerging new society. . . .

We are burdened with an educational system that, with few exceptions, does not prepare students to meet the direct challenges of their world. Students are swept downstream from course to course, year to year, amassing $50,000 to $200,000 worth of certificates, diplomas, and degrees, and then find themselves out on the street without an idea of what their lifework will be, or how to go about attaining it. Mass education is a failure when it comes to creating the context for a satisfying life's work.

However, once you have created your work goals, your knowledge of the system through which education and skills training are delivered can make a major contribution to your life. When you use education as a tool to support your life goals, the experience brightens considerably. When you know what you must learn to get what you want, a school or training course seems a natural place to be, and the material to be learned is like hot soup for the hungry.

As you develop long-term and short-term job targets, you will see areas where additional training or education is called for. If you use good location techniques and references, you can easily find out where to pick up the new skills you need for virtually any job area. In focusing on your education, always start with job targets first, and then find out with certainty what skills are required. Don't allow yourself to be talked into getting a master's degree in French if all you need to do is communicate with your Paris office. As we discussed earlier, a college degree is a technical necessity for certain fields. If you don't have one, see if you can work out a plan to obtain it with a minimal disruption of your work agenda. If you go to college full-time, find a way to stay in touch with a job target and employer along the way—through summer and vacation work, co-op programs (part work, part school), or other means.

And education, like nutrition, is a life-long need. To continue to grow, we must exercise our thirst for learning. We need to transcend simple information—that which is repeatable—and move to deeper understanding of the principles and concepts that stand under the "facts." And beyond understanding, we must translate what we learn into know-how; knowledge of practical, action-oriented things to do. Putting what we know to work for us is what keeps us moving.

Here are some informative sources of education and training to help you prepare for your first job, or to rise through the ranks toward your ultimate target.

On-the-Job Training

A very practical way to build your skills is to look for training opportunities in and around any job you have. Possibilities abound in almost every job for you to expand your skills while holding down a job. If you are a receptionist, improve your word processing skills. If you are a secretary, learn about bookkeeping and office management. If you are in personnel, go to night school for your MBA. If you are a media planner, learn more about account management. If you are an account executive, learn more about creative writing. If you are an attorney, learn computers. If you are a teacher, develop your physical skills. If you are a writer, learn word processing.

The American corporation is a new seat of learning of great scope and significance. This is not due to philanthropic motives, but to the pragmatic realization that in order to compete in tough world markets the employee body must know how to think, and what to think about. High performance requires high know-how.

According to Bud Paullin, Director of Learning Systems at US West, one of the nation's largest telecommunications firms: "Training is a powerful management technology which is gaining greatly in importance now. Corporate learning and training organizations must provide not only an operational support role, but also must be a strategic resource for the firm. Linkage with business plans and strategies, environmental trends, child-care issues, lifestyle characteristics, and public policy is essential." Among the issues Bud Paullin thinks are most important include:

- To promote a truly adaptive workforce
- To develop "intellectual capital" that is always relevant
- To prepare people for redeployment
- To champion and support—with time and money— lifelong learning
- To help people envision a world of greater possibility, not simply the acquisition of more skills
- To train people in ways that are innovative, cost effective, and which facilitate people in translating "theory" into action

ASTD reports that corporate spending for training in the 1990s will exceed 80 billion dollars per year. More and more often the nature of the training itself is shifting from the traditional and specific craft level training to more of what used to be called "soft" or motivational training: workshops in ways of thinking and working smarter. Leadership, coaching, career development, team building, and negotiating skills mix with technical symposia, executive retreats, wellness and exercise weekends, and multimedia software-based training processes.

Work for a company that promotes your learning and career growth. This is good for them and good for you. Set out your own training agenda to go along with career plans. Take advantage of tuition refund programs and special weekend courses cosponsored by employers and local government or union sponsors.

"How-To" Books

There is a massive crop of how-to-do-it books available in your local bookstore, drugstore, airport, and library. Most of these will not make you an expert. They will, however, give you a good introductory sense of the subject—a kind of preknowledge that will at least make you more comfortable with the subject, and will frequently give you references to more serious works. Ask practitioners in the field for the names of books they have found helpful.

Professional Class

Trade and professional societies abound. You can find a national organization dedicated to everything from the preservation of wildflowers to the expansion of hot-air ballooning. These groups usually have staffs of people who know what's going on in the field and can give you references on books and courses. Some offer career placement services.

You can find the names and addresses of associations in your field by going to the library and referring to the *Encyclopedia of Associations*. When you have identified an organization in your field, check the phone directory to see if they have a local chapter. Make contact by phone—you'll get more information faster than by mail—and you can ask questions.

Your Local Library

If you're interested in finding out more about any particular job target area, a stop at the library is mandatory.

Books, periodicals, reference works, and bibliographies will give you direction and insight into your job target field.

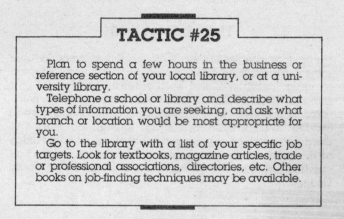

TACTIC #25

Plan to spend a few hours in the business or reference section of your local library, or at a university library.

Telephone a school or library and describe what types of information you are seeking, and ask what branch or location would be most appropriate for you.

Go to the library with a list of your specific job targets. Look for textbooks, magazine articles, trade or professional associations, directories, etc. Other books on job-finding techniques may be available.

Trade School

Most states have good adult training courses in the skilled trades. You can find out about these by contacting local community colleges, state employment services, and libraries. Check the white pages for local and federal listings. There are also over 7,500 private trade and technical schools in the United States specializing in occupations that don't require a college education—from electronic techniques to truck driver to dental hygienist to computer programmer to nurse's aide. Select carefully after a personal visit, and make a few calls to the Better Business Bureau. Contact a potential employer and ask if the school has a good reputation in the field. Most schools are professionally run, provide a good education, and will negotiate a very fair contract. The ones that make the news are poorly run, sell hard, and often push careers in which there may not be much of a future, or in which education can be obtained more effectively elsewhere.

As we've said, always select your job target first, based upon your own interest and skills and job market information, then look for the school. You can obtain a directory of private trade and technical schools by writing to the National Association of Trade and Technical Schools. The address appears at the end of the chapter.

The Midnight Oil

Home study courses are available for almost every possible subject, discipline, vocation, occupation, or fantasy. They are on video, audio, disk, and good old-fashioned print. Don't take the ''learn at home'' route unless you are *fully motivated*. Many start, but few finish. It takes fortitude and good eyesight to learn complex subjects through the mails. But there are valuable courses available that can give you much of the technical knowledge you need in many fields. You can find out more by writing to the National Home Study Council.

Apprenticeship Training

There are about half a million paid apprenticeships available through unions and nonunion shops, which are primarily for the younger members of our workforce who are willing to work hard for a minimal wage. Apprenticeships are the most direct and practical way to enter many crafts and skilled trades.

More than 300 job areas can be reached through the apprenticeship route, from aviation technician and bookbinder to carpenter and upholsterer. If you are interested, contact the local office of your state employment service.

Cooperative Work-Study Programs

One of the most practical and rewarding ways to get an education while furthering career goals is to locate one of the no-nonsense work-study programs available at many "reality-minded" colleges. Usually the programs are set up so that you report to work with a cooperating employer for a portion of the year, then play student for the remaining time. You get paid for your work time by the employer while you develop vocational skills that put you ahead of full-time students in terms of familiarity with and understanding of the work process.

Co-op programs are developed in close coordination with school officials and employers, and will be strongest in the more traditional work areas.

Internship Programs

Many colleges have made internships an integral part of the curriculum, to provide students with a wide experience in an industry that relates to the student's real or provisional career goals. Most of these are unpaid, but offer credit; they get you into highly relevant future work situations, open up doors to good contacts, and get your resume off to a very good start.

Community Colleges

The public two-year community college has taken on an important role in helping late bloomers or atypical students off to a good career start. Most of these colleges offer well-focused, practical programs with a high reality quotient and a strong relationship to career growth and development. Noncredit seminars for special interests of nondegree learners often present interesting and practical pathways for career development. Often these schools have effective career counseling and placement departments, in keeping with their orientation toward a stronger relationship between school and work. Community colleges in general have strong ties with the local community. They may have facilities for aptitude testing and counseling open to community residents who have not matriculated at the school.

The Adult Thing to Do:
Continuing Education

Your work experience is a lifelong affair, like it or not. The need for ongoing learning is also a fundamental part of the fabric. Work can be a constantly growing, expanding relationship, or you can find yourself repeating the same routines year after year, getting progressively more bitter as you wait out the final years of your career.

If this midcareer malaise strikes you, then the main way to break out is to stretch the mind with new challenges, new know-how, and new interests. Life is extended for those who keep on growing and learning. ''Being a self-directed learner is a richly satisfying and interesting thing to do,'' states Peggy Fincher Winters, Internship Director of the Fashion Institute of Technology in New York. ''Many of our students have previous degrees and have had careers in areas which are no longer exciting or challenging to them. They choose to come to FIT to develop new state of the market capabilities in writing and communications, technology, design; or to develop new product knowledge for a chosen industry.''

Visit any organization for a while and you will begin to notice the people whose careers have leveled off. They have that glazed over look that reveals that they have allowed themselves to stop growing. They are now living for weekends and vacation time. From that perspective school looks like one more black hole.

Complaint . . .

''Well, what else can I do? They won't promote a person around this place unless you play hardball politics. Sure, you'll get your 8 percent raise every year. Big deal. Doesn't even match the cost of living. Yes, I'd like to have more responsibility, but management plays favorites. They promoted that young black woman right over my head. I wouldn't want to look into *that* promotion too closely! They said it was because she learned how to operate the Macintosh Desk Communicator; went to classes on her own and all that. How's a person supposed to go to school three nights a week and raise a family too? If you ask me, her promotion doesn't have anything to do with that. Well, they can do what they want with their computers. I'll mind my own business and get my job done, and that's all they need to know about me.''

Beyond complaints . . .

Sour grapes are a product of sitting too long in the same place. If you don't continue to expand your skills, you will definitely reach a level where you are stuck. An ongoing expansion of your skills, abilities, and interests is almost a guarantee of expanded work satisfaction and pleasure. More work satisfaction and a bigger paycheck grow out of your ability to solve more problems, and your ability to solve more problems expands as you acquire more tools—more knowledge and skills.

Continuing education is one of the fastest-growing areas in the educational field. Our world is moving so quickly that people need new ways to supplement their knowledge or to obtain and retain highly marketable capabilities.

There are exciting continuing education programs in every city in this country. And the reasons for your enrolling are numerous.

Consider that you will be studying with people who are interested in the same field that you are. Consider that these co-students may already be employed or soon be employed in that field. A great place to make new additions to your network.

Establish good contact not only with your classmates, but with your teachers as well. The instructors in these courses are frequently practitioners or professionals who have come up against the very challenges you may find.

Who is enrolling:

- The very large and growing segment of our population who have discovered that their first rounds with the learning process did not prepare them for the ever more demanding workplace needs.
- Ex-homemakers who are looking for their first jobs and need direction.

- People who are looking to make a midlife career change.
- People who may be intimidated by large universities or who prefer the lower tuitions and smaller classroom situations of continuing education courses.
- Professionals needing to upgrade their credentials. (The National Board of Certified Counselors now requires 60 hours of continuing education from their members. New York State recently passed a law requiring all CPAs to have 120 hours of continuing education.)
- People like you.

Currently popular courses—subject to quick change—include:

- Communications/media arts
- Starting your own business
- Career seminars
- Computers—from spreadsheets to desktop publishing
- Personal growth (art therapy to Zen)
- Real estate (brokerage and sales)
- Paralegal

If you haven't been to school for a while, ease in by taking a course or two that grabs you by your interests, and gets you involved again. Once the gray matter is kneaded a bit, then find a good counselor or assessment center to test new aptitudes for further development. Basic Rule: If you keep the learning related to your interests, and keep your ideal career visions in sight, the learning/earning process will deliver a ten-to-one return on investment.

These are just a few offerings. The list goes on and on, involving everything imaginable from "healing foods" cooking to Chinese watercolor painting. The only limit is your imagination. If you can imagine it, then you should know that there are people out there studying it.

Contact your local board of education, community college, or four-year college. Counseling on the best program of study for you is usually provided free of charge. Find out what they have to offer.

Keep learning. Keep earning.

TACTIC #26

List your most recent job or jobs, or your entry-level job targets *at* the entry level. Below, list an expanded position you would like to be in three years from now, and below that a five-year goal.

To the right of these listings, write down some of the specific skills you feel you need to make your three- or five-year jumps. Then, on the far right-hand side, list where you think you can obtain the training or develop the necessary skills.

Reminders and References

REMINDER

Using education as a tool to support *your own* life goals is an entirely different experience from getting educated to do something that someone else wants you to do.

REFERENCES

New Horizons: The Education and Career Planning Guide for Adults. William C. Haponski and Charles E. McCabe. Peterson's Guides, Princeton, NJ, 1985.

Directory of Career Training and Development Programs. Ready Reference Press, Santa Monica, CA, 1986.

The Professional Trade Association Job Finder. S. N. Feingold. Garrett Park Press, Garrett Park, MD, 1983.

Happier by Degrees: A College Re-entry Guide for Women. Pam Mendelsohn, Ten Speed Press, Berkeley, CA, 1986.

Working Capital: Coordinated Human Investment: Directions for the 90's, final report of the Job Training Partnership Act Advisory Committee to the Secretary of Labor. 1989.

OTHER RESOURCES

For apprenticeship training, write to:
    Bureau of Apprenticeship and Training
    US Department of Labor
    200 Constitution Avenue, NW
    Washington, DC 20210

For schools offering co-op programs:
    Cooperative Education Association
    655 15th Street, NW
    Washington, DC 20005

For free directory of trade and technical schools:
    National Association of Trade and Technical Schools
    2251 Wisconsin Avenue, NW, #200
    Washington, DC 20007

For information on home-study courses:
    National Home Study Council
    1601 18th Street, NW
    Washington, DC 20009

6

Inside the Hidden Job Market

We all know what to do when looking for a job. You get the help-wanted section of your largest local newspaper, pour a cup of coffee, sit down at the kitchen table with pen in hand, and circle the advertised jobs that seem to fit your idea of yourself and what you should be looking for.

If you've ever looked for a job, you are familiar with your own version of the scene: the hope that you will find exactly what you are looking for, the mystery about some of the listings, the obscurity of many of the terms, the disappointment over jobs that seem just right but require more education or moving to another state, and the frustration of knowing that thousands of other job seekers are poring over the same newsprint, copying down the same names and addresses, mailing resumes to the same box numbers. The futility of it all!

This repetitious, passive, and unimaginative approach to your future worklife makes you feel powerless. But what to do, where to go, who are the right people, what are the right jobs? How do you get out of this rut? HELP!

Help is on the way. Put down your ballpoints, fold up your newspapers, gather around and listen to the secrets of the Hidden Job Market: a gold mine of jobs that haven't been advertised yet, but are very real—and, in many cases, are just what you are looking for. In this chapter we will show you how to locate specific unadvertised positions that fit the job targets you have selected. But first let's back up and look at the system by which jobs are created and filled in the first place.

The Employment Process

It's time to expand your thinking about jobs, what they are, and where they come from. How it happens that Bruce Kirkland calls personnel one Monday morning and asks them to help him find three new researchers, or why, after months of no employment advertising, IBM suddenly runs a full-page ad in *The New York Times* for a variety of technical talent. When you know how the employment process works, you will be able to discover openings long before they become public record.

What creates job openings? Almost any productive business activity does. For example:

New applications of technology
Increased consumer demand
Reorganization and leveraged buyouts
Opening new markets
Political realignments
New inventions
New legislation
Environmental challenges
Social trends
Plant relocations
Retirement
New management

Literally everything that influences this wild, wobbly world of ours is reflected in the workworld. If we discover that the Russians and the Mafia are monitoring our microwave communications system, within months 50 newly hired communications engineers are working on the problem. When a craze like skateboarding takes hold in upper Minnesota and receives national media exposure, stand back; within six months there are dozens of small firms designing, manufacturing, promoting, and selling skateboards, and 1,500 people are employed in a new industry.

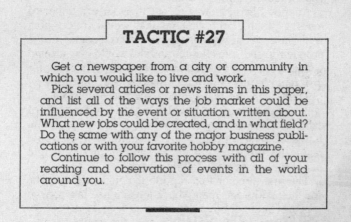

TACTIC #27

Get a newspaper from a city or community in which you would like to live and work.

Pick several articles or news items in this paper, and list all of the ways the job market could be influenced by the event or situation written about. What new jobs could be created, and in what field? Do the same with any of the major business publications or with your favorite hobby magazine.

Continue to follow this process with all of your reading and observation of events in the world around you.

Virtually anything you read about in the morning paper has influenced someone's job by the time you sit down to dinner that night. There is virtually no difference between this daily soap opera we call life and the job market; they are just different perceptions of the same thing. WORK IS LIFE. It isn't just today's classifieds.

Just as boxes on the market shelves reveal very little about the creation, testing, manufacture, and promoting of new products, help-wanted advertisements tell next to nothing about the hiring process. These ads are the final step in a sometimes long and involved series of events that you should know about. Tune in to this real-life work story:

HENSLEY CAPEHART—An Opening in the Hidden Job Market

Although Suzie lacked experience, I liked her. She had a terrific personality, worked hard, and paid attention when I talked or gave instructions.

I thought it was just a matter of some training. Looking back, I see that when I interviewed her I pretty much gave the job away. I didn't really probe to see if she had what it took to do the work.

Anyhow, her job was to put together a number of reports, graphs, and statistics that would reflect how well our division was doing. We would feed her all the production and sales figures and she would play around with them and give us pictures of how we were doing for different months in different regions. Stuff like that.

There was one major report she had to put out that was supposed to be in my boss's hands by the tenth of each month, which means that I needed it by the eighth. It was the most important part of her job, since we would read sales programs, inventory, and hiring plans right out of the information in this report.

The first three or four reports she did were fine. She was helped by the man whose job she had taken, who was moving to another department.

(January) In January I didn't get the report on time. When I finally received it, it was four days late, and had a few errors that took a day to correct.

(February) The next month's report was also late, and had some errors that, frankly, I also missed, but that my boss was quick to point out. I was beginning to get worried.

(April) The March and April reports made it on time, but were not organized according to the form we had decided upon. They didn't look good, but I passed them through rather than delay them. This is when I had my first serious talk with Suzie. I told her that she would have to do a better job. As I told her, I saw this glassy, defiant look come over her eyes, and I knew inside that the end was near. But I didn't really face it realistically.

(June) June was the last straw. Suzie was out sick on the day I should have had her report, and when I found it on her desk in rough form, I saw how confusing the whole thing was to her. It took us two full days to piece it together. Late again. For the last time, I vowed.

(July) It took me three weeks to tell Suzie that I was going to replace her in the job. I never have been very

good at firing people. I know I'm too much of a nice guy, but I don't like to put a person through that. I gave her one month's notice on condition that she work with me on the next report to make sure I knew all of the steps. The first thing I did was to put out the word in our department that we were in the market for a new analyst. I also dug out the applications from the past fall when we had last interviewed. I told a few of my friends, and posted the position.

(August) By the middle of August I had three interviews, and was interested in one person. I invited him back for a second interview, but he couldn't do it right away because he was leaving for a vacation trip. I decided to wait, and did the report myself, since Suzie was gone.

(September) I interviewed a few more people from the files, and the guy who had been on vacation still looked good, so I made him an offer. He thought about it for two weeks, and then surprised me by turning it down. I was really in a bind now, and damn tired of doing these reports myself, so I called personnel.

(October) Last week personnel ran an ad and today we are swamped. We've gotten 300 responses, and more arrive every day. This doesn't count the phone calls that my secretary has fielded for me. We've turned the whole thing over to personnel now, and they will do the initial screening. They should start sending me people to interview in about a week. I can't believe how long this whole thing has taken.

Making Contact Ahead of the Pack

It will normally take anywhere from six weeks to six months or longer for an organization to go from the realization of a need to actually advertising for the position. Most of the time they will have filled the position from within, or from an employee referral, or with someone's friend. This is true of a replacement, or for a situation where the organization is planning to expand, diversify, or move in a different direction.

Jobs exist as needs to be filled long before they show up in classifieds. As a matter of fact, *approximately 85% of the job openings or employment needs that exist on a given day are not advertised in public media.* This is an important piece of information for you as a job seeker, because if you can make contact with potential employers before the jobs get advertised, you have the field to yourself. In the case of Hensley Capehart, for example, you can see that if you had been a competent report writer and had made personal contact with him in April or May, or any time before the ad ran, you would have certainly had an interview, and if you had made a favorable impression, you could have had the job without any competition. Hensley didn't want to go through all that aggravation!

"Hold it," you say. "How do I know whom to contact, and when they have an opening?" A very astute question. Stay right here for the answer.

Turnover—Now and Into the 21st Century

Most organizations experience turnover (people who quit or are terminated) at the rate of 20 to 25% per year. When you add people who change jobs within the firm, the change rate climbs to between 30 to 40%. In corporations with 500 or more employees turnover has been traditionally somewhat lower, but with the massive rate of mergers and acquisitions among the Fortune 500 group, turnover is creeping up fast. *On the average, jobs change once every three years.* Add to this the fact that organizations are shifting and changing at an exponentially accelerated rate as we head into the new millennium. We hope you get the idea:

The employment picture is not static, but an ongoing flow of opportunity into which an informed, assertive, and confident job seeker can selectively insert her/himself at virtually any time.

But how do I do it?
Keep reading.

The Numbers Game

For example, you are job-targeted as a graphic designer with a particular skill and interest in boating. You estimate that the top 20 firms in the field (boat manufacturers, outboard manufacturers, boating suppliers) each have an average of two full-time graphic designers on staff and that these people probably change jobs around once every four years (25% turnover). Furthermore, you know that in all likelihood management will generally know about upcoming changes at least 90 days before they turn them over to personnel. For all this, you can make the following conclusion:

With a total of 40 positions covered, ten people (25%) will leave or be promoted each year. Because each position will be open for an average of three months, *in any given month* there will be (across the sample group of 20 employers) at least two projected, unadvertised openings with this job target.

If you are not clear about this, please go back and reread the figures.

An Important Conclusion

You can create a great advantage for yourself in your job target fields if you identify prospective employers not on the basis of employment ads, but by contacting enough of the right people in the right firms and uncovering opportunities that are not (and may never be) public knowledge.

Fear of Trying

People generally have a lot of resistance to being in the job market or changing careers or, for that matter, starting out in any new personal direction. The easy way is the popular way. The shortest route to a job—the one with the least effort and personal confrontation—is the way that most people take. And, as we have said, people don't "own" their jobs. They

TACTIC #28

Pick one or more of your job targets and call someone you've heard of in the field, or call the trade association. Ask them if they know what the general turnover rate in the field is. If they don't know, ask how you can find out. You might call the personnel departments of several employers (although they are often unwilling to admit to high turnover).

are there, frequently, because they *have* to be there. They are stuck with a lingering sense that, somehow, if they had looked a little further and challenged themselves with new experience and new outlook, they would have found something more satisfying—more related to themselves as real people.

GREG ROCKWOOD—A Not-So-Hard Transition

Word processing. Sure I was afraid. I knew absolutely nothing about computers.

Every time I called up a temporary employment agency looking for temp work they asked me did I know all these software word processing programs: Wordperfect, Multimate, Lotus, and on and on. All I could say was I was a good typist. Well, typists they *had* and didn't need any more. They said, "All offices have computers now. We're in the nineties and typewriters are out." Which meant that I was out. Out of work.

Then a friend who knew word processing said, "Why not teach yourself? It's very easy. The basics are in the manuals that come with the software. You can come over here and use mine, or, if I don't have it, we can go to the library to find them. There's even inexpensive books out on them, because everyone is using them."

She pretty much held my hand because even with all

her encouragement I was resistant. Frankly, I could barely find the "on" switch. But you know these companies do make their programs user friendly. Whenever you get stuck, there is always a help button that will show you how to get going again. The manuals are very easy to read and some companies even give you a telephone number to call in case you have any questions. What could be simpler?

Well, to make a long story not so long, I learned word processing in five days! That's right, only five days. And my value as a temp worker was increased by 60 percent. It had led me into learning more about new technology and I value myself much more. I didn't know I could until I did.

Job finding and career changing are high on the stress scale. They are human/social transactions that provoke fear and trembling in young and old, rich or poor, man and woman, successful and unsuccessful. Normally secure people become depressed, worried, and inert. Business planners who can map out corporate plans years in advance approach their own job campaign on a day-to-day basis, and wonder why they aren't seeing more results. Nightmares replace daydreams when people find themselves threatened with the possibility of failure in the job-seeking process. Every interview is a potential rejection. Every phone call holds the possibility of a turndown.

Unless . . .

Unless you are willing to turn the whole thing into a game.

"Some game," you say. "It's easy for you to feel that way. You're not looking for a job. You probably don't have to worry about your next paycheck, or paying the rent. Frankly, all I want is to get a job that pays well and doesn't hassle me so much."

Yes. We hear you. The job search is painful, it *is* threatening to people, it *is* hard work, *and* it is a game if you are willing to play it rather than struggle at it. The thing that makes it heavy is the point of view that jobs are scarce, and that if you are turned down at any stage it is an invalidation of you personally. Both of these thoughts are untrue. There is no scarcity of job opportunity, and most turndowns are simply part of the process. Let's examine the fallacies.

Scarcity

As one experienced employment counselor expressed it recently: "When someone asks me what the unemployment rate is, I ask in return, 'Are you working?' If he says, 'Yes,' I tell him that the unemployment rate is zero. If he isn't working, then I tell him that he's faced with 100 percent unemployment."

Unemployment or employment figures are irrelevant as measures of your own situation or of what you should do about it. As we expressed earlier, most people rarely look beyond the positions advertised in the public job market. When they don't find just what they are looking for, they feel that jobs are scarce. When they respond to an ad and find that there are 100 other applicants, they feel that jobs are scarce. The real truth:

- In the late 1980s the US job market expanded at the rate of over two million new jobs each year.
- Several million people retire from the labor force every year.
- Even with a minimum turnover rate of 20%, an additional 22,000,000 people change jobs each year. Total job openings per year: *over 25 million.*
- With the explosive growth of social, cultural, political, and resource-oriented problems, and the ongoing technological expansion, the range of personal opportunity is expanding daily.
- With a clear sense of your own skills and abilities and the techniques in this book, you can literally create job opportunities for yourself that not only pay you a competitive wage, but also provide you with a solid basis of priceless personal satisfaction.

Turndowns

This may be the most valuable part of the book for you.

Every job campaign looks like this:

NO NO NO NO NO NO NO NO
NO NO NO NO NO NO NO *YES*

If you are a middle-level manager changing careers, your job campaign looks like this:

NO NO NO NO NO NO NO NO
NO NO NO NO NO NO NO *YES*

If you are a housewife reentering the job market, your job campaign looks like this:

NO NO NO NO NO NO NO NO
NO NO NO NO NO NO NO *YES*

If you are a blue-collar worker changing from the construction industry to automotive repair, your job campaign looks like this:

NO NO NO NO NO NO NO NO
NO NO NO NO NO NO NO *YES*

Every job campaign will be a long series of NO's followed by a YES. That is the usual, standard, universal job campaign. And the more willing you are to explore new fields and directions, the more NO's you will create. The problem is that most of us see a turndown as a personal rejection, and are so determined to avoid the NO's that we get stopped between them. We slow down our job campaign to avoid what we see as inherent rejection. So, by resisting the inevitable turndowns, we stretch out the process.

You need to understand that there is virtually nothing you can do to avoid the series of NO's. They are inevitable. Repeat: THEY are INEVITABLE; there is NOTHING you can do. For a high-school or college student, you must be determined to go to *every* business on "Main Street"—not just three or four until you get discouraged.

The process of locating a new job—for anyone—entails putting yourself in a number of situations that will result in your being told "no." This is not a rejection of you personally, just a necessary part of the process.

Now for the key:

The best way to approach the job campaign is for you to actually accelerate the number of NO's you get. Yes . . . accelerate. Consciously set out to create more NO's faster. Get more turndowns by making more attempts. Consider the measure of speed and effectiveness of your job campaign the speed and the number of the NO's you receive. You will start getting YES's that much sooner.

You cannot be harmed by turndowns. There are over 400,000 employers in the United States who employ 50 workers or more; in your own job target areas there are probably thousands of employers. Don't be afraid to waste a few dozen by calling and being turned down. There are plenty more where they came from.

TACTIC #29

Get an 8½" x 11" sheet of paper and type, or have typed, ten rows of ten NO's each.

Post this over the work area from which you will conduct most of your job campaign. Every time you get a turndown or refusal, however slight, cross off another NO on the sheet. Obtain and cross off at least ten NO's per week.

Job Market Research

Here's where the ante starts to go up, because right in here is where you will have to venture outside the comfort of your home, or mountain retreat, or park bench, and start to interact with the outside world. You know, all those grim-faced people who are just waiting to reject you! (Actually, what you'll meet is probably the gray-haired librarian plus a half-dozen experts who are eager to tell you as much as you want to know about a subject, and then some.)

The purpose of job market research is for you to translate

the four job targets you came up with in Tactic #24 into real flesh-and-blood employers—people who can actually make you an offer you can't refuse. We call these people *employer prospects*.

An employer prospect is a person within an organization who, you suspect, normally has someone on staff doing the kind of work you are looking for as a job target. While obtaining prospects' names, you don't know whether or not they now have an opening or even whether they would normally hire someone in your category. You don't know, but you have a pretty good idea.

WALTER COLT—Getting On an Inside Track

I learned how to do it the hard way. I was a very qualified cameraman, I mean I still am a qualified cameraman, but this time last year, I wasn't quite sure. Two years ago I filmed a documentary that got several awards, and was shown at the prestigious Cannes film festival. I thought that would solve my job problems forever, but easy come, easy go. Within a year I was unknown from coast to coast.

The way it works in film is that people get to know who you are by what you've done, and when they are putting together a project that is similar they look you up and negotiate a deal. It's the old standby: ''Don't call us, we'll call you.'' It took me six months to wake up to the fact that the phone wasn't ringing so much anymore, and my friends were all asking me what I'd done recently.

My friend Sylvia, who was in the job market for a more regular-type job, dragged me to a career planning seminar at a local community college. I thought it might be dull, but it gave me some good ideas about my own profession. I decided that I wouldn't wait anymore for fame and fortune to beat a path to my door. I would break all personal precedents and initiate contacts in places where they could use what I have to offer.

I divided my professional targets into three categories: feature films, documentary and news work, and educational and training films. My first objective was to develop a list of at least 25 potential employers or producers in each category. I first contacted the publishers of the basic film trade papers, such as *American Cinematographer, The Hollywood Reporter, Backstage, Theater & Film Casting Weekly, The Filmmakers Newsletter,* and a few others. I visited their offices and got permission to read through back issues of their publications, and to look through their membership directories and other reference materials.

I made friends with one of the editors, and after some discussion he was willing to get me a copy of a mailing list of directors and producers that they had for special promotions. This was a real coup, since I recognized several people I had met before and had forgotten about, and a number of other well-known producers. Many were clearly at-home addresses, so whatever I sent them would probably get read.

The rest is history. I redid my resume, created a powerful cover letter to go with it, and had the envelopes and individualized cover letters typed by Sylvia.

I had this idea that, now that I look at it, was very bold: I decided to have a screening of my big film, and pieces of a few industrial things I had done, and invite producers and directors, and corporate training people, to the screenings. My friends said it wouldn't work, that I should just hang around like them and wait.

I went through with it. I mailed 125 letters and invitations reminding people who I was, and included a good professional resume. Sylvia and I spent four evenings calling people personally and asking them to come.

We had 38 or 40 people show up on two evenings, and it was really successful. I heard from five people over the next few weeks, and am still working on one of the projects. I know that there is a lot of business that will grow out of this naturally, and I'm thinking about doing it again next year. The breakthrough came when I discovered it was so easy to dig up the names of the people I wanted to reach. I'm convinced that with a little

research and some luck, you can find out almost anything.

Sources

The first step in your job market research is to identify the
specific sources of information that would be applicable to
your job targets. The task is to uncover three or four specialized sources, then to dig into these and pull out the names of
potential employers you can contact. After a while you will
begin to realize how many possibilities exist for you to
explore and exploit.

Here are some of the broad categories of source material
easily available and useful in your job campaign:

General Reading

Regular consumer-oriented news magazines and newspapers
in their routine coverage of the world's happenings often do
stories related to a particular growing industry or business, or
an area of technological change. As you read through *Time,
Newsweek,* and your favorite newspaper, clip out articles or
news stories dealing with growth influences in areas in which
you have an interest. Keep these clipping files up to date as
you go through your career and you will have an ongoing
reference of names, organizations, new products, and developments. From the scores of publications available by subscription or at your local newsstand, select those that are most
related to your career and life goals and keep up with them.

The New York Times and *The Wall Street Journal* are
national in scope and particularly strong in career-related
topics. The *National Business Employment Weekly*—published
by *The Wall Street Journal*—is a weekly magazine/newspa-
per with all *Wall Street Journal* employment advertising for
the entire week by region.

Books

There are more books being published now than ever before.
Hundreds of new titles are released every week, and your

local all-purpose bookstore or library can be a major source of information in virtually any field. Nonfiction titles abound, and you will probably find one or more books about almost any area in which you are interested in working. You won't find specific work references in most books, but you will get information about new trends and directions, and the names of people (including authors) who are experts in the field. There are people you can contact.

Trade Publications

Just about every profession, skill area, occupation, or other cross section of human activity has a magazine or newsletter. These trade publications are probably the most valuable single source for finding out what's going on in a career field. From trade journals and other related publications you can find:

Names of key people (authors, editors)
Names of organizations active in the field
New projects
New legislation directly or indirectly related to the area
Classified employment ads
Descriptions of new processes or inventions
Business and financial reports

—and, of course, more personal contacts. You can get the names of publications related to thousands of topics by looking up the subject area in *Standard Rate & Data,* published by Standard Rate & Data Service. Copies are generally available in advertising agencies, and sometimes in libraries.

TACTIC #30

Locate a copy of *Standard Rate & Data, Business Publications,* in the library or borrow an old one from an advertising agency media department.
Look up the topic area of your four job targets, and for each list three or four related publications as sources of information.

Back Issues

By surveying the most recent issues of a trade journal, or by canvassing old newspapers going back as far as a year or two, you can build up a large file of information about potential employers, products, trends, etc. This use of back issues is equivalent to a mini-education in the field.

Some people have had great success contacting employers about last year's or two-year-old job listings. The job was filled 18 months ago, but now the person is being promoted, or he is not working out, or the job is expanding. Certain employers will advertise and fill the same position year after year.

Membership Associations

There are as many associations of people organized around a common interest as there are specialized publications. Those associations directly or indirectly related to your self-selected job targets can be a major source of information, direction, and even inspiration in your search for employer prospects. Depending upon their size and purpose, associations can provide you with membership directories (people you can call), publications, booklets about new developments, career information, a resource library, lists of employers in the field, and in some cases people who will be willing to sit down with you and answer your questions, give you leads, perhaps even guide you to particular employers.

National associations tend to be headquartered in major cities, but many of them have local chapters or affiliates in smaller cities or towns. Check with someone who is in the field, and she/he can probably steer you to the nearest location. A call to the headquarters office will get you membership information and a list of local chapters and/or members. When you have identified the local group, find out when the next meeting is, and see if you can be invited on a trial basis. At the meeting, collect some phone numbers and permission to call the people you meet at a future time for a 30-minute conversation. Once you have met people personally, the doors start to open faster and wider.

TACTIC #31

Contact your main local area newspaper offices and ask how you can obtain or review back issues of the paper (most keep microfilm files of every issue). Look up several employment sections that are at least a year old and select employment ads for openings in your job target areas. Write down at least 15 of these, using as many back issues as necessary.

Then telephone the potential hiring authority in each of the advertised firms. Without making reference to the ads, present yourself as a person who can contribute a particular value to the job target area. Keep doing this, and you should be able to average one interview for each eight or ten calls. You can do the same research with trade journals.

Directories

The easiest work-related research source to tap into is usually a directory. There are thousands of directories published that can give you an organized listing of almost anything. Once you have located the most appropriate directory, discover how the information is organized and pick off the names and addresses of potential employers. If you have established an intelligent and willing information source in your job target field, ask him or her for the names of some of the most useful directories in the field. But don't stop there; probe further. You will undoubtedly find out about some publications that even your contact isn't aware of.

The three most used business directories are *Standard & Poor's Register of Corporations, Directories & Executives; Dun & Bradstreet Million Dollar Directory* (or *Dun & Bradstreet Middle Market Directory*); and *Thomas' Register*—but don't let your imagination stop there.

Super Directories

There are three volumes that are unknown to perhaps 80% of the job seekers in the land that contain such an immense range of information sources that they can literally turn your job campaign around. These are the *super directories:* master references that you can use to pinpoint other materials that are right on target for your job campaign. The super directories do not provide employer leads of their own, but they will lead you to the publications and groups where you can find the specifics you seek. Do whatever you can to locate these directories, and see how much they will expand your job market research, and thus your entire job campaign.

- *Guide to American Directories* contains complete information on over 5,200 directories in over 200 subjects.
- *Encyclopedia of Associations* lists over 1,200 associations in virtually every field.
- *Standard Rate & Data* has the names and addresses of the trade publications in thousands of fields, listed by topic.

Stand Up and Stretch

In our workshops, when we get to the part about job market research and take out the super directories and other information sources, a marked change starts to come over participants who heretofore have been conscious, attentive, and eager to press through personal barriers and resistance. Eyes start to glaze over, one or two people start to nod. The collective consciousness seems to retreat.

The thought of going to a library for a few hours to thumb through back copies of trade journals, or to look up employers in directories, reactivates old school images of long, boring weekend homework assignments grudgingly pursued while the other kids are outside playing.

We know that right now you would like to look for shortcuts. Ways that you could just make a few phone calls and find out about a terrific job that meets all your standards, and is just down the block. You're tempted to skip this part and move on to resumes and interviews. Anything, as long as you don't have to handle this dull stuff. Right?

We understand. Job market research is like being down at mission control instead of flying high among the stars. Maybe job market research has no sex appeal, but it does have challenge.

And, it works. People who back themselves up with lots of research always cross the finish line laps ahead of those who were too busy answering ads to take the time. In the job search, as in almost every other area of endeavor, nothing pays off like preparation.

We invite you to look upon the research assignments in this book, not simply as homework that has to be done, but as steps in a treasure hunt, tasks that will bring you closer to the hidden job gold *you* want. No one will grade your work, no one will scold you if you don't do it. And we want you to know that *we* know how strong the temptation is to skip ahead. If you are willing to go through the research stages now and build the kind of opportunity base we recommend, we want you to know that it is you who make these pages live, that we wrote them to be used by you, and that we are working together.

Now let's all go back to work!

Yellow Pages

The classified telephone directory is an amazingly valuable research tool. Through it you can uncover an amazing number of things about your job target areas. Not only will this free gold mine of information give you contacts and resources in your city, you can also request a free copy of the classified directory from any other city in the country.

Let's follow the pattern of Sally Archer as she embarks on her telephonic research campaign toward her new job target, as an artists' representative or talent agent:

First ring: Sally discovers that her telephone directory has no listings for talent agents and momentarily considers giving the whole project up.

Second ring: After scanning the index, Sally discovers

three categories that seem to fit: "Theatrical Agencies," "Artists' Agents," and "Theatrical Managers and Producers." "Well, that was easy. They're all here," she thinks.

Third ring: Time for the first phone call. Sally gets up, walks around in a circle, pets the cat, picks up the *TV Guide* and puts it down again. She's anxious, but she *perseveres.* Sally selects a theatrical agency from the listings: International Attractions, sounds good. She dials and then, as the phone starts to ring, quickly hangs up. "Damn, I don't know what I want to say," she mutters to herself.

Fourth ring: Sally writes down three things she wants to find out on her first call: 1) Is there a trade association that she should know about? 2) What publications would be most logical for her to read? 3) What are the qualifications that agencies look for in a talent agent? That's clear. "Okay, let's go." Dial. What's that? A recording! The number has been discontinued! "Grrr-r-r-r . . ."

Fifth ring: Same questions, another agency:

SALLY: Hello, may I speak to one of the agents, please?
VOICE: What's it in reference to?
SALLY: Um—well, I just wanted to get some information.
VOICE: Yes, well perhaps I can help you.
SALLY: Well, I don't know. I wanted to find out about your professional association.
VOICE: Our what?
SALLY: Oh, never mind. (Hangs up.)

Sixth ring: Many more thoughts about this calling project: "Why go through this hassle? People aren't going to give out information. They don't know or care about me. On the other hand, what can I lose? I want to get this information, and I really can take a few more no's. It can't hurt."
Contact

SALLY: Hi, this is Sally Archer. May I speak to one of your agents, please? Someone who specializes in dinner theater engagements.
VOICE: That would be Mr. Este. Can I tell him what it's in reference to?
SALLY: Sure, I'm writing an article about dinner the-

aters in this area, and thought that he could give me some information.

VOICE: Of course. Just a minute please.

ESTE: John Este here.

SALLY: Hi, Mr. Este, this is Sally Archer. I understand that you specialize in dinner theater casts, and this is a field in which I'm doing some personal research, and I wonder if you have a minute.

ESTE: Sure, what do you want to know?

SALLY: Well, frankly, I'm most interested in the process you go through to line up your people. Not just the actors, but, for example, the people in your agency. How does someone get into your business? It must be very difficult to break in.

ESTE: This business? First of all you have to be crazy, and then . . .

(fade out)

EPILOGUE:

Sally got the information she wanted. She wasn't too encouraged at first, but after she made three or four other connections, she started to see that it wasn't at all hopeless.

She learned about the publications, *Billboard* and *Variety,* and the three main unions, Screen Actors Guild (SAG), the American Federation of Television and Radio Artists (AFTRA), and Actors' Equity Association (for the stage, which includes dinner theater). She met three or four people along the way, and talked herself into a good beginning job with an agency that specializes in casting commercials for ad agencies. Even now, she is starting to move toward her target.

Networking Works

Many people keep the fact that they are in the job market a secret. Embarrassment about being unemployed or dissatisfied is part of our work-ethic culture. (Although the wide swath of the corporate raiders has made the fact of nonemployment a more distinguished situation—almost a status symbol—in recent years.) When we let this obsolete attitude take over, and hide the fact, we lose out on one of the most powerful job search tools: personal networks.

When you drop your reticence to talk about your active work search, and instead pass the word loud and clear, you will discover that the majority of your most productive job target leads come from your communications with others— often people you never heard of before the networking. For the 1990s the all-points bulletin is a much more appropriate career strategy than any other.

Networking is the art of connecting yourself through phone, letter, and personal contact to a large number of third-party contacts who might be able to further your aims for research. "Third party" means any person, other than yourself and your ultimate employer, who can aid you in any way to find out about and locate your job targets, and make contact. Third-party networks include your family and close circle of friends, a second-level cadre of people with whom you have a professional relationship, and still yet another outer circle of people whom perhaps you don't even know but can help you put together powerful connections. Let's look at each of the three levels.

LEVEL 1: SUPPORT SYSTEM NETWORK

Blood is thicker than unemployment. Your husband, wife, mother, father, children, uncles, aunts, and cousins all pulling together in the same direction could probably get you elected to public office if you really wanted it. They are eager to see you get what you want. Besides, they are probably tired of hearing you complain about the upcoming job search, and are more than ready to assist you. Here are some of the things your family and circle of close friends can provide. (If you're really clever about it, you'll let them read this section.)

Organizational support: Assistance in setting up a specific day-by-day, week-by-week job campaign plan, and then help you to follow it (with a few nudges in the ribs).

Moral support: Reminding you that who you are has nothing to do with your job title, and nothing to do with whether you are working or not. They can help unplug you from the automatic culture shock that accompanies unemployment or career change.

TACTIC #32

Figure out a suitable weekly budget (not necessarily an austere one) and calculate how long it will realistically take for you to locate a new position that will nurture you.

Add up your liquid assets, subtract your current liabilities, and divide the remainder by the weekly budget. Then compare the number of weeks you are financially prepared for with the number of weeks you estimate your directed job search will take.

If you have a shortfall, rather than try to rush your job campaign (it usually won't work), find a group of relatives who can each put up a small amount every month, which will lessen the load for you and not burden them. Let them see how you have prepared your budget; it will give them confidence in your intentions.

Financial support: Don't be afraid to ask, as far in advance as possible, for the specific financial support you will need to carry you completely through your job campaign. Please don't make the mistake of "sparing" everyone your financial problem and rushing into a crummy job to get the payroll started again. Don't sacrifice long-term satisfaction and fulfillment for short-term financial gain. You and your family will end up suffering for it. If you don't budget for the necessary costs in advance, the financial pressures will grow to the point where they will preoccupy you, resulting in a need for last-minute emergency aid that will put everyone on the spot.

Personal feedback: Your family support system is probably close enough to you that you can get them to keep you in touch with what and how you are presenting yourself to the outside world.

This means telling the truth to you about you, even when it is not what you want to hear. To accomplish this is a major achievement that will pay dividends for you and your family for years. Let your family know that you are willing to know—indeed, that you insist upon knowing—how you can improve your self-presentation. *It is crucial to this level of communication that you do not defend or explain yourself, even when you don't agree with the critique. Just allow the communication to get through to you.* Sample:

YOU: How do you think I am coming across to employers? How can I improve my presentation?

WIFE: Your suit always looks just a little mussed when you go out.

YOU: Thank you, I understand. What else?

WIFE: I think you could use a new haircut.

YOU: Okay, I'll do that. How about the rest of me? Is there anything else?

WIFE: I have never liked those shoes. I think they look old-fashioned.

YOU: All right. What else?

WIFE: I can't think of anything.

YOU: Take another look. How can I improve my appearance or presentation?

WIFE: Well, I really think the whole suit should go. It's four years old, and as I remember it was a cheap one to begin with. You don't look successful in it.

YOU: Great, you're probably right. I appreciate your comments.

And so forth. You must know that all of us have set up such a defense system that it is virtually impossible for our friends to critique us at all. Many of them have tried, and been stopped short by our explanations and justifications.

Once you get the truth detector going in your family, you can feed it questions about your resume, your verbal and nonverbal communications, your assertiveness, your budget, and your overall purpose.

Logistical support: A spouse or parent can help a lot in library research, preparing card files of contacts, canvassing organizations in advance, typing letters, keeping records, scheduling your travel, and keeping you to a time/money budget. Family members can make survey phone calls, take part in role plays, and critique accordingly.

TACTIC #33

Identify one or two people in your life who you feel would be able and willing to critique your personal presentation, and from whom you would be willing to accept feedback.

Write five or six questions to ask, such as: How do you feel I can improve my resume? How would you suggest that I improve my personal appearance to look more successful? Where do you feel I am selling myself short? What do you feel my strongest job-related strength is? What is my weakest point? How can I improve my communication?

After you have organized the questions you want to ask, contact the two people and ask if they would be willing to give you an objective critique even if it involves some negative information. If you sense that they won't do it, find someone else.

An organized work flow with the assistance of a support system member is an inspiration to you to keep the job information flowing clearly.

Scheduling: A family support team can help you keep to your self-imposed schedules and goals. This is best done by positive acknowledgment when the schedule is kept, and a specific critique when targets are missed. The schedule in question should be your *own* schedule that you agree to in advance. Your supporters don't need to berate you if you go astray; they can simply remind you to keep your own agreements.

Role-playing: Later in the book we are going to set up a game for you to play that will give you direct feedback on how you present yourself in interviews. To do these role-play interviews you should enlist the aid of at least two others, one to play the role of employer representative, the other of observer and critic. Start now to think of who these two people might be.

LEVEL 2: THE PROFESSIONAL NETWORK

By "professionals," we mean people whose work carries a certain standing or credibility. For example: consultants, executives or managers, professors, and authors of books or articles in the chosen field.

Professionals have many contacts in their fields. They can generally open doors, get meetings arranged, and questions answered. Because of their positions, personal recommendations can open up many avenues that might not be accessible to you otherwise.

Warning: Treat your professional contacts as though they were face cards in a poker hand. Don't waste the contact relationship with sloppy communication. Resist the temptation to turn them into substitute parents, or to lean on them too heavily with your problems, unless that is already the nature of the relationship.

Do your homework first, have a specific objective in mind, get to the point, and don't waste time. When they have assisted you, acknowledge them with an appropriate thank-you for the information, contacts, and contributions they have made.

Here are some of the kinds of assistance you can get from the professionals in your life:

- Introductions to executives in firms related to your needs
- Knowledge of organizational changes that are not yet public knowledge
- Arranging introduction interviews with authorities in your fields of interest
- Names of growing organizations and the challenges those organizations face
- Knowledge of openings that are about to be announced
- Suggestions about career choices
- Referral to specific information sources
- Resume review and critique
- Recommendations and referrals to particular employers

By staying in touch with the professionals in and around your life, and by letting them know what you are looking for and what you need to know to put your job campaign together in a straightforward and organized way, you will almost invariably increase the range of your work search campaign. Of course, you will still get your share of NO, NO, NO between the YES's, just as we promised you would, but stay with it. If the person doesn't have the information you seek, see if she/he can recommend someone else. Ask if you may follow up with a phone call or letter to them later on. Keep the relationship going, and don't forget to acknowledge the person for his/her time and assistance. Sending flowers or a small gift is not inappropriate if that person helped you in a big way on the road to your job target. People will remember your appreciation.

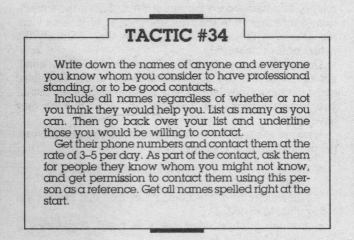

TACTIC #34

Write down the names of anyone and everyone you know whom you consider to have professional standing, or to be good contacts.

Include all names regardless of whether or not you think they would help you. List as many as you can. Then go back over your list and underline those you would be willing to contact.

Get their phone numbers and contact them at the rate of 3–5 per day. As part of the contact, ask them for people they know whom you might not know, and get permission to contact them using this person as a reference. Get all names spelled right at the start.

LEVEL 3: OUTER NETWORK

There's more. As you are beginning to see, there is a universe of outside contacts through which you can expand your knowledge of and contact with the vast hidden job market. A third group of people who can serve as information sources are persons with whom you do not have a personal link. They are people who, by the nature of their business are in daily touch with changes in direction and opportunity in different fields and industries.

This group includes, but is not limited to:

Salespersons
Personnel managers
Editors and publishers of trade publications
Brokers (real estate, financial, insurance)
Employment service employees
Career counselors
College placement officials
Computer users groups

Also include private employment agents, career counseling firms, and executive recruiters.

Picture yourself in the center of a vast information network that includes virtually everyone at any level who has a connection to your job target field. Literally anyone you can reach by phone or mail or in person is a potential source of information from which to develop the names of prospective employers. A major part of the strategy is to grow the networks. One good contact can/will lead to two more—which leads to four, which leads to eight . . . and soon—the universe.

Contacting network members will take some assertiveness on your part. For example, you know that the Aztec Electronics Company in Phoenix, Arizona, is doing the exact kind of work in CAD/CAM components that you have selected in your own job target. Fearlessly you call the sales manager long-distance, person-to-person. You get his name and the call is put through on the first attempt. You introduce yourself as one who is trying to learn more about the field, conducting some research or finding out who's who in the industry. You use the three questions you have prepared in advance and get the information smoothly. Whew. Wipe your brow!

The key to tapping outer circle networks is your willingness to give up your thoughts about why it might not work, such as the fear that you might get rejected (you will, sometimes) and the variety of other excuses that will occur to convince you of the futility of the task.

The job market information you require is out there waiting for you now. The sources are at hand, the third parties are at their desks waiting for the phones to ring, operators are standing by. All is in readiness. Are you willing to do it? (Answer yes or no.)

You have acquired a set of keys for unlocking the hidden job market. By selecting and using these information sources, you will have initiated a process that will result in your discovering and creating rewarding work opportunities. With this knowledge and the experiences it will produce in practice, you can shape your future time after time. What you've learned is the first step. Here's the next step:

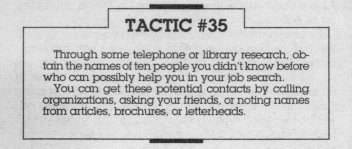

TACTIC #35

Through some telephone or library research, obtain the names of ten people you didn't know before who can possibly help you in your job search.

You can get these potential contacts by calling organizations, asking your friends, or noting names from articles, brochures, or letterheads.

Putting It Together

From all the research sources we have described, you will now start to obtain the names and addresses of prospective employers in your job target fields.

At this point you are simply collecting names and addresses. Except for the occasional stroke of luck, you have no idea whether these employers have jobs available in your target field or not. Soon you will know, but now you are at the broad end of the research funnel. The idea is to build up a quantity of raw material for the refining process that follows.

Make an organized campaign out of this job market research, or you can get swamped in confusion.

1. Decide on a half-dozen or so prime sources from the selection you have gathered, and plan to work on three or four at a time.

2. Purchase the necessary directories and publications, or use them at the library.

3. From your research sources, start a file of 3 x 5 index cards with the names, addresses, and phone numbers of the employers and organizations you plan to contact.

4. Be as specific as you can about each source selected. For example, from a directory of businesses in a particular field, extract only those names located in the geographic areas that interest you, or select only organizations of a particular size or quality.

5. On each employer card, make a note of the source so that you can find out which sources work best for you.

6. Create a *minimum* of 50 cards, 50 potential employers, for each of your job targets before you start the actual calling.

7. When you discover that a particular source is not producing the names you are looking for, switch to a more productive one or change from one job target to another.

When you have 50 employers' names, addresses, and phone numbers for each of your job targets, *stop*.

YOU DID IT. Congratulate yourself. Treat yourself to a day off—go to a movie, bring home a bottle of champagne, take a bubble bath, go to the beach. But only when you've gotten the job done. If you're still getting around to doing your research, sorry, you'll have to save the celebration for later.

TACTIC #36

Set aside ten hours, in three different sessions, for the sole purpose of contacting or using the various sources you have come up with to uncover the employer prospect names you seek. Keep going until you have listed at least 50 employer names in one of your job targets. Enter the name of each employer prospect on a separate 3 x 5 card.

The Hiring Authority

Q: Whom do I want to contact in my job search?
A: The person who can make the decision to hire you.

Q: Whom do I want to send my resume and cover letter to?
A: The person who can make the decision to hire you.
Q: Whom do I want to talk to on the phone about how I might fit into the organization?
A: The person who can make the decision to hire you.
Q: Who is the person who can make the decision to hire me?
A: The person who can make the decision to hire you.
Q: Is it personnel?
A: Sometimes. Not usually.
Q: Is it the company president?
A: Sometimes. Not usually.
Q: How do I find out who it is?
A: Good question. We'll try to help you answer it.

In most organizations, with the exception of government or highly bureaucratic firms, the hiring decision is made by the line supervisor with whom you will work on a day-to-day basis plus, generally, the approval of her/his boss and a recommendation from personnel. In most organizations, if you have the solid backing of the line supervisory or department head, you will get the offer unless someone turns up some skeletons in your broom closet.

This means that the person you want to identify within an organization is the manager or supervisor in charge of the function you wish to perform. In a small organization it may be a department manager or even a vice-president. In a larger firm the supervisor will be further down the line, depending upon your own reporting/salary level. We can't give you a hard-and-fast rule to follow. You will have to find out on your own who the hiring authority is.

How to find out: If you are familiar with the working situation in your job target field, you probably have an idea of the title you seek. If not, call the company switchboard and do what you need to do to get it:

YOU: Hi, this is Louise Derry. I need to know the name of your, uh, I think the title is installation engineer.
SWITCHBOARD: What?
YOU: What is the name of the person who is in charge of the engineering for all your new ventilating installations?

SWITCHBOARD: I'm sure I don't know.

YOU: Do you have an engineering department?

SWITCHBOARD: Just a minute, I'll connect you.

YOU: (Under your breath) Damn . . .

VOICE: Engineering.

YOU: Oh, hi there. This is Louise Derry. Could you give me the name of the person who is in charge of the engineering on all new installations?

VOICE: Would you want military or commercial installations:

YOU: Uh, let's see—commercial.

VOICE: Yes. Well, that would be Mr. Sadek.

YOU: Could you spell that?

VOICE: S-A-D-E-K. Mr. Dwight Sadek.

YOU: Oh, thank you. By the way, could you give me his exact title?

VOICE: Let's see—it's contract manager.

YOU: Thank you very much, and while I've got you on the line, do you know if he reports directly to the marketing manager?

VOICE: I think so. That would be Mr. Alvo. A-L-V-O.

YOU: Great. Thank you.

VOICE: You're welcome.

TACTIC #37

Allocate at least one day's phone calls either by you or someone in your support network, to get the names of the specific hiring authority of each of the firms you have written down on a 3 x 5 card.

Make the calls professional and polite. Avoid talking with the person directly, just get the spelling of their name and their job title. If someone asks why you want to know, say you have some material to send and you want to make sure it gets to the right person.

If you have any difficulty at the switchboard level, have the call transferred to the department itself, or even to the president's office, where you are sure to find someone who knows who is in charge of what.

An Urgent Message From Personnel

"Your tactics appear to leave us out of the hiring process, where we actually play a very valuable part. Please explain or correct this oversight immediately."

Yes. We will.

Personnel departments are very valuable, almost indispensable. They are part of the employment process in virtually all major organizations. In recent years their importance, and the value of their contribution, has expanded considerably in light of sophisticated hiring practices. Their goal is to develop the human resources within the company's organization. They are an absolutely essential support and provide valuable services that are sometimes not fully utilized.

"But wait a minute," you say, "just one minute ago you told us . . ."

Yes. Here's the distinction. In the recruitment and hiring role, a large majority of personnel departments are concerned primarily with filling known or recognized positions that have been forwarded to them by departments with clear needs.

In the system we are presenting here, where you are not chasing after advertised positions but looking for ways to uncover opportunities that haven't been announced, you are more likely to uncover these situations at the line level rather than through personnel.

Eventually you *will* have to meet with someone from personnel in your job search. This might be required even before you meet the person whose interest you stimulated on the phone, or most likely, after a successful meeting with that person, you will be scheduled to meet with personnel.

In some cases, when you are calling in to find out about needs to be filled or unadvertised positions, a secretary or assistant might ask you to call personnel. Try to keep from doing this if you can, and stay with your intention until you talk with the person who would make the hiring decision or would know about future situations.

Q: So, whom do I call?
A: The person who can make the hiring decision.

The Developmental Interview

BRAD JENNINGS—Interest Generates Love

Brad Jennings went to MIT for his undergraduate work in engineering. However, by the time he finished his undergraduate degree it was clear to him that he would not be satisfied being an engineer. He went on instead to Harvard where he obtained a master's degree in English Literature. Shortly thereafter he got a very comfortable job teaching English Literature in a fashionable private boys' school in Connecticut. But even then, with all his success, he still felt restless.

Please don't get me wrong. I've very much enjoyed teaching at the school. I've enjoyed the students and I've always enjoyed the subject. The money has been fairly reasonable and the working conditions very nice. I don't regret for a minute teaching the young; it is very valuable work and we should all become aware of how much better it could be.

But you know, I just reached a point in my life that it was limiting and I realized it was just not for me anymore. It had been, but now it wasn't. I'm one to think that there is no good reason why a person can't do many things in a lifetime. I like challenge, and I like to push myself.

I've always had an interest in computers ever since they exploded on the scene way back in the early eighties. And I've always wanted to try my luck at business. Wasn't there a way to bridge the gap between the two? It seemed others were doing it. I had been reading all sorts of things in the papers about some of the companies marketing new software and hardware. So I finally made the decision to go ahead.

I didn't quit the school right away. I stayed there one

more year while I investigated ways into the market-place.

First I needed information. And I knew I should be talking to people and start learning again. But, I didn't want to go to "regular" school again; I had enough of that. My schooling was to meet the people who were doing it.

I got some basic books and magazines on current computer merchandise and skimmed through them to see what was some of the common terminology. When you go to see people they like it if you've at least made an attempt to learn something on your own.

Not only did I find new words to learn about computers. I found names and addresses of companies marketing different packages in my area. That was a surprise! Why not start from my own backyard?

I made a list of seven companies in my area and notes on the different products they sold. I then made a list of specific questions for each company. I wanted to know how they did things and what was involved. Questions like: How did that get developed? And how is it marketed? Are you developing anything new?

Once I felt prepared I called them up and asked to speak with their marketing director. Or sometimes I just asked for the name of the marketing director and sent off a letter. It all depended on how large the company was and how busy I thought these people would be.

Well, I got three interviews from that initial work and one in particular was interested in my background. She informed me that the computer and technological industries were now growing at a phenomenal rate. In her opinion she thought anyone who had an interest, motivation, and could think for themselves could find a place in that industry. She then proceeded to give me all sorts of information and guidance. She seemed to be having more fun than I was!

I left that interview feeling very positive and with a lot of education about how things work in that industry, in that firm, and with that person. Out of that one interview I had enough to study for the rest of the year that I was still teaching.

The next year when I was officially unemployed I stayed very busy looking for ways to gain experience as a "software marketing analyst." This is someone who identifies and studies the problems involved in bringing new software into the marketplace.

And it was in that year that I discovered that I was not only totally suited for this kind of work, but that I was actually quite valuable to these companies.

It was this recognition that made me decide to start my own consulting firm. I'm not really an expert in computers, or marketing for that matter, but I now know how to put the right technical people together to get a job done. I get to work with many different kinds of people, on a variety of projects; and I get to learn more and more every day. This I find rewarding. But who knows . . . maybe I'll find that in 15 years I'll want to do something else. Did I tell you about my interest in marine life? It's absolutely fascinating. It all started . . .

This story really illustrates a very important point that the European artist Joseph Beuys once made:

"Interest generates love and love generates interest."

Brad didn't go into his career change with the attitude that he was owed anything or that he was looking for more money. He went in because he was truly interested in what he was doing and how he could be of service to others in that way. In doing this he was "infor-mating." He was finding out how to use his information to become part of a community of workers who in turn are part of a larger community.

This conclusion has been confirmed by many in the counseling field. Ultimately, you will find ways of structuring your "infor-mating" interviews, but as you begin, keep the following in mind:

- Find out who the most successful people and organizations are in your job target field.
- Meet as many of them as you can.
- Always have particular questions prepared in advance.
- Never initiate discussions of your job search.

- If they start to talk about possible job openings, appear interested but not needy.
- In every meeting develop the names of at least two other people you can meet.
- Keep your energy and enthusiasm up while remaining professional.
- Be appreciative and respond in a manner appropriate to the assistance you have received.

If you haven't uncovered a particular job possibility that interests you, you have at least gained experience and made valuable contacts for the future. TRY AGAIN. Reorganize your list. Let each person know that you have decided to go for a particular job target where you feel you can make a contribution. Inform them that you are available to them if they are in need of assistance. Keep it light, but remain firmly in control. Communicate as equals.

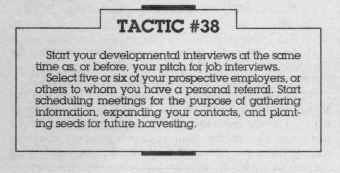

TACTIC #38

Start your developmental interviews at the same time as, or before, your pitch for job interviews.

Select five or six of your prospective employers, or others to whom you have a personal referral. Start scheduling meetings for the purpose of gathering information, expanding your contacts, and planting seeds for future harvesting.

Savoir Faire

To successfully handle the developmental interviewing cycle, you will need to reinforce your natural ability to be with successful people.

Sometimes the tendency, particularly if there is some degree of panic in your job campaign, is to want to throw yourself at the feet of the nearest expert and ask for help. This is a natural and understandable tendency. However, it doesn't help to do that. In fact, that behavior has the opposite effect to what you are trying to do.

Acknowledge your feelings, yes. However, try not to let them overwhelm you to such a point that they put you in a bad light. Showing instability does not inspire confidence. But as you will learn, confidence can only grow out of being challenged, which includes all those moments of doubt and anxiety. It's natural, it's healthy, and you will be the better for going through them. Eventually you'll learn to control them.

Here are some specific steps you can take to offset the pressures associated with the "failure syndrome," which frequently accompanies many people's work search:

- Make an anxiety list. List all the thoughts and feelings associated with yourself and your work search that come to mind, even if you aren't certain whether or not they are true. Don't stop to analyze. List emotions, attitudes, self-images, fears of failure and rejection, and anything else. Stand back and let them flow.
- Redo your list frequently. Anytime you feel stopped or blocked, take a look at your experience and list what you find. Don't repeat things that were on last week's list if they aren't true today.
- Communicate. Find someone in your support system to whom you can communicate your anxiety list, who will be willing to just listen objectively to it and not reinforce it with exaggerated sympathy and pity. Let those persons know your purpose is not to set them up as parent figures, but simply to communicate in an honest and sobering way. Their only role is to receive your communication and acknowledge it.
- After you have written your list and communicated it, ask yourself this question: *Am I willing to allow all of these things to be true in my experience today, and to express myself powerfully anyway?* Don't lie. If the answer is no, then you need to go back and do some more communicating. You need to become the "observer" of your anxieties rather than the victim of them. Once you are able to observe and describe anxieties truthfully and accurately, you won't have to act them out.
- Stay with the process until you feel released.

- Relax before going to the phone or on an interview. Consciously set yourself up for a five-minute silent period in a comfortable chair with a minimum of outside distractions. Uncross your arms and legs and remain in the same position for the entire time. Try it with your eyes open or closed. Don't try to do anything in particular. Just observe your breathing and let your thoughts go by.
- Allow time before career-related meetings to clarify your purpose.
- Dress to win. Put yourself in the best business or work-style clothes you have. Get someone to tell you specifically how you look. Clothes must be fresh and clean, and match the occasion.
- Monitor yourself in meetings. You don't want to talk too much. When you ask questions, stay alert for the answer. Keep your mind from wandering. If you aren't clear about an answer you receive, admit it and ask the question again. Occasionally pause to consider and observe yourself: How are you holding your body? Where are the tensions? Lean back, let yourself go, and

R E L A X.

- Acknowledge the other person in an interview or meeting. Compliment them if it's appropriate, let them experience your appreciation, but not your dependency.
- Consider yourself an equal (you are) in the relationship, and notice any tendencies to play yourself down. Watch out for bragging, which is generally a manifestation of insecurity.
- Hint: do your first interviewing in a geographic location away from your area. You can afford to "blow it" a few times at places you're not really interested in, using what you learn in later interviews that you really care about.
- Refresh your vitality. Get sufficient rest, and don't think about or work on job search-related tasks more than five hours a day. Keep your mind engaged in other areas.
- Make a game out of it.

TACTIC #39

List at least five personal characteristics or attitudes that you feel could get in the way of a fully effective developmental interview campaign.

Be very honest with yourself, and include things about your appearance, your attitude, your emotions or self-image, and any other personal factors that could inhibit you in this cycle.

Job Creation

Jobs are a scarce natural resource to be allocated to a favored few and held back from the young, the old, women, and various minority groups. True or false?

False. This is what "slots" are about, not jobs. A slot is a budgeted opening for a job that has somehow lost its inherent value and become a number on someone's long list. It is work reduced to its most mundane and dehumanized level. Slots can be allocated and distributed by government agencies and other bureaucracies, and parceled out apolitically or charitably. When the president asks Congress to create jobs, he is actually talking about slots.

The people who work in slots hate the work and the people they work for. The people at the top don't have much respect for the people down in the slots either. Slots rob people of a working job.

This book is not about slots, it is about a satisfying work-life.

A job is an opportunity to solve a problem, to create value for others and satisfaction for yourself. A job involves a relationship with the world you live in. A job isn't the duties that describe it, it is the results that are produced.

As we move into the 21st century there is absolutely no limit to the jobs to be done, and those who would have you believe there is a limit are either lying or don't understand the truth about jobs. By the way, most government agencies and many economists and educators don't know about jobs. They look at them as something created by government or big business, rather than as a reflection of the productivity and value of a group of individuals. But all you need to know is that the number of jobs, not slots, available in today's workworld is unlimited.

Q: I don't get it.

A: Good. Is there a limit to the number of jobs available today?

Q: Yes, there is.

A: Great. Who sets the limit?

Q: I don't know, but it's obvious; otherwise more people would be working.

A: What are these people doing to locate jobs?

Q: I don't know. I guess many of them have given up; others are waiting for jobs to be advertised.

A: Yes, so there is a limit to the number of *advertised* jobs.

Q: Right.

A: Now do you see any areas of our economy right now that are experiencing problems?

Q: Are you kidding? It's all screwed up: pollution, prices, energy, health, education. There aren't any good movies around. Even TV stinks.

A: Exactly. But doesn't that mean that there are jobs?

Q: Not as far as I can see.

A: Oh, no? Think of any industry.

Q: Okay, I got one.

A: What is it?

Q: Health food. I got fired from a job in a health food store. They said that there was a recession. Not enough people buying health food these days. At least around here. I tried several other stores—same story.

A: Good example. No jobs in health food stores because of low sales. So what is a problem they face?

Q: What do you mean?

A: What is a problem faced by the health food stores in this area? You just said it.

Q: Oh, a problem they face is low sales.

A: Right. Did you look for a job in sales?

Q: No, I was in purchasing.

A: Do you have any ideas how the stores could increase their sales?

Q: Oh, yeah. There are a lot of things they could do. They don't do any promotion at all. They are very unimaginative in how they display and package their stuff, how they . . .

A: Hold on, do you see that if you got very clear about how a particular store could increase its sales, you could get a job as a salesman or sales manager?

Q: You mean go in and tell them I'm a salesman?

A: Yes.

Q: I hadn't thought of that.

A: That's right. There are an unlimited number of jobs around if you are willing to see them as problem-solving opportunities.

Q: Even in big industries?

A: Particularly in big industries. These guys need all the help they can get. They may lay off ten thousand workers who all end up sitting around waiting for someone else to figure out what to do next.

Q: Well, how come the people who don't have jobs aren't out looking for problems they could solve so they could get back to work?

A: Most of them don't know how. No one ever told them that they could.

Q: Really?

A: Really.

Reminders and References

REMINDERS

- Your future worklife is not in the "help wanted" columns. Believe it.
- Identify prospective employers not on the basis of ads, but by contacting enough people in firms to uncover opportunities that are not public knowledge.
- Every job search is a series of NO's followed by YES. To get what you want, create more NO's faster.

Question: Are you willing to put in some work to get the job that works for you? The investment in job market research will pay you back bountifully in increased job satisfaction and earnings.

REFERENCES

How to Get the Job You Want in 28 Days. Tom Jackson. Hawthorne/Dutton, New York, 1981.

The Network Book: People Connecting with People. Jessica Lipnack and Jeffrey Stamps. Methuen, Portsmouth, NH, 1986.

Business Week—Top 1000 Companies, published annually.

Job Creation in America. David Birch. Free Press, New York, 1987.

Guide for Occupational Exploration. US Government Printing Office, Washington, DC, 1979.

SUPER DIRECTORIES

Guide to American Directories. B. Klein, New York, 1989.

Encyclopedia of Associations. Gale Research, Detroit.

Business Publication Rates & Data. Standard Rate & Data Service, Wilmette, IL.

DIRECTORIES

Standard & Poor's Register of Corporations. Standard & Poor's, 25 Broadway, New York, NY 10004.

Dun & Bradstreet Million Dollar Directory, and *Dun & Bradstreet Middle Market Directory.* Dun & Bradstreet, 299 Park Avenue, New York, NY 10171.

Thomas' Register. Thomas Publishing Company, 1 Penn Plaza, 250 West 34th Street, New York, NY 10119.

7

The Universal
Hiring Rule

The Automatic Work Machine

Most of us are taught to believe that a job is a gift bestowed by society in honor of our having passed successfully from childhood to adulthood. The job is our way of knowing we made it.

When no job is "awarded" we fall into the other side of the equation: feelings of remorse, self-doubt, apathy—common childhood attitudes; the experience of being fired or terminated can turn grown men and women into babies.

Schools relentlessly drive home the message: "Dropouts don't get jobs"; "If you don't study, you won't get a good job." Go to college, study hard, wash behind the ears, do your homework, marry the boss's daughter. A good job is the prize. In counseling circles the underlying message is frequently the same: If you don't have a job, you are in trouble. It's parent/child, doctor/patient all the way. Public service counselors, whose own worklife is frequently entangled in red tape, zero feedback, and next to no acknowledgment, bestow job possibilities like charity. It is not surprising that in the view of a "disadvantaged" applicant, work ends up somewhere between remedial reading and reform school.

This is to let you know that the system is rigged. Work is not the prize. *The reward is the game itself.* And like any other game you play, you will experience a far greater degree of satisfaction and reward if you enjoy playing it than if you are only concerned with keeping score.

Although it has been foretold that the 1990s will produce a strong change in attitude to the role of work in our lives, the fundamental attitudes that drive the work ethic still spring in large part from the Industrial Revolution, when a person's ability to have a fulfilling relationship with the economic world was usurped by an economic system that supported machines more than people. Anyone could tend to the steam engine or loom, or mine the coal, or lay the tracks, or carry the cement, or file the unending flow of paperwork. The age of craft was waning. A job was a job was a job.

The educational system quickly fell in line with the needs of the new factory system. Workers' kids were taught to be workers. Bosses' kids were taught to be bosses. And, unfairly, whole communities of children learned that work was a burden, bore, drudge, or pain.

So, you generally stayed put. Too many job changes were a sign of instability or a disagreeable temperament; and employers weren't looking for *that*. Whatever you did, in the manufacturing-based employment system, you didn't want to get fired. As little as a generation ago, being fired from a job could literally be the end of a career and of the opportunity to participate in life in any terms other than poverty and failure.

In short, the foundations of the employment/education structure that operates for most people today were laid down to support a factory job-oriented system at a time when the prime motivation was increased production and maximized profits, with little concern for worker satisfaction.

New Ways of Working

As a result of generations of conditioning, few of us realize how completely the rules of the game have changed. Particularly if you have experienced any of the recent down-sizing or restructuring arising from the "age of leverage," it is hard to grasp the idea that it is now reasonably easy to identify and locate jobs that combine personal satisfaction and reward and create strong value for both your employer and for you. The old work ethic is being supplanted by new concepts of Career Entrepreneurship—looking at your worklife as an opportunity to go beyond simple job-seeking to opportunity creation. This approach can translate the strongest values of your life into values to others.

Here's one story of two people who just made a lot of "bread" doing just that:

Robert and Gail Go It Alone Making Bread

ROBERT: It was a combination of things that made us move to the country to set up our own bakery, but one kind of experience in particular was the deciding factor: walking through wheat fields. That's right. I love those fields. When you walk through them you see partridges and pheasants—imagine, in a wheat field! And I'm not talking about the wheat fields that have been put to death by pesticides and chemical fertilizers. When I walk through one of these, the ground is hard and unyielding, cracked and dry. But when I walk through a really healthy field, the earth gives under my feet like a sponge. It lives. We wanted this in our lives. I want the bread we make to be made with healthy wheat, and to have this "aliveness" be what others tasted and felt when they bought our loaves.

GAIL: It was hard when we first moved out here five years ago. In the city, Robert was a chef in a restaurant and I was a captain at a hotel. We have two children, and at that time Melissa was four and Jamie was five. We were doing fairly well where we were, but something was missing. Something very real that we both had experienced when we were in these fields or when we lived simply. And we wanted that for our children. So, we moved.

ROBERT: We took over this small vacation house. We love that it is surrounded by mountains. We furnished it with things to make us comfortable in a simple way. We were thrilled to have a real wood stove in the kitchen. We poured our life savings into our lifestyle.

We built the bakery out back with the help of friends. And then borrowed everything we could to make the enterprise work.

GAIL: From that time on, our lives became about creating our own workstyle. It was not easy, and we had to learn a new way of living but we grew to love it. The work itself is its own reward. We can see that what we do matters.

ROBERT: Work starts at 5:00 A.M. The dough is made from stone-ground wheat which has had the bran sifted off to make the powdery cream-colored flour. It feels like grainy silk and releases a nutty aroma when it bakes. The dough rises slowly over a minimum of five and a half to six hours. And we use the traditional method of baking: loaves are cast directly on the floor of the masonry oven, which uses an intense, even heat and steam.

GAIL: You know I've seen Robert work now for over five years making bread six days a week, 40 weeks of the year, and he's still as excited as ever when those loaves come out of the oven. It's not satisfaction with work, it's true love! And when his work is finished, my love affair with the bread can begin. It's my job to get the loaves to market and handle all the millions of details that that involves.

We are not a small operation anymore. We now have 15 employees and sell over 10,000 loaves a week. So any stereotyped image you might have of us with a few loaves peddling them on street corners for loose change is not the case here.

ROBERT: I think our success is in a number of factors. First of all, people have a need for real bread. One taste and you can tell the difference between ours and the stuff that is made in large corporate ovens. In these factories, they accelerate the rising of the dough with chemicals and then pump preservatives into the loaves. Because we can build our own personal values into our work, the only thing we pump into ours is a lot of time and love.

We take it very seriously, not only because it gives us a healthy lifestyle and lots of joy, but also because it is work we feel helps bring balance into the world.

It is important for you to become very, very clear about the opportunities that exist around you, in your own fields of interest. It is your conscious awareness and ability to spot these problems that enables you to navigate the employment market with confidence. That's why we keep coming back to it. It is through the employment process that the world's human resources (or our human resourcefulness) are deployed to address the world's problems and needs. It is the failure of this process that allows the world to remain deep in problems and at the same time have countless millions of people in many nations out of work.

TACTIC #40

There are an enormous number of jobs to be done in the world. A number continually expanding beyond the ability of people to even catalog, let alone fill. Select one of your job targets—close your eyes, and see how many different connections you can make. Then list every specific problem or task you can think of that would be involved in this job target. In other words, analyze the specific components of the job target in terms of the problems that are solved by it.

Q: **May I ask a question?**
A: Yes, what?
Q: Is this supposed to be a book about how I can get my worklife more together?
A: Yes.
Q: I thought so. Well, why are we dealing with all this stuff about world problems, hunger, environment, and so forth? I read the paper. I know that things are all . . . screwed up. I really do. What I want to know about is what to do for me.
A: Okay. You want to get practical.
Q: Yes, I'm getting sleepy with all this stuff.
A: Okay, I'll move on, but we really need to make one more important point first.

Q: All right, but please keep it short. Then I want to know about this universal hiring rule you promised.

A: It's a deal.

One More Important Point

Individuals, schools, government agencies, counselors, and others need to help expand the ability that all people have to deal with their personal career campaigns. The lack of education and understanding in this area, whether it be on the part of lower-class black youths or blue-chip executives, is appalling. It is also costly in terms of the unemployed resources as well as the human downtime, suffering, and economic costs.

The demonstrated fact is that the more trained a person is in the "delivery system," the more able that person is to effectively devote full time to personal job search needs, and the more likely he or she will be to achieve a job that produces personal satisfaction and a contribution to the growth of the society.

The Universal Hiring Rule

Any employer will hire any applicant as long as they are convinced that the hiring will bring more value than it costs.

It's as simple as that. Employers will hire people who they feel will produce value for them. Let it sink in for a minute. Now put it in terms that will make sense to you in light of the problems you have already identified in your job target area:

Apex Videochip would hire me if they felt I could design an attractive box that would cut their shipping costs by 20 percent.

Perry Productions would give me an interview in a moment, and probably hire me, if I showed them how to get new business from the airlines.

Mr. Blax would definitely offer me the job if I could

somehow show him how to have the digital processing team function better. We could probably even earn back my salary by more efficiency on the night shift.

Ms. Goodwin would probably pay me $8.00 an hour for not only babysitting for Kyle, but tutoring him in math and helping him with his homework as well.

TACTIC #41

Think of a potential employer in your job target area (real or imagined). Think of three problems that he probably experiences. Then write down a solution for each problem that you could provide with your own skills.

The Bureaucratic Exception

Let us quickly tell you that there are, unfortunately, a few exceptions to the Universal Hiring Rule. Large governmental structures, and other organizations where hiring is controlled by civil service, or where the ultimate user of your service is not involved in the hiring process, can present obstacles to your communicating the true value you offer. The Universal Hiring Rule works here if you can reach up to a high enough level so you are communicating to someone with the authority to respond to the application and an appreciation of the value you offer. But in many bureaucratic agencies this can be a long hard fight.

If It's So Simple . . .

Listen to what some top corporate recruiters say about the applicants they see:

> I'll swear that this woman I interviewed didn't even have the first idea of what we *did*. She spent most of the time trying to find out about the benefits.
>
> Bruce Bradon, Personnel Interviewer
> Southern Infocom

Seventy-five percent of the college kids we interview never get around to letting us know what they can do for us. They do a good job talking about their future interests and goals, but they forgot to relate them to us.

Alvin Zerkain, Purchasing Manager
Asset Management Corporation

People call me all the time on the phone. "Do you have any openings?" is about standard. If they don't at least have an idea of what they could do for us, I give them the brush-off.

Helen Charles, Owner
Rite Style Boutique Chain

Please tell people, particularly if they are entering the job market for the first time, to read up a bit on what the employer does so they can at least show that they care a little.

Peter Jones
MCI

I guess what happens is that people get all mixed up in their fears and needs. It doesn't help them much. The ones who get the best offers are those who put a little sell in their presentation. Value added is key.

Don Winkler, Director
Citicorp Europe

It is simple. But most job seekers haven't gotten the word that the way to excite interest is to communicate how you, the applicant, can assist the potential employer in achieving results: literally, to communicate how the employer will easily benefit from your association. It isn't necessary for you to have uncovered the secret to an extremely complex problem—just plain old garden-variety problems will do, unless you are in the upper tax brackets. It is the fact that you are willing to deal from a position of support and contribution that makes the biggest impression. This is music to an employer's ears.

Old Favorite Problems to Solve

As we said, the value you communicate doesn't have to be highly technical or represent an ingenious breakthrough in a complicated problem (although if you have it, flaunt it—without, of course, giving away your secrets). You may not even have to do any research, as there are a number of standard problems and needs that apply pretty much across the board:

Cut costs
Make it look better
Get it done more quickly
Increase sales
Expand (virtually anything)
Make the boss look good
Provide more information
Improve the profit picture
Open more territories
Diversify the risks
Cut staff costs
Get government support
Turn around a bad situation
Preserve competitive advantage
Improve the packaging
Avoid potential problems
Organize it
Expedite the workflow
Get faster delivery
Use old things in a new way
Cut downtime
Provide a tax advantage
Meet deadlines easily
Reduce inventories
Put it on computer

TACTIC #42

Back to you and your problem-solving abilities. List three achievements or accomplishments that you have been responsible for in your life—each one at the top of a page. Under each achievement, list all the problem-solving skills that contributed to it. Keep expanding the list of things you can do to produce value for others.

You are, indeed, a unique combination of skills, qualities, interests, abilities, education, training, and accomplishments. There has never been a person just like you, and there never will be another. You have the ability to excel in one or more areas, perhaps in directions you are not even aware of.

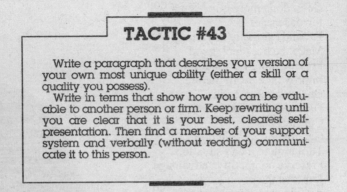

TACTIC #43

Write a paragraph that describes your version of your own most unique ability (either a skill or a quality you possess).

Write in terms that show how you can be valuable to another person or firm. Keep rewriting until you are clear that it is your best, clearest self-presentation. Then find a member of your support system and verbally (without reading) communicate it to this person.

GINNY BOWEN—Hiding Her Pot of Gold

I remember what my dear ol' mum used to say whenever I just got fired from yet another job: "Ginny, you got the luck of the Irish, just like your father; and one day you're going to get that pot of gold. You just keep lookin', luv." And she said it with that thick Irish brogue of hers. Ah, how I miss it. I have a feeling that she's looking down from heaven now as we speak and I can hear that very thing.

And, she was right!

In the eighties, when I was younger and not yet settled in what I really wanted to do, I got those jobs working in offices. Sometimes typing, sometimes filing, sometimes answering phones. It was awful. I wasn't very happy and obviously it showed. I lasted maybe six months. One time on one job I went to lunch and never went back. I just couldn't take the office politics and some of those clowns . . . you know the type: people who get ahead by stepping on the heads of everyone under them. Grrr-r-r-r. It made my blood boil. And I'm not one for holding my temper.

The problem as I now see it is that I thought something would eventually come along on its own. I was drifting, with no direction. In the back of my mind I knew I'd get married (which is what eventually happened), but in the meantime one has to make a living. And I was having a struggle doing that.

Thank God I had a hobby to relieve the pressure. Since I was a little girl, I always enjoyed sewing. I used to sew just for the fun of it; I'd sew little pieces of bright cloth together or I'd make a funny looking animal from cotton and wool. I could sit for hours with a basket of thread and some scraps of cloth. I'd finish something of God knows what and then I'd pretend with it, or I'd wear it, or I'd give it to Mum or Dad or a friend. Sewing was something I never gave up. It was my outlet. And as I got older I'd make hats and clothing.

Well, one fine spring day my friend, Betty, comes over and lays her eyes on this quilt I'd just finished. I was going to give it to a friend for a birthday present. "Where did you get that?" she said. "I made it." "You did?" And she got all excited. She said (and I kid you not), "So this is where you've been hiding your pot of gold, you little red-haired leprechaun!" Obviously, she was saying some magic words. And I didn't stop her. "Why are you wasting your time typing when you could be making quilts for a living? I know hundreds of people who'd die for a handmade quilt like this. I'd pay $500 for a quilt like this." I took her up on the offer.

From that first sale, from that revelation that what I had in my love for sewing was valuable to someone else other than myself, I gained enough insight and confidence to go out and peddle my wares: quilts, scarves, hats . . . you name it.

At first I still had to hold down a regular job, but then that became part-time, and then eventually no job. Slowly I built up a clientele, a career, and I continue to this day because I still love it. The money is like an added bonus. I'd still sew even if there wasn't the money. It would just mean I'd have to get another (ugh) job, because with three little ones around we can't manage on Jamie's paycheck alone.

So I hope that answers your question.

You know it's as my mum used to say: "When you do find your gold, luv, it won't be in anyone else's back-yard; it will be there at the end of the rainbow . . . inside yourself."

What is that thing you can say about yourself that no one else could say quite so clearly? You may not be in touch with it. It's probably covered over with some other skills you think are more practical, or maybe you haven't seen this side of you fully expressed.

Returning to Earning

One of the most important dynamics of the past ten years has been the explosion of women returning to the job market after years away rearing their children.

Many come with feelings of inadequacy. Many have told themselves (or have been told by others) that they are best for raising kids. Many homemakers do not realize the wealth of skills gained in raising a family: organizing, managing, teaching, communication. When faced with an interview, many immediately make a point of saying they don't have any work experience or skills, or that what little they do have is rusty. It often takes a serious confrontation with a trained job counselor or work therapist to push past the illusion of powerlessness to the still valid skills and abilities under the surface.

Feelings of inadequacy are not only experienced by mothers returning to the workforce, but also by recent high school and college graduates. The newly graduated taken as a group, and with growing exceptions, probably hold the record for the lowest levels of self-esteem. It is amazing that after many years of education, many do not have a sense of personal worth and are unaware of their ability or lack of ability.

It's important to get in touch with the aspects in you that can make a unique contribution to the workworld, and to develop ways to let people know about them.

TACTIC #44

Write your own obituary. From your alive and healthy vantage point right now, think of the things you feel you would most like to be remembered for when you pass on.

Write the obit in the past tense starting with the words, "She (he) is most remembered for her work in . . ." and write at least half a page. *This exercise might seem a bit morbid, but it is a good way to gain a fresh perspective.*

The Universal Hiring Rule (Applied)

Here are six specific steps the following of which will result in your obtaining relevant job offers.

1. Be clear and certain about your job targets.

2. Research the names of all the employers related to your job target areas. There are probably thousands.

3. Find out what problems or opportunities exist within these employer types.

4. Define your abilities in terms that address the solution of the recognized problems.

5. Identify the persons most concerned with the recognized problems/opportunities within the job target area.

6. Clearly communicate your relevant problem-solving abilities (#4 above) to this hiring authority in a way that gets him or her to recognize the specific value you offer.

These six important steps are a major foundation for this book. They are also the foundation for a system that will allow you to move comfortably and effectively into any workplace.

Let's follow these six steps in more detail:

1. Be Clear and Certain About Your Job Targets

By this time, if you have followed the tactics concurrently with the text (if you haven't done the tactics yet, stay with us here anyway), you will have looked within yourself and located elements of personal interest and satisfaction leading to several specific job targets you are willing to pursue. You must make these targets real for yourself so you can focus your energies on them.

Without a job target to go after, you will be tempted to change your direction each time you run into an obstacle. And unless you confront obstacles with energy born of certainty, you won't get through them.

2. Research the Names of All the Employers Related to Your Job Target Areas

We live in the world's most populous job market, one in which thousands of new work opportunities are created each day—365 days a year. This economic engine is fueled by innovation, imagination, and entrepreneurship. As inventors of the free economy, we continue to surprise ourselves with the fresh new ideas that nurture growth. As a career entrepreneur, you will uncover thousands of new employer possibilities in trade publications, directories, and other research sources.

3. Discover What the Employers in Your Job Target Field Care About

This area of problem identification has been discussed several times, and will undoubtedly show up again before we are through. If you can go beyond the language into your personal experience of this proposition, you will vastly expand your ability to master the workworld, or in practical terms, *to make more money and have more fun.*

It is important to get away from the idea that problems are "heavy" and to be avoided. *All human endeavor exists in the context of problems to be solved.* That's the name of the game. Without any problems to solve, there is no game.

Where we get stuck is in staying with the same old problems year after year. It's as though we were afraid to give them up and move on. Look around you and you'll see that in our private lives, as well as at work, we are tenaciously clinging to the same old patterns:

- After five years together, Mary and John are still trying to work out an agreeable way to make household decisions.
- Brad and Harry still haven't resolved their boyhood struggle to beat one another in sports.
- Helen Sparkes is still trying to lose weight. She's on her tenth diet.
- George Siegel is handling the same accounts he had three years ago.
- Ozzie and Sue are still looking for work as a comedy team. They go out on four or five auditions a month, and haven't had a gig in six months.

When you solve a problem, wrap it up, and put it away, you have completed your involvement with it and can move on to another more challenging game. New energy is released.

As a problem solver, your task is to identify a problem, systematically, disregard the elements of the situation that *are* working properly, then objectively examine the parts that aren't working. Close to 75% of the movement toward solution is identification and narrowing down. Once the key misalignment, or break in communication or unconsciousness is clearly seen, the solution is often rather easy to uncover or design.

A problem is not necessarily something that is going wrong. It can be the realization that things are not working to their optimal usefulness. A desired condition may not be realized and those involved may "learn to live with it." However, this can lead to complication further down the line and it is best to address things when they are in a manageable state rather than when they get out of hand. Always working toward the betterment of conditions is a way of remaining fluid.

You don't have to know about the particular problems of a specific company to be able to communicate your value, although it helps. If you know what is going on in the industry, you can make an educated guess as to the issues that are facing a particular company or individual involved in that industry.

Telephone people who are knowledgeable about the job target field. Find out from them what is going on, what issues people are talking about, what new strategic directions or market shifts are occurring. Talk with trade association executives, editors of publications, experts, teachers, veterans, newcomers. Listen and take good notes.

Once you have identified information leads, the key to getting expert information is your willingness to place an intelligent phone call. Consider in advance how the person on the other end of the line will be able to assist you. Yes, it will frequently take several calls to get the information you want. Persevere. Remember how the job campaign looks: It's NO NO NO NO NO NO, ditto 20 times, and then a big YES!— eventually you will be placed in contact with someone who knows what you are looking for and can help. This one internal resource person is all you need to make the whole task worthwhile.

We are discussing life management skills. They will increase your ability to control your life while you integrate with a larger community of interesting and interested people. Eventually, you in your turn will become that "other" person on the end of the line as someone calls you for information and assistance. People helping people.

TACTIC #45

Gather the names and locations of at least ten experts in one or more of your job target fields. Do this by phoning someone you were referred to or whose name you found in a reference article.

Ask that person for the names of others with expertise in the field. Don't stop until you have the names and phone numbers of at least ten experts. These names will be a strong backup resource for you when you need to know where to find something or someone in your field.

4. Define and Acknowledge Your Specific Ability to Contribute to the Solution of the Recognized Problems

We didn't say *solve it,* we said *contribute to the solution.* You don't need all the answers before getting on with the job campaign. The mere fact that you are willing to demonstrate an interest and ability in the area will put you ahead of most others, whose primary communication to employers is need and dependency. What works is for the potential employer to realize that your purpose in the relationship is to assist him in reaching objectives.

To accomplish this, you need to be clear about your own capabilities and skills, and learn to frame them in words and phrases that you can communicate powerfully.

Barrier: *People generally don't know all they can do. We are not fully in touch with our abilities.* "Don't boast," our mothers said. "Won't you ever learn?" said Father. "How many times do I have to tell you?" the teachers repeat. "You're stupid!" we hear.

We live in a culture that doesn't know how to acknowledge small everyday accomplishments and achievements. As a result, many of us have lost sight of them in ourselves. This is particularly true of those of us who are entering or reentering the job market. Self-esteem is in the pits. We've got it set in our minds that somehow the people "out there" with good salaries, attractive secretaries, private offices, and generous expense accounts have all the answers. "They know!"

Secret: They don't know. It would shock and alarm you to find out how much pretense is in front of how much ignorance in the workworld. People who look like they know what's going on don't necessarily. It is more and more frequently proven that experience is not a measure of potential work success. Many people are stuck at a level of competence in which their jobs become replays of the same record. Their job is to find answers, to put out fires, to end failure, and they need all the help they can find.

You are able. Yes. You are able and competent and skilled and proficient, and probably perfect the way you are. Of course, you may not see it that way. You probably think that you *will* be just right—or perfect—only after you have completed five more courses, or gotten a promotion, or practiced your shorthand, or finished a training program. Or when you've managed to find the right mate, or saved enough money, or found the right job. No. That's not it. If you keep looking at all of the next things you need to do to be perfect, you won't ever make it. The list is too long. Your demands are too high. *You are, right now, in your prime.* You will never be more ready than right now to move on. You are reading this book at exactly the right time. The perfect moment.

Q: **There is a part of me that doesn't want to believe you.**

A: Okay. What do you say that?

Q: Because I know I am not perfect and I doubt that I ever will be the way I want to be. But what does it matter? I'm interested in what my next step is and what I can do now. Something practical.

A: Like what?

Q: Like getting a better job.

A: Any job?

Q: No. I did my homework. I know what my targets are. You made sense in that part.

A: Thanks. You have your job targets. That's good. Have you identified potential employers?

Q: Sort of. I've started the research, and I'm making progress. It's pretty boring though, as you said it would be.

A: Yes. Let me ask you something—what do you have to offer an employer?

Q: I think I'm very competent. I communicate well. I don't mind hard work. But I know that there is a lot to learn. I don't think I'm perfect. I don't think this is my prime. Not yet. I've got a lot of good years left.

A: I agree. As I see it, you are at a place where you have developed your skills and abilities to a point, and are getting clear about what you want to do, and what it will take to do it. Right?

Q: Right.

A: Well, that's what perfect looks like for you right now: being willing to be exactly where you are when you are there.

Q: I still don't get it. I haven't arrived, I'm still in the middle of it.

A: What you don't see is that when you are in the middle of something, the perfect place to be *is* in the middle of it.

What you will present to potential employers in your job target field is *the strongest possible description of your skills and abilities, described in terms that relate to solving problems the employer experiences.*

Incorrect: "I'm looking for a job. Do you have anything?"

Correct: "I'd like to show you some designs that you could probably use very profitably."

Incorrect: "I've always been interested in publishing."

Correct: "My layout experience might help you in your new PC series."

Incorrect: "I'm an excellent designer."

Correct: "I can get your manuscript designed with very high quality and right on budget."

Probing for relevant skills: One of the things you will learn in your working experience, if you haven't already, is that even the most complex positions can normally be broken down into relatively simple, easy-to-understand skill components. Of course, the manager or executive holding down a $150,000-per-year position will probably be the last person to admit this. He or she has built up an immense wall of jargon and complications to render the position virtually indecipherable to outsiders. Beneath the facade lie the basic elements of most work transactions:

Planning
Feedback
Correction
Verbal and written communication
Interpersonal relations
Research and analysis
Measuring results
Selling or presenting
Delegating
Organizing

On top of the basics we have just described are, of course, specific technical skills and information.

But in most jobs, the actual application of these technical skills usually accounts for under 20% of the work done, and (be prepared to get a lot of argument here) much of that has been so specifically organized, so fragmented, that new people can pick up the techniques in a very short time. (Obvious exceptions abound: airline pilot, physician, semiconductor designer.)

- A well-paid, experienced office manager confesses that she could teach someone virtually everything he or she would need to know to do her job in six weeks.
- Paramedical and paralegal workers are handling tasks previously done only by doctors and lawyers.
- Technicians are frequently able to handle engineering assignments within particular areas where there has been good on-the-job exposure.
- People who have not been schooled in management techniques frequently turn out to be better qualified to supervise others and produce results than the most prestigious MBAs.

Keep probing for your innate capabilities. These are the building blocks with which even the most elaborate job structures are erected.

Once you have clearly identified and inventoried the basic skills, and are aware of the particular problem areas you wish to address, your task is to clearly express the skills in a way that directs them toward solving the problem.

TACTIC #46

List three activities that you will have to assume in the targeted job position that you don't feel qualified to handle at this time.

Analyze the work that these activities entail. Do they require technical expertise or basic work skills? Separate the technical requirements from what you know you can probably learn within a short amount of time.

5. Identify the Persons Most Concerned with the Recognized Problems/Opportunities Within the Job Target Area

For each problem area within your job target, there is at least one person who cares, one person who would be willing to go out of the way to solve that problem, and seize the opportunities it represents. You may have to track through miles of organizational spaghetti before you reach the place where someone acknowledges responsibility. It may be someone whose own career is tied up with the problem, but it is not always the most obvious person.

We have seen people who you would think would have a strong interest in cleaning up a problem actually perpetuate it—perhaps to sabotage their boss, or to hold on to their jobs.

But someone ultimately takes responsibility for that problem. It is your job for the moment to know the players involved and how the problem can be approached. When you find that person in the organization, you may discover that you are a vital asset to him or her (and *vice versa*).

ELENA TAYLOR—The Importance of Implied Referrals

Elena Taylor knew she had what it took to become a first-rate actress and director. She was a prize winner at college, and in two years of local community theater before she married and had children.

From time to time, over the 18 years during which she raised her boys Andy and Chris, she'd fantasize about that career she almost had but gave up to have a family.

But with the boys grown, she had new time to herself. It didn't take her long to decide to make a real effort to return to the stage. Elena said she felt rusty and, except for the odd school production, hadn't done anything serious in a very long time. However, she knew it wasn't experience that really counted in the theater but basic know-how and creativity. And as a mother of two imaginative children she felt she had all the creativity one could need. Much of the know-how she remembered and refreshed by a local community college theater course.

She had kept abreast of current productions and subscribed to a number of important theater journals and reviews. Through the years it remained her hobby: reading theater, seeing theater, and once she even wrote a play. Now she was ready to unleash what she put on hold 18 years ago.

Elena researched for six months looking for small theater companies that hired guest directors for their summer theater seasons. She knew that if she could get some work during the summer season when the competition isn't so great she could then work her way up. She realized she needed to prove herself first, even to these smaller companies.

Elena found six companies in the upstate New York area that did popular shows in the summer, and found out everything she could about these companies: how and why they operated; who was operating them; and how well they were doing. She knew that most companies that are doing really well stick to people who they already know can do the job or to guest artists who have established names, so she narrowed the list down immediately to two companies: a new one that catered mainly to tourists, and another company that had once had a following but because of some poor seasons was having a hard time paying the bills.

Elena crossed the first one off her list because she wasn't interested in a "formula" play. She wanted to be creative and she knew that the tourist attraction play would be very limiting. That left one. She had actually seen this company perform two years ago and remembered not liking it very much. The costumes seemed inappropriate for their performing space and the set crowded the actors too much. The lighting was not good. It was this company she felt she could help and could be a proving ground for her.

Elena wrote to the assistant manager asking for a list of plays that the company had produced since it began in 1985, and copies of reviews, good or bad, from those seasons. She did this without mentioning her intentions. She studied these carefully and then set to work choosing a suitable play for the company, writing up a budget, a three-page description of how she would stage the piece, how she would use the lights, with a simple sketch for scenery. She put this all together in an attractive portfolio.

Elena next contacted three very well-known stage directors she had met on a casual basis years ago. (Two didn't remember her, but she went on anyway.) She met with all three for a short interview, explained her intention, and asked if they would take a look at her portfolio. Two obliged her but the third apologized because he was too busy. The two directors that did take a look both contributed good input.

Elena was now prepared to meet the general manager of the company who was responsible for hiring guest directors. It was a sensitive part of her attempt to return to the stage because if she came on too strong she would alienate, and if she didn't come on strong enough she would miss her opportunity and nine months of work could go down the tubes. In spite of tremendous stage fright, she went on.

She wrote a very short letter to the general manager stating that she was a director and that she was requesting a meeting with the general manager because she was interested in the company. She worded the letter in such a way that she could mention the two well-known directors without seeming to be name-dropping.

Surprisingly, the general manager seemed almost eager to meet her. She attributed her reception to the names of the two directors she included in her letter. From there she said it was a piece of cake. She outlined how she would approach everything. She was prepared for all the questions, and showed an insight into problems that had been plaguing the company for some time.

Two weeks later, Elena was asked if she would like to stage her project for the company's pre-summer season. Without revealing her incredible excitement on the phone, she cordially accepted the offer. She hung up, screamed, laughed, and cried with joy for almost two days!

Implied referral: Something to notice in this last example is the power of having a referral or "implied referral" from someone in the field. It is often necessary to drop a few names to unlock doors that are instinctively closed to outsiders. But these names don't have to be people you know intimately or personally. Look for natural relationships—a supplier, a customer, a higher-level executive in the same firm, a noted authority, a friend, a school chum, a social connection—to reveal to you and introduce you to the power source you need to contact.

TACTIC #47

Accumulate some "power" in your job search. Discover the names of some of the people who can make a difference in you getting what you want; these are people at, or close to, the top in your particular job target.

Follow up on the names you accumulated in Tactic #45, or use other sources to identify two or three influential or recognized people in your area. Then call them and set up a personal meeting at which you can get to know the person and obtain support, information, and referral to potential employers.

6. Communicate Your Relevant Problem-Solving Abilities (from #4 above) to the Appropriate Hiring Authority in a Way That Gets Him or Her to Know the Value You Offer

We are engulfed in the hardware of communications. We have at our fingertips the most elaborate and advanced technologies ever conceived to move information around: video telephones, car fax, high-definition TV, person-to-person Walkmans, modems, microwaves, lasers, satellites, and all the endless products of the communications industries. And still it is almost impossible to get a clear answer to a simple question.

It is obvious that bigger and more complex communications systems have not contributed to a better understanding between people, whether they be parent/child, teacher/student, boss/subordinate, or job seeker/employer. As a matter of fact, with so much information flowing back and forth, it is virtually impossible to hear yourself above the noise.

Employers and job counselors are agreed that the one area in which most job seekers make the poorest showing is in their ability to communicate. Of course, applicants are pretty well agreed that the people who can't communicate well are the employers and job counselors.

Unfortunately, little of what goes on in the employment

process (or in life on the job) is grounded in effective communication. When we review videotapes of employment interviews, for example, what we find is:

Questions that were never answered
Wasted words, taking too long, saying too little
Automatic, careless conversation
Wandering from subject to subject
People not listening
Time taken up with irrelevancies
People not asking directly for the thing they want to know
People only "hearing" the things they already agree with
Applicants not communicating value, but primarily demonstrating their needs

But Is It Communication?

We are so deep in the middle of the communication process that we take it for granted. We never challenge the process itself. At workshops and lectures we often ask the participants to give their answers to the question: *What is communication?* Here are some replies. (As you read them, think to yourself which, if any, *you* feel describes or defines communication.)

Transmitting information
Expressing your feelings
Talking
Understanding another
Telling someone something
Relating to someone
Observing nonverbal signals
Knowing what you want to say, and saying it
Listening

What would you add to the description above? Take a few moments to answer the question from your own experience: *What is communication?* If you have a piece of paper handy, write your answer down; then look at it and see if it is adequate to describe your experience of communicating.

What It Isn't

Talk is not communication: it's just talk. As a matter of fact, if we reduced the amount of talking we did, we would probably experience a marked increase in our communication.

When you examine people's speech in work and social settings, you realize that most talking conveys very little information, is not connected to any clearly defined purpose, and accomplishes very little except to reinforce or remind people of each other's presence. If you mentally step back and observe people at a party or business conference you will begin to see that most of the chatter that goes back and forth is without purpose.

We are talking machines: Jane tells Steve about her skiing trip to Aspen. While Jane is talking, Steve is thinking about his trip to Mount Snow, and deciding what he will say when Jane is finished. When Steve gets to tell his story, Jane is thinking about what she will say to top Steve's story and bring the subject back to herself. After 20 minutes of this they separate and within a quarter of an hour neither knows much, if anything, of what the other party experienced. Little was accomplished in the verbal ping-pong match.

The same noncommunication often occurs in interviews: an unprepared interviewer asks questions. While the applicant is answering, instead of listening, the interviewer is anxiously thinking up the next question. Job seekers, not sure of their footing or preoccupied with their own thoughts, frequently miss important clues in an employer's statements, or do not recognize the real questions underlying the superficial questions of an interviewer.

What, Then, Is Communication?

Communication is the process of being responsible for ensuring that a message is received and re-created.

Read that aloud, and then follow through the elements below.

. . . THE PROCESS OF . . .

Real communication is not automatic. The process takes development, feedback, correction, and adaptation. You must be willing to realize where you are not effective, and improve on those areas.

. . . BEING RESPONSIBLE . . .

This is the key element. A real communicator does what is necessary to get the message received. Most people blame others for not having received their communication: "He never listens," or "She's too stupid," or "You can't talk with anyone over there." This irresponsible approach to communication is like a pilot blaming the wind for a poor landing.

. . . FOR ENSURING . . .

A first step in the communication process is to determine what you must do to get the communication through. If the other party is asleep, awaken them rather than blame them for not listening. If the other person doesn't get your message, take a look at where you failed to penetrate the resistance. Then correct.

. . . THAT A MESSAGE IS RECEIVED

The message is received when the intended party can *re-create* it exactly. That is, if it were repeated to the sender, it would all be there. A message is not necessarily received just because it is transmitted. If you tell an interviewer the details of an accomplishment that you feel was relevant, you may find that only part of the story got through. By obtaining good feedback, you will be able to find out what has been received and what has not. You can then repeat or paraphrase what was missed.

As we said, communication is a *process*.

The 100% Rule

You are 100% responsible for your communication. It is not a 50/50 deal where you get to blame some other person, event, or set of circumstances for your lack of results.

In the 100% game, you tell how well you communicated from what the other person "gets," or receives. If it isn't what you aimed for, you know you need to take corrective action. Be willing to admit it when you don't communicate. In the game of responsible communication, from your point of view the other party has zero responsibility for getting what you want to communicate. You have all of it, and must play from this position. It's 100% to 0%, and you are never the other party.

Listening and Hearing

The flip side of the rule is that *as a listener or receiver of communications you are also 100% responsible.* Yes, we know that appears contradictory. How can you be 100% responsible as a sender of communications and also be 100% responsible as a receiver? Because what you are totally responsible for is the context of the communications. You must be willing to do whatever you need to do to ensure that communication happens.

If you miss your mark, so what! Just go back again. Correct your aim and repeat the communication, or if you are the receiver, ask for the statement to be repeated or restated.

It is virtually impossible for most of us to hear exactly what is being said by another party. We miss the nuances and the subtext, the unarticulated assumptions. In training workshops where interviews are videotaped and played back for review, managers and supervisors who have considered themselves accomplished interviewers are often shocked to see how much they have missed hearing or seeing. The same is true among college students who consider themselves very articulate after several years of post high-school education.

It has long been known in psychological circles that people tend to hear what they want to hear. We pick out of a conversation those things that tend to justify or support our own biases or stereotypes.

Werner Erhard and other authorities on the communication process have observed that the mind is constantly subvocalizing. A "little voice in the head" is constantly judging and evaluating what is in front of it, shuffling hundreds of generally unrelated thoughts, ideas, pictures, suggestions, and reasons, forming an active voice-over on top of our apparent purpose.

Right now, without thinking further about it, close your eyes and, without effort, listen to the voice in your head for a few moments. Go ahead! Do it.

What did you get? Probably the first thing that came up was the question: "What voice?" That was it.

Stop again, and this time, with your eyes open, take a moment to observe the voice-over you carry around in your head.

This mind chatter goes on all the time at conscious, subconscious, and unconscious levels. It is always there—in everyone. There is nothing you can do to stop it. All you can do is acknowledge that it is there and still do whatever is necessary to receive another person's communication. Recognize when your mind wanders, when you don't understand something, or when you miss a point, and clear it up. Asking questions, "Would you mind asking that again? I didn't get all that," is a perfectly acceptable way to clear up missed communications. Do this in your work search and in your personal communications as well.

TACTIC #48

Start to monitor your communication during social conversations or business discussions with co-workers and friends. Observe the "voice in your head" evaluating and judging and pulling your attention from the content of the communication.

Also notice how much unnecessary information you add, and how it dilutes the clarity of what you want to convey. Since it is very difficult to remember to watch your communication, try this: carry a small polished stone or small solid metal object in your pocket for a few weeks. Every time you feel it or see it, use that experience as a trigger device to remind you to observe your communications.

Use good communication techniques to present a particular problem-solving skill, or set of skills, to potential employers in a way that lets them see how they will benefit from your skill. Start to develop these techniques early. If you are in high school or college, don't wait until you're in the work-world! You can start to develop powerful communication skills immediately. Start by rehearsing key phrases and words that will let your listener hear your ideas clearly and concisely. Here are some important guidelines to follow:

- Have a clear idea of the results you wish to produce.
- Prepare key phrases in advance and list them on 3 x 5 cards. Know thoroughly the points you wish to make, but don't read them or repeat them from memory.
- Use direct-action words such as verbs to lead into accomplishments and results. Avoid lengthy windups and introductions.
- Eliminate from your vocabulary tentative expressions like "well," "maybe," "I think I," "sometimes I can," etc.
- If possible, refer to some specific past achievement that will support and add credibility to your presentation.
- Give the person you are talking with the opportunity to get your communication. Don't rush! Remember to pause to allow questions and to LISTEN to the other person. By what they say to you, you can tell how well you are getting through to them.

TACTIC #49

With a tape recorder at hand, identify a real or imagined employer prospect in your job target field. Get a good mental picture of what he or she is looking for, and then turn on the tape.

Ask yourself the question, "Why should I hire you?" and then answer it into the tape. Repeat the process three times, giving different answers, and then play the tape back and listen to it as an employer. See how you, the candidate, communicated to you, the employer. What benefits did you communicate, and how well did you communicate them? Develop your skills to communicate confidence regarding your benefits. Keep repeating your description of your abilities until you hear authority and confidence in the tone of your voice.

The Employment Triangle

There are three parties to the hiring negotiations. You are one. The employing organization is another. The third party is the particular individual who interviews and makes, or influences, the hiring decision. Each may have very different motivations in the negotiation process.

Personal likes and dislikes usually enter the game at some point. In reviewing hundreds of hours of taped interviews, we have heard very few people who can totally put aside their personal biases. Knowing something about the way people react to you will help you to present an appropriate behavior or help you realize why you were rejected. (Don't forget: being rejected may not have anything to do with you.)

Be prepared to provide the right information at the right time without "steamrolling" the person interviewing you. Remember it is a two-way street and you are there to find out as much about them as they are trying to find out about you. Ask a well-thought-out discovery question at the beginning of the communication to avoid making the person feel that you are just a fast talker.

Don't threaten the interviewer. Listen for telltale signs of how things are going. If you feel you have lost the interviewer's attention, ask them that. Your communication to a potential boss or coworker should make it clear, as should your subsequent behavior, that if you are on the team, the team will win. Of course, one of your primary objectives is to make the boss win. *Bosses love to win,* and if they are clear that their relationship with you will let them experience their own victories, then you will find the Universal Hiring Rule working at full power in the direction of good job offers for you.

The Universal Hiring Rule is a statement of reality. It is an important tool that you can use in your job interviews. When employed in the right way with the right information, it is a logical method of making an offer the employer can't refuse.

Reminders and References

REMINDERS

- Name one thing that you can do better than anyone else you know.
- **THE UNIVERSAL HIRING RULE:** *Any employer will hire any individual as long as the employer is convinced it will bring more value than it costs.*
- *Real communication is being 100% responsible for ensuring that a message is received or re-created.*

REFERENCES

Skillful Means—Gentle Ways of Successful Work. Tarthang Tulku. Dharma, Berkeley, CA, 1978.

The Way of the Ronin: A Guide to Career Strategy. Beverly A. Potter, Ph.D. Amacom, New York, 1984.

Winning the Job Interview Game. Jo Dana. Palamino Press, Jamaica, NY, 1985.

The Road Less Traveled. M. Scott Peck, M.D. Simon & Schuster, New York, 1978.

8

The Way In

Checkpoint

Whether you are reading this book to redirect your work-life, to acquire new life skills, or just to confirm what you already know, it is time to take a look at what you have (or haven't) accomplished in the book so far, and evaluate your progress.

In Chapter 1 we examined your worklife as an opportunity to express yourself in a way that creates satisfaction and aliveness for you and contributes value to others. We gave you some updated ideas of what success is and how to have your worklife support your life working. You had the opportunity to see how you could fit into the worklife revolution of the 1990s.

In Chapter 2 you took inventory of your unique problem-solving skills and defined important personal interests. You saw how these both can be combined within your work situation to provide you with challenging new directions and an exciting payoff. You saw that work can satisfy all of you without compromising the values of integrity and dignity. We hope we got through to you that people usually make more money from work they find satisfying.

In Chapter 3 we gave a quick outline of the historical development of jobs and we provided you with informed predictions for the future of the job market. You learned some valuable tools for dealing with the changing world around you and how to take advantage of this change.

In Chapter 4 the focus shifted to specific job targeting. The tactics presented showed you how to apply your interests and skills to the kind of work you would most like to do. We also showed you how to keep in touch with people either in the local neighborhood or globally who can help you find jobs in your target area. You were given advice on how to make and maintain those valuable personal contacts.

In Chapter 5 we showed how the role and place of education and training is changing radically in this decade, along with the changing nature of work itself. We pointed to the necessity to make learning an ongoing lifetime growth relationship—and to keep as much attention on capability development as on career development. The two are interrelated.

In Chapter 6 we led you to the hidden job market, where 85% of the available jobs on any given day can be found, and showed you how to tap into these jobs through job market research.

In Chapter 7 we presented the Universal Hiring Rule, the successful approach to communicating value that few job seekers truly understand. We explored new ways to understand the context of communications, in day-to-day work and everyday life.

In each of these chapters you have had the opportunity to go beyond the printed word and put yourself in the picture—with action. You have had the choice of simply reading the text, and putting it to use as appropriate, or when called for. You have also been invited to use the numbered action tactics step by step as you go along. Perhaps you have chosen a combination—to read several chapters to get the sense where we were taking you, and then go back to do the tactics.

Either position is valid; however, when you get inside the process and practice the tactics you will make this material real for yourself.

At this stage it is important for you to get in touch with the barriers that get in the way of your progress. You are now reaching the stage (that is if you are doing the tactics this time around) where you will move from the introspective, research phase into the action phase of your campaign. You are ready to start contacting people to set up meetings, and you will soon be taking part in interviews, following up to get offers, negotiating a salary, making phone calls, and meeting experts. You will be out in the world and in the job search game. Use the following tactic to crystallize what you have achieved to date and discover what barriers are getting in the way.

TACTIC #50

Get in touch with your resistance to taking action in your job search. List five action steps you now see as necessary in your campaign (making phone calls, seeing people, asking for interviews, etc.).

Under each, indicate the barriers or reasons you have found to avoid taking this action. Now list specific things you can do to overcome this resistance.

Targets, Resume, Action

It has been our experience with thousands of job seekers that a job-finding campaign without the foundation of good personal life planning and job targeting is a waste of time.

Job seekers end up getting into areas that don't interest them and that are dead ends for personal development and growth.

It is a mistake when facing a job change or a new job to simply sit down, crank a sheet of paper into the typewriter, bang out a resume, have it reproduced, and mail out scores of copies. It is also a mistake to do all the introspective work, research dozens of work areas, uncover the names of potential employers, and then lean back and wait for opportunity to knock. It won't. *Opportunity does not knock!*

A well-managed worklife campaign has two different aspects to it: *research* and *action*. Research without action is like a well-planned military campaign in which the troops forget to fire. Action without research brings the troops storming to their feet and running off in different directions. Both action and research are required.

This chapter brings you to the action stage in your job campaign.

Now is the time in the job search process when you first put yourself in a position to be rejected. That's right: *Rejected!* The word sends a shiver down every spine. We all have a serious problem about feeling rejected, ignored, passed over, told "NO." It doesn't matter who you are: the negative power of a potential rejection is virtually universal.

It's valuable here to reinforce the picture we drew earlier of a typical job campaign. Regardless of who you are or what your level of achievement, discipline, age, sex, or race, the standard job campaign looks like this:

NO NO NO NO NO NO
NO NO NO NO NO NO   YES

That's exactly the way it is. The job campaign, by its very nature, is about people not being available, not returning phone calls, not inviting you back, not wanting to talk, and so forth. What you must know in advance is that NO is what you should expect, and that this is not a comment on your worth as a human being. *Rejection is a basic part of the employment process.* The way to really get your campaign going is to *accelerate* the speed at which you are told "no!" Get the no's to happen faster. There is no scarcity of no's; you can get dozens of them, and still have room for lots of yes's. Feel excited and productive when you knock three more no's off your list! You are that much closer to "Yes."

TACTIC #51

Keep a record of the first 10 or 20 turndowns, rejections, or refusals you get.

After each, list your feelings and emotions. Also write down what you see as the "net" practical effect on your job campaign. What behavior does it tend to inhibit? Are you willing to transcend these inhibitions and create new results in your job campaign?

It's worthwhile to stay with this discussion of the "direct action" phase, since this is an area where most of us get stuck. Your assertive step out into the world with your new career direction, along with your hopes, can change to a timid retreat if you aren't willing to handle the inevitable disappointments along the path.

It can be tough to go after what you want. Our "child" selves keep coming through hoping that someone will do it for us. "Uncle Sam will take care of us." "Perhaps the school counselor has the answer." "Perhaps the entry-level job we are in now isn't so bad after all." "Maybe we should listen to the employment agent."

The temptations to quit the game can be severe and deceptive. When there is something you don't really want to face, the world conveniently comes up with a lot of reasons to delay: "There isn't enough time this month." "What about our re-modeling?" "The winter doesn't seem like the best time." "I deserve a short vacation." "I should probably wait until the kids get a little older." The list is endless.

TERRY HARLON—Action Pays Off

I don't know what went out of my life at that point. I was 35 and suddenly the "oomph" of my ambition was gone. I had reached the job in the company I always wanted but it was nothing like I had imagined it would be. I thought the money would be fabulous, but you know, it really wasn't. Sure it sounded like a lot; but now that I had a house, a husband and child to support, there wasn't much left. I felt trapped and growing old quickly.

Thank God for my understanding husband. If Doug hadn't supported me during those days, I'd probably be defeated by now. When I came to him with my decision to quit the firm he put his arms around me and said, "Honey, through thick and thin." What a man!

Next day I went in to see my boss, Henry, and simply told him the truth: I didn't want to find myself at 40-plus doing the same thing I'm doing now. Well, blow me over with a feather, he said, "You know, I don't blame you, Terry. Things have changed a lot since I got into this business. For a young person like you there's a lot of opportunity out there; I'd like to see you take it." Imagine "Horrible Henry" saying something like that!

I was psyched. My boss, my husband, and all my friends were behind me. If my little girl, Jennifer, was old enough she'd probably say, "Whaddya waiting for, Mom. Go get 'em."

Well, I took some time off and did a lot of research into something that I had wanted to do for a long time: design concepts in home electronics. I thought for sure there would be a future in it, especially with my background in architecture and engineering.

When the first rejection letter came I wasn't all that surprised; I figured that it might be a month or two before I landed something that was decent. I waited and patiently read the next three rejection letters with the conviction that I was making the right decision. However, after eight months on unemployment benefits and 35 rejection letters I was wiped out. I had had six interviews in the meantime and not one of them paid off. I was either over- or under-qualified. One firm almost got me at half my current salary because I was beginning to feel desperate.

I'd never felt so unsure of myself. What was wrong? I had done what I thought was expected. I sent out dozens of resumes, but no luck. I had no serious prospects in sight. Things became so bad that I decided to see a job counselor to find out what I was doing wrong.

At first this counselor starts telling me that it wasn't what I was doing *wrong,* but what I *wasn't doing.* I needed to contact more prospects. She then pointed to several areas that I had completely ignored. It was obvious once I heard it from her.

Well, I felt very foolish. I knew almost everything she was saying to me was true. In fact, over the last few months, at one time or another, I had thought my job targets were too restrictive, I just hadn't wanted to expand the risk. If all these things were so obvious, why didn't I follow through with them?

I wrote down everything she said and went home

even more dejected than before. I went right upstairs and poured myself a stiff drink, turned on the tube and just stared at it.

Doug came in, took one look at me. "I said 'through thick and thin,' not through vodka and tonic—what happened?" I told him how awful I was feeling.

He snapped off the TV, dragged me to my desk, literally made me write 100 times, "take action daily," and then watched over me as I made a list of what I needed to do to get the ball rolling again. He said, "No job search, no TV." We laughed, and somehow the cloud over me evaporated.

I stayed with our schedule for 60 more tough days, with Doug and the job counselor coaching me. I simply followed their instructions to the letter, and set aside my feelings. The results were truly amazing—120 new contacts, 15 first interviews, 10 second and third interviews, and 4 good offers. I picked the job I wanted with a small high-tech design firm that I never would have even known about if I hadn't searched deeper into the market. With the right support, and coaching, the barriers seem to disappear, and what seems impossible becomes just a matter of time. Whew!

Working the network.

You know someone, who knows someone, who knows someone who can get you an introduction to almost any employer you want:

- Your cousin Janice went to school with a man who is now a world-class banker with access to many of the financial organizations you are trying to contact.
- Your ex-husband has a customer who is the head of one of the city's top ad agencies. This person could undoubtedly get you introductions at the local newspapers for your job target as a copy editor.
- Your college placement director knows several managers at the local IBM division and could give you the name of someone to call.
- The congresswoman you campaigned for can reach any executive in town, and will do so if properly approached.

• Your sister's co-PTA board members are in touch with many organizations you might wish to contact.

Most people's initial reaction to using personal referrals is the idea that they don't know many "important" people. With a little probing it becomes obvious that they've been very limited in the people they are willing to approach. They have restricted their contacts to direct family or close friends.

When you expand your contacts from personal friends to the friends of your friends, and then the people that these folks know, the numbers start to get interesting. Asking your friends to get in touch with people they know is the key to effective networking. Insist on it. Don't be shy or heroic or try to deal with the world single-handed. Once you've asked them, follow up. Did they make the calls for you? Ask when. The more direct and indirect contacts you create for yourself, the further your network will take you. If you don't believe it, observe the people who are really producing results, and notice how they create and use their own far-flung networks. Powerful people are supported by others.

Some embarrassment creeps in when we think about letting others know we are in the job market and looking for leads. You may not want to look as if you have a problem, but you *do*. However, it's *not* a heavy problem. Everyone else in the job market has the same problem, and the same opportunity for a solution.

Test

If you want to know how your friends will react to your request for assistance in your job campaign, try the following test:

Imagine a specific person, one you would consider calling, *calling you* on the phone and saying: "I'm calling to ask if you would do something for me. I'm thinking of switching careers and want to explore some ideas in your field. I wonder if you can give me the names of some people I could call to get information."

How would you react? Would you cooperate? Do you feel imposed upon? The golden rule to apply is: ask others for the same kinds of support that you would be willing to give them if they asked you.

Our guess is that when approached by someone else you feel no threat. You want to help. People want to help you. People are *very* willing to give information if they are acknowledged and treated with respect and consideration.

TACTIC #52

List five specific job search tasks or problems you feel you could be assisted in by others.

Then list two people from your immediate network who could assist you in accomplishing these tasks or problems. Are you willing to approach these people for their assistance?

Fight Phone Fear

In the eyes of most job seekers, the telephone is a small modern instrument designed to say "no." Competent people seeking jobs are often very reluctant to use the phone to arrange interviews. For instance, salespeople (usually very talkative) all of a sudden turn shy and can't find "the right words," or high-powered executives with lots of experience become nervous and frightened even when talking to receptionists.

Telephoning strangers is considered by many to be hard sell at its worst. All the times we have been turned down for a date, refused admittance to a club, told that the flights were all filled, that a show was sold out, or that our daughter was not accepted by a private school are associated with the phone.

And yet, mastery of the telephone is essential to the success of your work search. The issue needs to be faced squarely and realistically: *Are you willing to make the calls necessary to your job search?* How many? No one can tell in advance. Be prepared to make a *minimum* of 50 to get a sense of the variety of opportunities available to you. And there is no maximum. You will set your own standards and reach for your own goals and targets. The fact is: *the more exploratory calls you make, the more potential job opportunities you will make for yourself.*

Please keep a few things in mind:

- There are almost as many ways of identifying people to contact as there are people to contact. One especially good way is to use mailing lists. These are available from firms that prepare direct mailing lists for targeted products and/or services. You can usually find the names of these firms in the telephone Yellow Pages under mailing-list brokers. There are lists for everything. What follows are the numbers taken from one typical list broker's catalog. Listings for US organizations:

Manufacturing firms	210,646
Management consultants	203,405
Cemeteries	8,591
Dentists	122,643
Greeting card stores	11,116
Interior decorators	19,753
Insurance executives	26,440
Lithographers	3,897

- If you are successfully communicating a potential value to someone, three out of five people will take the time to speak with you.
- When you receive a negative response, it is not directed to you *personally*, it's just part of the process that everyone goes through (NO NO NO NO NO . . . remember?).
- If you organize your contact information in advance, you can easily *complete* 15 calls a day. In ten days this means 150 possibilities for interviews.
- The more calls you make, the more interviews you will get. The more interviews you get, the more job offers you will receive. The more offers you receive, the better the job you can select.

Phone Strategy: Thoroughly complete a good segment of

your research on the names of firms and people you wish to contact *before you begin your calls.* List 25 (minimum) to 50 employer contacts in each of your job target areas on 3 x 5 cards. Plan to do intensive calling—half-day periods minimum—with a day or so between major efforts to refresh, follow up on the results of the calls, take interviews, etc.

Schedule your calling to begin at a particular time, preferably at 8:30 or 9:00 A.M. Set it up so that you are not interrupted or distracted. Call until you have reached five persons, then take a 15-minute break for a cup of coffee or a walk around the block. Return to your calling on schedule, and stay at it for the targeted time. Keep track of the time it takes you to contact people and how long you talk with them. Evaluate how effective your time is being spent on the phone. Learn when to leave a message or stay on the line. Find out the best ways to command the attention of the other person without imposing on them. Go for the interviews.

Make notes on each of your calls and review them often. This will reveal to you what you are doing well and not doing well. Above all, improve your technique with every call you make instead of becoming a machine repeating the same thing over and over again, and getting nowhere fast. At the end of the day review your progress, make notes on the follow-ups or further actions required, congratulate yourself, share the results with a friend or supporter, and then plan the next calling session.

TACTIC #53

Set up the time and space for your calling program.

Allocate sufficient time for you to do the research to list at least 50 employers to call. Follow the instructions detailed above, and make 25 calls. Continue this procedure throughout your job campaign.

What to Say

At this point in your job campaign you should be interested in only one thing: *interviews*. You have done all the preliminary work you need or wish to do. This is it. It is time to set up face-to-face visits with employer targets.

The message you need to communicate to the "prospective" employer is, quite simply, that you have the potential to help him meet his objectives in a way that could be valuable both to his organization and to him personally. *In other words, you will bring him more value than cost.* (The Universal Hiring Rule.)

Here are the steps:

- Preparation: Before the call, have a clear idea whom you're calling, by name and title, and what you want to say. Note this on the 3 x 5 card.
- When the person answers, assuming you get through directly, make sure that she or he is the right individual and that she or he has a few moments to talk. Don't rush into a speech; first establish a two-way communication.

  "Hello, Ms. Marks. This is Bob Rich. Do you have a few moments?"

  If "No":

  "Fine. When would be a good time to call you back to talk to you about your new fisheries contract?"

  "If "Yes":

  "Fine. Is it correct that you are taking over the new fisheries contract?"
- Then, within one minute, say something about yourself that you feel is directly related to a problem or need of that particular employer.

  "I would imagine that this new contract will require people with good underwater photography experience. I have done some work in a very similar project and would like to meet (don't talk about interviews, talk about meetings) in order to show you how I might possibly assist you with this contract."
- At this point, pause to allow the person on the other end of the line to have a reaction, to ask a question, or to raise

an objection (see below). When this occurs, address yourself to the response, restating the main point you wish to make, the benefit you offer. If you note any annoyance or antagonism, don't respond to it argumentatively, simply accept it and continue to communicate your support as clearly as possible.

- Establish credibility. If possible, use the name of a person or organization you know the employer will recognize. Or use facts and figures to strengthen your short presentation.

   "I worked directly with Donna Waracki, the director of the underwater research project, and together we developed a new technique."

- Don't volunteer that you are looking, or have been looking, for a job. Avoid the temptation often displayed by nervous job seekers to lead with negative information: "I've been out looking for work for nine months . . ." or "I don't know much about _____ but would be willing to find out." We're not telling you to lie, simply don't advertise the things you are worried about. You will have one minute to communicate a clear, *irresistible* value.

- Ask for a "meeting" (interview) at a specific time. Do this as lightly as possible, with the intimation that the employer could have a productive, simple half hour with you. Eliminate the "need" from your voice.

   "I would like to meet with you this week, if it's convenient, so we could explore this further. Are you available for coffee Thursday morning?"
   or:
   "It might be a good idea for us to get together next week when I could describe this in more detail. Are you free on Tuesday afternoon?"

- Don't stop at the first NO. There is a popular sales motto that says, "The sale begins when the customer says No." Follow this. Realize that the initial response to almost any new proposition is negative. Allow the response to occur, then restate the benefits or answer the objection clearly and ask again for a meeting.

Meeting Objections

Every step along the way in your job campaign, you will meet resistance from others in the form of reasons why they can't do what you want or grant what you ask for.

These objections are an expected part of your campaign. They are the rule, not the exception. They are virtually automatic. The majority of people, when confronted by an objection from another, will stop in their tracks, apologize, and back off. That is what you will want to do. Don't.

Here is how to handle an objection:

1. Accept it. Don't pretend you didn't hear it or that it is untrue. Don't argue about the objection. Allow the person on the other end of the line to experience that you accepted it.

2. Respond to it with a clear communication of benefit or value that can overcome the objection without denying it.

3. Reintroduce the original request.

Here are three examples of what we mean:

YOU: I'd like to stop by to discuss this with you further at your convenience.

EMPLOYER: Well, to be perfectly honest with you, we are cutting back our staff and I don't think we are looking to hire anyone at this time.

YOU: I see. How unfortunate. I wasn't aware of the cutbacks; however, I know that you are a viable company with a great future, and I know that I could make a good contribution. I have some ideas about marketing you might find valuable; I'll put some information in the mail, and next week I'll call. We could at least meet, and consider the long-term possibilities.

* * * *

YOU: Would it be possible for us to meet next week?

EMPLOYER: I don't think so. You don't have the qualifications that we need right now.

YOU: I see, What are you looking for? I thought my background might be relevant.

EMPLOYER: Well, you don't have experience with the data-base system we use here.

YOU: You know, I have considered that. I believe that the two systems I listed on my resume are very similar to yours and I feel confident in saying that I am a quick learner. And I could even say that by the time of our meeting next week—if you are open to having one—I could review the manuals for your system and have a handle on my ability to learn them in a short time. Are you willing to give this a try?

* * * *

YOU: I think my organizational skills could get your department to work even more effectively than it does now.

EMPLOYER: Well, we've already interviewed enough candidates and we have a couple who seem to be just what we're looking for.

YOU: I can understand why you wouldn't want to interview anyone else. But I'd appreciate having the chance to meet with you briefly just so we can both be sure we're not missing an opportunity, and maybe there is the possibility of working together in the future.

TACTIC #54

List three objections you feel will be raised during the course of your job campaign. Then write down two answers to each objection. When you are satisfied with these answers, role-play them with someone.

The Secretarial Blockade

Many healthy job campaigns have met their abrupt ends when encountering a formidable obstacle: the efficient secretary. The two classic show stoppers—right after you've asked to talk to the potential employer:

"What's this in reference to?"

or

"May I help you?"

can strike fear into the heart of an unprepared caller. Take heart—the secretary is not a monster, and good communication skills will build the right bridge over the obstacle. First: Do *not* blurt out that you are looking for a job, unless you are responding to an advertisement listing the name of the person you are calling. (For most of these strategies, we assume that you are following the approach of creating your own job, out of your self-discovered personal targets.)

Consider that the purpose of your call is not just to look for a job, but to talk to a particular person about a specific topic. So when the secretary says: "What's this in reference to?" simply say: "I want to speak with Mr. Webb about the new cold fusion research project."

When the secretary says: "Can I help you?" instead of saying "No," say, "Yes, perhaps you can. I'm interested in knowing what kind of sampling techniques you will be using," or some other technical point. Chances are you will be referred to the boss for the answer. If the person does know the answer, thank her and ask if you can talk to Mr. Webb about it further, and if this isn't a convenient time, what would be?

The most effective way to get through is to sound as though you *should* be talking to Mr. Webb. In other words, sound professional and confident. After practicing calls to "important" people, you will soon find that your tone of voice will get you through much of the time. Other techniques are:

- Call just before or after normal office hours. Sometimes the boss is in earlier or later than the secretarial staff.
- Ask the organization's switchboard for the direct dial number of the person you want to reach.
- If you don't know who to talk to, call the president's office and ask, "Who would I talk to about _____?" Use this referral to get you past the secretary. When

he asks why you are calling, say Mr. (the president's name)'s office said you should.
- Don't leave your name and number; say that you plan to be out and will call back. This keeps the initiative on your side.

Keep On Trying

The way to get interviews is to keep communicating value to the right people until they start to get it. There are two successful patterns to follow that use the phone call in connection with the cover letter and resume (next chapter). In the first case (most recommended) you call first and then send the resume if you can't get the interview. In the other you send the resume first, then start calling.

Most recommended scenario:

1. Collect the names and phone numbers of 25 firms that you know could hire or have hired someone in a position that is equal or is close to one of your job targets.

2. Identify the hiring authority.

3. Continue to call until you reach that particular person.

4. Communicate a clear value and ask for a meeting. Listen to any objection and answer with a benefit. Ask again for the interview.

5. If the answer is yes, take your resume with you to the interview.

6. If the answer is still no, after you have met at least one objection (you can go for more if you're up to it), ask the employer if you can send a resume. Most will say yes to this. If no, go on to the next prospect.

7. If yes to the resume, prepare a well-thought-out cover letter detailing your specific value, and send it with your resume.

8. Five working days after you have sent the resume, call again to verify if the employer has received it. Quietly repeat the benefit and ask again for a meeting.

Q: **Wait a minute! I'll get the phone slammed on my ear if I do all this calling. Why would anyone hire someone who can't understand the meaning of the word "no"?**

A: Have you tried it?

Q: No, and I doubt that I will. It might work in New York or with sales personalities, but not in the rest of the country and not with shy people like me.

A: How do you know?

Q: Well, if he liked what I had to say, he wouldn't say no.

A: That's not true. People frequently say no at first to almost any new idea. Ask any salesperson. They hear "no" all the time. And they know that their job is to change the "no" to a "yes." You must know that.

Q: Yes, but that's different. They're selling a product, not themselves.

A: They are selling neither. They're selling a benefit and they are communicating through a wall of doubts and skepticism.

Q: But how do you know it's a wall? They might not really need me.

A: The approach we are recommending deals with the projection of value and benefit. The alternative seems to be to dramatize your needs. Which would you rather do?

Q: I don't know. I'm still doubtful. I was never taught to project my value, only my needs. I could project a better image, I guess.

A: Exactly.

TACTIC #55

Establish a definite written schedule for your interview "set up" campaign.

Allocate specific dates and times in advance, and the number of calls you plan to complete on each date. Keep to your schedule. Acknowledge yourself when you meet your targets and note when you don't. If you are consistently missing your schedule, adjust it downward to a level where you can experience success.

Dropping In

It is possible to go into an office building in the center of a busy downtown area, look at the directory of tenants, write down a dozen of their names, get on the elevator, stop by the offices, get brochures, and read them, return and ask for an interview with a particular person, present your abilities, and get a job offer before lunch. We've seen it done. You might even want to try it. It's a little like doing a dozen laps in the swimming pool with your tennis shoes on. It builds muscle. And it can be a rewarding, expanding experience.

Developmental Interviews

It is easier to get interviews for the purpose of obtaining information than for selling yourself. So go after interviews with people in the field who wouldn't mind telling you how things work. Before the interview, prepare a list of questions you need answered. Keep track of the information obtained. Be flattering but not cloying. By building up contacts through an information network, you set yourself up with good contacts and referrals. It is a good first step to actual job interviewing.

The Agency Game

There are many thousands of profit-making placement agencies interested in helping you get a new job. Most of them have an equitable system for charging for their services. If they don't get you placed in a job, there is no fee. In many cases the fee is paid by the hiring employer. Check this first.

So what can you lose? Plenty. If you don't manage the relationship well you could end up in a job that the agency prefers to see you in, not the job you would choose for yourself. Conduct your relations with employment agencies with the same degree of conscious intention as the rest of your job campaign. Otherwise you will lose time, direction, and the personal satisfaction that comes when you are in charge of your own career destiny.

If you manage it properly, however, you can establish a relationship with replacement agencies that expands the dimensions of your self-directed career search. Here's how:

1. *Don't relinquish the responsibility and energy of your job search to a third party.* The employment counselor will often encourage you to leave matters in her or his hands. You may be tempted, but don't do it. Apply the professional standards to all job possibilities whether you found them or the agency found them.

2. *Use placement agencies as* part *of your support system.* To do this, you must identify the areas where they can be most helpful to you. For example, they can usually offer you knowledge of local market conditions, ability to make employer contacts, knowledge of current salary offerings in particular areas, feedback on your resume, and knowledge of specific employers.

3. *Make certain that the employment agent is clear about your job targets.* Don't allow a counselor (who may have an immediate job interview to send you out on) to convince you that you would be better off by changing your target to something more readily available. The temptation can be very strong. Resist it in favor of your own satisfaction-centered targets. If the agency can't or won't support you in *your* goals, find another agency.

4. *Work with the best.* If you feel upon initial contact that an agency or counselor is not providing the top-quality support you expect, tell them. If they don't come up to your standards, find someone who will.

5. *Support the agency that supports you.* Don't dump your job-finding problem in the agency's lap and walk away. Find out what you can do to make their job easier and better. Provide the counselor with copies of a good, well-printed resume. Provide a list of potential employers from your research. Develop a clear statement of your unique selling propositions, the things you offer potential employers that create a clear, irresistible value, and give a copy of it to the counselor.

6. *Keep your agreements.* Stay in communication with the agency and counselor and show up at the interviews you agree to take. Call back and report when you have a change in status or direction. Acknowledge to the counselor the things that he or she has accomplished for you. With acknowledgment and thanks, you can create miracles and motivation.

TACTIC #56

Use some imaginative research techniques to uncover the best personnel agency to work with you in your search.

Do this by calling the personnel departments of several employers in fields related to your job targets and asking them for the names of agencies they work with. Then ask them for the names of specific counselors at these agencies.

Call the agencies and counselors and tell them they were recommended to you by the organizations from which you got their names. This implied referral can get you meetings with the best agency people in your field.

The Executive Suite

Executive search firms specialize in the identification and placement of top-level personnel in salary ranges generally exceeding $75,000 per year.

They charge large fees for their services to the employers who retain them. Executive search firms are not usually considered part of the normal marketplace. They do not provide the depth of job orders or referral information that might be available at an upper-echelon employment agency.

The search firm customarily handles each new assignment separately. Through investigative research techniques similar to those for locating employers described in this book but used to locate applicants, they go after people who are already well employed and entice them to consider new and presumably better opportunities with their client employer.

It is clear that the search firm's client is the employer, and that the employers who are signed up for searches at any particular moment in time are looking for very highly specialized talent. Search firms usually report to the board of directors of a firm, the president, or the vice president. They don't generally work with the personnel department.

You probably won't get specific job referrals from an executive search firm unless you are in a special high-growth area or have impeccable qualifications. However, a relationship with the specific purpose of helping you put your job search in perspective can be valuable, since many of the search consultants are quite knowledgeable in specific fields.

If you are qualified in a high-level professional area, you can possibly establish a conversational relationship with an executive search firm by using a technique similar to the one we discussed above for the identification of placement agencies.

Contact an executive with a firm in a field similar to your own job target. Tell the executive or the executive's secretary that you are interested in getting the name of a search firm and the name of one of the principal search consultants working with the firm. With the names of three or four search firm executives available to you, it should not be too difficult to arrange a meeting in which you can pick the brains of an expert in your job targets field. This meeting will occur because of your ability to use the implied referral technique, a bit of flattering, and the search firms' natural tendency to want to meet people who are "up and coming" in their field.

If you set up such a meeting, go into it with a list of specific questions that someone at this level can help answer for you. You may find it hard to get the names of particular employers; however, indirect referral to reference sources and a good knowledge of which firms are expanding and which are cutting back can speed up your work search.

A good tool to use for finding a firm is the *Directory of Executive Recruiters,* published by *Consultants' News* and revised annually.

Executive Counseling

A frequently asked question: ''Are the services of a private career counselor worth ($750 to $5,000) to assist me with my job campaign?''

We don't know. We've heard from people who have experienced a successful working relationship with career counseling organizations or individuals, and we have heard from people who have been taken in by big promises and small delivery.

Career or ''executive'' counseling firms specialize in assisting job seekers, particularly those who are having difficulty in their job search campaigns, to implement a self-marketing program to employers whose names are provided by the firm itself. The services are provided for a flat negotiated fee, which usually is payable whether you get a new job or not. The services provided vary considerably from firm to firm and from client to client. They can include testing, career planning, resume and cover-letter preparation, identification of employer prospects, and mailings.

The services of an individual—on his or her own—will often be more cost-effective than a counseling organization, since the individual doesn't need to support a high-powered sales organization. Service will vary widely from individual to individual, so definitely check references.

All this can provide a most valuable support to your job campaign if you have been unable to mobilize these activities on your own, but for the average worker it is an expensive substitute for his or her own organized campaign. If you have experienced difficulty getting your job search together, and feel that the organized push of a career counseling service is worth the cost, take the following steps before deciding:

1. Contact two or three separate firms. Compare services and professionalism.

2. Ask to meet the people you would be actually working with in your campaign. They may not resemble the salesperson who signs you up.

3. Find out *specifically* what you will get for your money. If, for example, they promise an employer mailing, find out how large it will be and where the names have come from. If the counseling firm plans to redo your resume, ask to see others they have done.

4. Once you have obtained a clear description of what the firm—or individual—plans to do for you, get it in writing.

5. If the counseling firm boasts of good contacts with employers in your field, ask for the names of some of the firms they have worked with recently and contact one or two employers at random to verify.

6. If you have any suspicion that the career counseling firm is promising more than it will or can deliver, check with your local Better Business Bureau to see if it has received any complaints.

7. Negotiate. It is frequently possible to get the same services for a reduced fee if you are reasonably tough, or eliminate parts of the program that are less valuable to you. Also, see if you can pay in installments, with an agreement that if you change your mind partway through the program you will not be obliged to pay the balance.

8. Do not stop being responsible in your job campaign just because you have engaged someone to assist you. Cooperate fully with the counselor you are working with, assist with whatever supportive research you can do, communicate whatever barriers or problems you face, and do your homework.

College Placement Offices

Schools are becoming increasingly involved in the process by which their students make the transition from academic life to the world of work, although we feel that many programs remain at a level far below what is called for.

Many schools have traditionally split the responsibility for career planning and placement into two departments: *counseling*, testing and measuring aptitudes and values, and assisting with vocational and academic choices; and *placement*, the actual job-match process—scheduling interviews on campus, providing referrals for full-time and part-time jobs, and maintaining career information facilities. The trend now is to combine these services into one career planning and placement department.

There are many career planning and placement offices that are very good. The placement and counseling functions work closely together to support the student in identifying and obtaining work situations that will provide the individual with personal satisfaction and growth. At worst the two functions operate competitively, doing a poor job of expanding the student's understanding of her real work potential and concentrating primarily on the "placement rate," that is, on how many students get jobs of any kind. This narrow view of the placement function can make the school look good—"95 percent of our students get jobs upon graduation"—and leave the student with a very narrow range of choice for the important entry into his or her worklife: "I interviewed three companies, got one offer, and the placement counselor recommended I take it."

Many schools will allow people from the community to get assistance from the facilities of the career planning and placement departments, so even if you are not a college graduate, or if you went to college elsewhere, check out the career planning and placement departments of the schools in your area. Here are some of the resources you may be able to use:

Vocational and aptitude testing

Qualified guidance and placement counselors

Access to immediate available job listings

Information about firms that are recruiting for specific fields.

Reference materials on specific career fields (books, trade journals, etc.)

Employer materials—many schools maintain extensive libraries of employer information, such as annual reports, product information, and position descriptions

Business directories

Career guidance materials—books about the job search, sample resumes, etc.

Lectures, workshops, career fairs

Computerized career information

TACTIC #57

Consult the Yellow Pages, the public library, or someone very familiar with the community colleges and four-year universities and colleges in your area. Through investigatory phone calls, determine the names of the placement directors at these schools.

Next, find out what kind of community involvement the school has had in the past. Call the school president's office, find out from his secretary or assistant the name of the person at the school in charge of community relations and programs. Contact her or him to find out if the facilities of the placement/counseling center are ever made available to selected individuals from the community. (Don't scare her or him into thinking that helping you will open a floodgate.) If you get a green light, contact the placement director, give your referral, and lay out what it is you want to accomplish. If the community affairs director is not encouraging, thank her or him for the time spent and contact the placement director directly.

Organize your approach to create minimum disruption and maximum acknowledgment and thanks for the value you have received (including a thank-you letter to the president of the school).

Try several schools until you have established a supportive relationship with one.

State Employment Service

Your local state employment service office can assist in your job search if you are seeking employment in an entry-level, industrial, skilled or unskilled trade or craft position. In some cases, depending upon the local office, they may handle professional and white-collar jobs. The state employment service office will also have information about a variety of government-sponsored skill-training and counseling programs.

The employment service agency is another resource you can tap to support you in your work goals. They will not invest much time in assisting you in identifying positions that support your life goals and personal aliveness. That is not their function. It is essentially a large-volume clearinghouse of lower-level jobs and supportive training and counseling activities.

If you are unemployed or looking for some needed upgrading of your skills, pay a visit to your local state employment service and ask for brochures describing the variety of services they provide. Pick out the specific programs that appear to be most valuable and then, having armed yourself with the details, visit the office and meet a counselor to learn how the service applies to you and how you can employ it.

In your relationship with the employment service, don't lose sight of the fact that *you* are responsible for getting the kind of job that works for you. The government won't do it for you.

Reminders and References

REMINDER

Communicate past accomplishments, not merely duties.

REFERENCES

How to Get Your First Job. Max Elsman. Crown, New York, 1985.

The Job Search Companion: The Organizer for Job Seekers. Ellen J. Wallach and Peter Arnold. Harvard Common Press, Boston, 1984.

The Managerial Woman. Margaret Hennig and Annie Jardim. Anchor, Garden City, NJ, 1977.

Director of Executive Recruiters. Consultants' News; revised annually.

Liberal Arts Power. Burton Jay Nadler. Peterson's Guides, Princeton, NJ, 1985.

OTHER RESOURCES

For a list of executive search firms, write:
American Management Association

135 West 50th Street
New York, NY 10019

For a list of employment agencies, write:
National Association of Personnel Consultants
1432 Duke
Alexandria, VA 22314

Question: Are you completing the tactics that we provided throughout the book? They represent solid, proven ways for getting what you want.

9

Building the Perfect Resume

Fallacy: A good resume will get you the job you want.

Fallacy: Your resume will be read carefully and thoroughly by an interested party.

Fallacy: The purpose of the resume is to convince an employer to hire you.

Fallacy: The more good information you present about yourself in your resume the better.

Fallacy: If you want a really good resume, you should have it prepared professionally.

Fact: Hundreds of thousands of unsolicited resumes cross employers' desks each and every working day.

Fact: Your resume probably has under ten seconds to make an initial good impression.

Fact: Most resumes, at every employment level, do not communicate clearly.

Fact: A majority of resumes actually do a disservice to the job seeker.

Fact: You should have a perfect resume.

The resume is a specific, written, directed communication with one very clear purpose: *to present your accomplishments in a way that convinces a potential employer to want to meet you personally.*

Let's tune in again to our panel of employment experts and see what they have to say in answer to the question: "What are the most common faults in the resumes you see?"

Employer No. 1: "I read hundreds of resumes most weeks, and I must say that there are very few that are clear. I have to dig to find out what I need to know."

Employer No. 2: "Too much meaningless, redundant information. Most are poorly written and too long."

Employer No. 3: "Maybe two out of every five resumes I receive are intelligently prepared with a clear sense of organization. The balance are hard to read; they don't get much consideration."

Employer No. 4: "Much of the information appears irrelevant or unclear. I can't relate it to what we are looking for."

Employer No. 5: "I would suggest that applicants spend less time mailing out dozens of resumes, and more time making the ones they do send out relate clearly to practical requirements."

A perfect resume is like proper attire for a job interview: If you are improperly dressed, you certainly *won't* get the job. However, the fact that you *are* well-dressed doesn't guarantee an offer.

The biggest problem associated with resumes, in our experience, is that applicants frequently use the resume as a substitute for a job campaign. They will put lots of time and attention into it, print up 300 copies, mail them out, and then sit around and hope for responses. This waiting time will get them into trouble if they are using it to avoid handling the next steps in their job campaign. Procrastination is the enemy, because the longer you wait without accomplishing movement in your work search, the harder it will be to get moving again.

Resume Writing Rules

RESUME RULE 1: *Know your reader.* Picture a tired recruiter facing a stack of 50 resumes on a busy day filled with a myriad of duties, hassled by phone calls and other interruptions. Your resume is stuck somewhere in the middle of the pile. This is your audience. Your resume will only have a few precious seconds to make a first impression. The recruiter has no interest in figuring out what you are trying to say or probing beneath the surface for hidden skills that you have not clearly communicated. If your message is well organized and communicates direct, relevant value, you may get a more thorough appraisal. If not, a form rejection will be on its way to you.

RESUME RULE 2: *Take inventory.* Don't start your resume until you have listed your skills and accomplishments. You will have done this in earlier parts of this book. If you haven't done this yet, and you need to push ahead with your resume anyway, follow this shortcut (or, better yet, go back to the earlier chapters and get to work on the tactics): on a large sheet of paper record everything you can think of about past work or personal endeavors that has produced identifiable results. Use this written inventory as a resource from which to pick and choose the most relevant aspects of your background to use in your resume for a particular job target. (You will generally want to use a different resume for each *major* job target area). Don't write your resume until you have completed this inventory. For high school and college graduates (or students) with limited work experience, write an expanded paragraph about an accomplishment you're proud of, then read it aloud to two good friends, or family members, and have them help brainstorm the skills, qualities, and characteristics they think were needed to accomplish that. Use this date for your resume inventory.

RESUME RULE 3: *Select the appropriate format.* Resumes are typically organized along one of three common formats— each with a particular purpose and strength.

• **The Chronological Format.** In this format, experience and accomplishments are organized by employer worked for, starting with the most recent job, and working backward to the earliest since completion of your primary schooling. Dates, employer names, and job titles are shown as a lead into each major time block. The most recent employment experience, unless very brief, is given greater emphasis than earlier work. If more than three or four jobs are represented, the earlier ones can be lumped together to avoid repetition.

The *advantage* of the chronological resume format are that it highlights the most recent experience, is easy to follow, and is most widely used and understood.

The *disadvantage* is that it will tend to call attention to a spotty employment record and stress recent experience, which may be a hindrance if you are planning to change fields. It will also highlight any lack of experience.

• **Functional Format.** In the functional resume, you do not organize the accomplishments according to dates, but under functional or topical headings. The functional area (design, production, office management, purchasing, retailing, etc.) in which you have the most personal interest is at the top, followed by at least two other functions. You include identification of employers and dates, as secondary information in this approach, which allows you to downplay an irrelevant or poor work record.

The *advantage* of the functional resume is that you can organize information about your background focused on your currently most interesting job targets, and stress areas of experience and interest in which you might never have held down a regular job. If you are reentering the job market, changing fields, or going after your first position, it can be ideal.

The *disadvantage* is that the resume can be suspected of hiding information and it could be confusing.

CHRONOLOGICAL RESUME

JACK DEUTSCH
2714 Third Avenue
New York, NY 10035
(h) (212) 555-1699
(w) (212) 555-3006

EXPERIENCE:

1985–Present GOODSON APPAREL INDUSTRIES, INC.
New York, NY 10019

Divisional Controller

Reported directly to the chief financial officer. Managed cash funds, prepared consolidated corporate tax returns for seven companies and financial review of major subsidiaries. Designed and prepared a monthly sales comparison report for corporate executives. Co-supervisor of a twelve-member staff that handled all facets of accounting for a $25.0 MM company.

1984–1985 MACY'S, INC.
New York, NY 10019

Corporate Auditor

Reported directly to the Assistant Corporate Controller. Conducted operational and financial audits within the Treasurer's office and five operating divisions. Developed a report with findings and recommendations for the chief executive officer of each division and numerous management personnel.

1977–1984 PRICE, WATERHOUSE & COMPANY
Certified Public Accountants
New York, NY 10012

Supervising Senior

Joined the professional staff as an assistant accountant. Reported directly to partners and managers. Planned, supervised, and completed numerous audit assignments.

AWARDS, ACCREDITATIONS, AND MEMBERSHIPS:

Peter K. Ewald Award in Taxation—June, 1977; Certified Public Accountant, New York State—April, 1971; American Institute of Certified Public Accountants; New York Society of Certified Public Accountants.

EDUCATION:

1977 HOFSTRA UNIVERSITY—BS in Accounting

FUNCTIONAL RESUME

ELLEN MESINE
279419 Sepulveda Boulevard
San Francisco, CA 94310
(415) 555-9842

SALES MANAGEMENT: Sales Representative: Planned and implemented phone, mail, and public sales presentations that increased business 30%. Developed and led over 100 presentations in the US and Mexico to over 1000 people.

Conference Service Manager: Booked 17 local and national conferences within three months. Initiated and researched conference sales campaign. Created multimedia sales presentation. Negotiated all fees and contracts; supervised staff of 20 in handling all conference services.

PROMOTION/ ADVERTISING: Introduced successful promotional phone campaign to create magazine articles, newspaper coverage, and radio interviews. Worked with artists, writers, photographers, and layout people to create initial promotional material. Promoted college sportsmanship program to entire student body first semester.

PROGRAM DEVELOPER: Created, developed, and managed sportsmanship program for children and college students. Directed women's center; initiated counseling services and special courses. Codeveloped newsletter for over 1000 readers. Responsible for designing and delivering training sessions for groups of 10 to 150 people.

EXPERIENCE:

1988–1991   FOX FOREST RESORT—Reno, NV
Conference Service Manager/Sales Representative

1985–1988   CALIFORNIA STATE UNIVERSITY—Petaluma, CA
Director of Sportsmanship Program
Department of Physical Education

1983–1985   MANAGEMENT CONSULTANTS, INC.—
San Diego, CA
Head, Department of Enrollment/Assistant to President

1982–1983   LOS ANGELES WOMEN'S CENTER—
Los Angeles, CA
Administrative Assistant

EDUCATION: Claremont Business School—Associate Degree

TARGETED RESUME

JASON HEILBRON
10420 Sharewood Avenue
Ypsilanti, MI 48197
(313) 555-0985

EDUCATION: BA, University of Michigan 1991

JOB TARGET: BOOKING AGENT

CAPABILITIES:

- Create, develop, and manage jazz and rock groups.
- Develop and implement well-planned budgets and schedules for bands.
- Scout talent for purpose of creating new groups.
- Establish and direct showcase presentations to expose new talent to the public.
- Write press releases and album covers.
- Negotiate fees.

ACCOMPLISHMENTS:

- Promoted five concerts in 2000-seat auditorium for college audiences.
- Created and managed two progressive jazz groups that traveled nine states in 60 days.
- Supervised spring concert series featuring new talent and attended by over 1200 students.
- Wrote numerous reviews on new album releases for college newspapers.
- Booked jazz bands on several campuses and in local clubs.

WORK HISTORY:

1989–1991   University of Michigan

                Chairman, Concert Committee

1988–1989   The Student Chronicle
                University of Michigan Newspaper

                Music Critic

1987–1988   The Brothers Three/The Music Students

                Manager/Agent

• **The Targeted Format.** Whereas most other resume formats emphasize the past, the targeted resume looks to the future. Where the previous two resume types don't require "job objectives" here a clear, specific, target is essential. Following the listing of a specific job target, the opening section is headed <u>Capabilities</u>, and lists 5–8 things that you "can do." This section allows you to include things you know you can do, that are related to your jar target, even if you haven't actually done them before.

The next section is called <u>Accomplishments</u>. This is where you select from your store of past work and nonwork accomplishments and achievements, those 5–8 that could be most related to your "Capabilities" section.

The strongest *advantage* of the targeted resume format is that it allows you to get the reader to picture your success in tasks in which you might not have yet had experience. This is not presented as hyperbole or invention, but as an honest presentation of how you see your ability to translate what you have done to a future opportunity. By keeping the objective specific, and the following sections custom tailored, you can maintain interest in the reader who is interested in this target area.

The *disadvantage* is that to get the most from this format you should keep the target highly specific (e.g., "counselor to homeless children" as opposed to simply "counselor"), and distribution of each targeted resume will be limited to a small group of potential employers. This means more resumes. With some good resume software or a word processor, this task is lightened considerably.

TACTIC #58

Reread the advantages and disadvantages of the chronological, functional, and targeted resume formats. Then analyze your own needs and objectives, and decide which format will best represent you.

RESUME RULE 4: *Present your accomplishments.* Let the potential employer know about past accomplishments that could relate to his needs, not just the job titles you have had or the duties you were supposed to perform. People can comprehend tangible results far easier than sterile sounding job descriptions or duties. Use quantities and specifics to create a picture of what you produced. Include percentages, money amounts, everything that could give an employer a *precise* picture of your capabilities. Consult the lists you created in Tactic #42 (Chapter 7) and select the accomplishments that are most relevant to the job target in the resume. Incorporate them in your resume.

RESUME RULE 5: *Start with action.* Begin sentences and paragraphs with verbs that convey actions, such as:

Designed	Directed	Organized
Produced	Managed	Edited
Started	Controlled	Built
Researched	Sold	Learned

Be concise in your writing. Don't use long wind-ups. Communicate your abilities and your accomplishments directly. The more you bury your real talents in a maze of qualifiers and connectives, the less they will be recognized.

Your writing style should be more terse than descriptive. Edit out words and phrases that repeat points you have already made. Strange as it may seem, the more you repeat (in a resume), the less clear the communication.

Don't use fancy or cute writing styles unless you are in a field where this is acknowledged as appropriate, e.g., public relations or advertising copy writing.

RESUME RULE 6: *Keep your resume short.* The object is to communicate the most information possible per unit of reading time. The best length is *one page.* Do everything you can to stay with this length. If you have a long list of publications, inventions, or memberships, you can prepare a page two addendum. When you go to the second and third page, you risk losing the reader's attention.

RESUME RULE 7: *Make a rough draft first.* Do not attempt to produce a finished resume on the first pass, or you will probably represent your abilities poorly. What follows is a proven step-by-step procedure for drafting your resume.

1. Get a separate sheet of paper (preferably legal size) for each *function* you plan to include—if you are using the functional format—or each *position* you plan to discuss if you are using the chronological format, or each specific *job target* if you choose the targeted format. List one function, or position at the top of each sheet. Then draw a line across the sheet one-third of the way up from the bottom. You are now ready to start writing.

2. On the top two-thirds of the sheet write down *everything* you can think of related to that function, job, or target. Pour out as much information as you can, related to your accomplishments on the job and other relevant skills and duties. Don't worry about organization of structure at this point, but don't write on the bottom one-third of the sheet.

3. After you have written on the top section of the paper everything you can think of related to each skill, function, or target, go back over it and underline the most powerful, least redundant, most descriptive statements, that is, those you would want to include in your final resume. Then use the bottom third of each sheet to rewrite the key information on that function or position, condensing and writing clearly and powerfully.

4. After you have written a very tight paragraph for each function or position, cut these paragraphs from the sheets and position them in order on top of a fresh sheet of paper with tape or a stapler. This will allow you to have an overview of everything you want to include and let you see how it all works together. You can also see how long the resume is and whether you have to cut it to fit on one page. Leave room at the top of this sheet to list your name, address, phone number, and education.

5. Now write a fresh new draft from the information you have organized so far. Cut and edit as appropriate to fit on one page.

RESUME RULE 8: *Eliminate extraneous information.* After you have drafted your resume, go over it again to eliminate extraneous information. Take out everything that does not directly present your accomplishments in a way that clearly demonstrates your ability to produce results.

You should *leave out* or reduce to a minimum most of the following information:

Age and gender
Height and weight
Hobbies and awards (unless related to job target)
Race or religion
Military service (unless it was a career)
Part-time jobs (unless related to job target)
References
Your career objective—except in the targeted format (To keep your resume flexible, communicate "objective" in your cover letter—see below.)
Salary
Reasons for leaving last job
Any self-evaluating or self-serving statement (such as "I am a good leader" or "I am very dependable")

RESUME RULE 9: *Have the resume critiqued.* Once you have prepared a draft resume, have someone review it. If possible, find someone with experience in reviewing resumes: a personnel manager, a recruiter, a placement counselor, or someone with experience in your field. Be sure to set it up so you will get real feedback, not just approval. Don't ask: "Say, how do you like my resume?" Instead ask: "How do you think I can improve this?" and then *listen* to the feedback. Here are some of the things that should be checked:

Spelling and grammar
Clarity and organization
Lack of redundancy
Basic layout
Presentation of accomplishments

You might want to ask the person who will critique your resume to read this chapter first and then be as hard on you as possible. Obviously it's better to have someone critique the resume before you send it out than to have the employer do it when it's too late to change it.

RESUME RULE 10: *Make it attractive to the eye.* The appearance of your resume is as important to your presentation as the way you dress is to your interview. If you are not a top-notch typist with a good, clean electric typewriter, or you don't have a great word processor with a laser printer, or computer resume software, have someone else type the final version. Make certain that the layout is attractive, with enough white space so that it is easy to read.

Unless you have access to a laser printer, or very high quality photocopy machine, have your resume offset printed on good quality white, buff, or ivory bond paper. Don't get into flamboyant colors or binders unless you are in a field where this is appropriate. Don't include a photograph with your resume.

The Computerized Resume

Much of the hard work in vocabulary choice, format, layout, and design has been eliminated from the process by intelligent resume writing software. *The Perfect Resume Computer Kit*™ by this author is one such program, designed to allow you all the features of a word processor, resume consultant, and print shop. For further information on how to order this extremely helpful kit, write to Permax Systems, 5008 Gordon Avenue, Madison, WI, 53716-0455; or call (800) 233-6460. Other programs are appearing in stores regularly.

TACTIC #59

Set aside two three-hour periods to produce an effective one-page, professional-looking resume. Assemble any earlier resumes you have produced, and any other work references or resources that can help you.

Be willing to stay with an all-out concentrated effort that will result in a well-written, effective resume. Use your support system to critique and assist you.

The Custom Cover Letter

A well-done, individually prepared cover letter sent with your resume is almost equivalent to a personal introduction for an interview. It personalizes the communication in a way that a printed resume could never do on its own.

After 20 years of involvement with tens of thousands of resumes and hundreds of employers, we strongly believe that a well-prepared custom cover letter will make a major difference in the number of interviews you get as a result of your resume mailing.

The custom cover letter is a personal, individually prepared communication that should go with every resume you send. It is designed to relate the information about your background to the needs of a particular employer. Here are the rules for preparing a cover letter:

1. Each cover letter should be addressed to a specific person (the person who could hire you) by *name*.

2. Each cover letter should indicate, in the first sentence, something that will show the potential employer you know something specific about his or her activities. This establishes that the letter is not a form letter.

3. In the opening paragraph you should state, or at least imply, that you are aware of what the organization needs or wants to accomplish. This does not need to be highly researched information; rather, it can usually be based on your own common sense or general understanding of the field.

4. In the next paragraph, you should communicate something about your background that could be valuable to the employer, particularly in relation to the implied problem of the opening paragraph. A simple statement of your ability or accomplishments with a reference to the appropriate section of your resume is sufficient.

5. The final step in your cover letter is to request an interview at a specific time and place. By going after a specific interview date, you help to accelerate the decision-making process.

On the next two pages are examples of custom cover letters.

TACTIC #60

Write a few actual or practice cover letters to different prospective employers. Follow the above steps carefully and remember to include some relevant piece of research that reflects your understanding of the needs of the potential employers.

SAMPLE COVER LETTER

1736 D Street, NW
Washington, DC 20006
(202) 767-8192

Mr. Robert Olsen
President
Vendo Corporation
1742 Sunshine Drive
Fort Lauderdale, Florida 39642

Dear Mr. Olsen:

I was intrigued by the write-up of your new portable
vending centers as described in Sales Management
magazine. Frankly, I think it is an extremely good idea.

As you will note from the enclosed resume, my market
planning and sales management experience could be of
great assistance to you at this early stage in your project.

Because of my familiarity with the types of locations and
clients you are seeking, I am sure that if we were able to
work together in this new venture, the results would
reflect my contribution.

I have roughed out, and am enclosing, some specific
marketing ideas that you might like to review, and would
like to make arrangements to meet with you in Florida
during the week of February 15th.

I am looking forward to meeting with you. I'll call you
sometime next week.

Very truly yours,

Leonard Hardwick

Leonard Hardwick

Encl.

SAMPLE COVER LETTER

204 Palisade Street
Olympia, Washington 96403
(206) 843-2971

Dr. Warren Stanton
President
12 Foxhollow Road
Seattle Heights Junior College
Seattle, Washington 98101

Dear Dr. Stanton:

My experience on the administrative staffs of two colleges
could be of interest to you in your new drive to centralize
administrative functions of SHJC.

The enclosed resume will illustrate my ability to handle
the specific administrative problems of a college
department.

I am moving to Seattle at the end of this school year. I
will be in Seattle from April 10 to 14. If possible, I would
like to arrange an appointment during that period to
discuss your new organization and how my experience
could make a contribution to your program.

Yours very truly,

Christine Williams

Christine Williams

Encl.

The Resume Alternative Letter

There are several situations where it may not be appropriate to put together a standard resume: for example, when you have no work experience; when you have been out of the labor force for a long time; or when you have had far too many job changes. It may also be inappropriate when you are making a radical career change. In these cases, one approach that may work to get interviews is to send an expanded cover letter instead of a resume.

To be effective, this resume alternative letter requires more detailed research than a regular cover letter, to make it clear to the reader that you can contribute real value to his or her organization. This letter should provide enough information of your background so there will be no need for the employer to request additional information. You should state your education, your general experience and provide the name of one or two references, preferably people whom the employer may know. You can sometimes use the name of a casual acquaintance, but get their permission first.

Above all, the resume alternative letter should be clear about the specific value you are offering the prospective employer. Research each employer thoroughly! The more time you know about the organization, the more specific you can be about how you might help them. Here is a sample of the resume alternative letter.

RESUME ALTERNATIVE

1011 Orange Court
Pasadena, California 92318
(213) 787-2724

Mr. Herbert S. Gruen
Medical Laboratories, Ltd.
425 San Marco Boulevard
Pacific Dunes, California 92316

Dear Mr. Gruen:

Dr. Paul Beneson at the USC Graduate School suggested that I contact you about the studies your firm is currently making into the utilization of nursing homes in this country. He also remarked that you might be thinking about hiring someone to coordinate the field investigations that are part of your study.

As an officer of our local Women's Community Center, I have had a great deal of experience with the operation of day-care centers, which, as you know, are quite similar administratively to nursing homes. This experience includes familiarity with the financial and administrative aspects of the centers as well as knowledge of the programming and educational considerations. I have met with the staffs of most of the day-care centers in the county, and am certain that my ability to work with these professionals would enable me to facilitate the execution of your study.

In addition to this experience, I have had two years of administrative work on an important research project in health care at USC while working on my master's degree in education.

I plan to be near your office next week and wonder if we could get together on Wednesday or Thursday for an interview. I'll call you to explore if or when you might be available.

Yours truly,

Norma Ridgewood

Norma Ridgewood

TACTIC #61

Have your cover letter and resumes critiqued by
a member of your support team, or by an expert in
the field. Encourage them to be as professional with
you as they would be with themselves. Explain to
them that the harsher the criticism, the better your
resume will work for you.

Reminders and References

REMINDER

The purpose of a resume is to get you interviews. It has to be
excellent even to be read.

REFERENCES

The Perfect Resume. Tom Jackson. Doubleday, New York,
revised 1990.

The Perfect Resume Computer Kit™. Tom Jackson and Bill
Buckingham. Software. Permax Systems, 1990.

The Well-Tempered Sentence. Karen Elizabeth Gordon. Tick-
nor & Fields, New York, 1983.

Getting the Words Right. Theodore A. Rees Cheney. Writer's
Digest Books, Cincinnati, 1983.

10

The Power Interview

Fresh Start

Everything you have done so far in your job search has led to this moment of truth in the employment process—the meeting between you and a potential employer. Regardless of how sloppy your job campaign might have been up to this time, or how long your job search has taken, and despite the fact that you may not be satisfied with your resume, or may not have done as well as you would have liked in previous interviews, the next interview you have rolls the scoreboard back to zero.

The employment interview is something like a courtship in which the parties are interested in each other, but wary of hidden flaws, uncommunicated concerns, or questionable past history. Everything—or nothing—is possible.

We asked our employer panel for suggestions of ways applicants could improve their performances in the interview. Here's what they said:

"Candidates need to know more about us and to be able to converse easily about the basics of our business. They don't need a detailed history of our company, but they do need to know something about our products and our goals."

- "An applicant should come to the interview ready to tell me what she or he can do for us. If the candidate is a telemarketing expeditor, I want to hear how he organizes and meets volume targets. If she is a salesperson, I want her to have at least thought about our product. I get tired of hearing only what the applicant *wants* from the job.''

- ''One very important factor in an interview is how the person is dressed; the way he or she presents herself. Neatness. It sounds rather basic, but you'd be surprised how many good applicants get turned down because of a sloppy appearance, or by being overdressed. Do a little research to see what the dress code is at the place you want to join . . . it makes basic sense. Simply wearing your Sunday best doesn't do it.''

- ''The candidate should be willing to ask questions, to let us know what his or her standards are and what he or she wants to know about us. It doesn't make a good impression for an applicant to just sit there and wait for me to ask all of the questions.''

- ''Many applicants are so nervous that they come across as far more timid than they really are. It's okay to be a little assertive in the interview—take some risks. It would help if applicants would practice before they went out for interviews. It would loosen them up.''

- ''I think that what we've all been saying is that an interview is a sales situation, and the applicant has to present himself or herself as the product in the best light, and that this takes a bit of planning in advance.''

TACTIC #62

If you have previously looked for work, think back over any of the interviews you have had and list the ways you could have been more effective.

The Irresistible Message

Most job seekers envision the interview as a minor inquisition; they think the employer's purpose is to prove how bad they are in order to screen them out. As fear of rejection is frequently the overriding element in the candidate's approach, it is helpful to look at the meeting from the interviewer's point of view.

One thing becomes clear rather quickly: The goal of the interviewer is not at all like the images in the candidate's fearful expectations. For one thing, *the interviewer is usually very interested in hiring someone for the job as soon as possible.* After all, the purpose of the organization is not to be in the employment game, but to get the job done. The sooner they identify and hire the right person, the sooner they can get on with their real work.

Employers are not doing anyone a favor when they hire them. In the most basic terms, they are making a purchasing decision: identifying a capability and capacity that will fit their needs, and then hiring the person who has it.

Employers profit by hiring. That's why they do it. The employer you are nervously waiting to see is probably just as nervously hoping you are going to be the one he can hire so he can give up interviewing and get back to "real" work.

In most cases, an employer is waiting to hear a simple positive statement from the candidate that expresses clearly what the employer is looking for. The transaction is not as involved and complex as most job seekers think. It is simply the answer to the question: *"Why should I hire you?"* Although rarely asked just that way, this is the underlying context for the employer that the candidate must satisfy before an offer can be made.

The problem is that most candidates don't really address themselves to this question at all. Most candidates are dramatizing an almost opposite communication: *"I need a job. . . . Can you help me?"* And so the interview frequently becomes a game in which the employer is forced to dig for the reasons himself.

Something else observed frequently in interviews is the tendency for applicants to put out communications that almost thwart their objective of getting a job offer. This is surprisingly common, and shows up in the frequent tendency to lead with negative information: "I haven't worked for a while, but I think I could do it," or "I don't know if I can handle it or not, but I'm willing to try." These communications dramatize uncertainty and reveal lack of confidence. Fear or resentment can also show up in a variety of unconscious ways, such as sullenness, lack of communication, low energy, and even caustic comments masquerading as superiority.

The message that is irresistible to an employer is the message that makes him or her feel confident of two things:

- Your ability to contribute to the solution of the problems he or she faces; your skills or aptitude.
- Your willingness to do what's necessary to get the job done. In other words, your attitude or motivation.

TACTIC #63

If you are now working, or have done so recently, list three activities or tasks you perform that make a direct measurable contribution to your employer. Write them in terms of accomplishments rather than duties. If you are not working, think of an employer you know of and would like to work for, and list three ways you could contribute to that employer. After you have written these, practice communicating them verbally to someone in your support system.

Managing the Interview

There is no guarantee that employers you meet will ask the right questions to enable you to present the information you want that person to know. Often the employer representative (if he or she comes from outside personnel) will know very little about good interviewing techniques. He or she may be a good socializer or spend the interview looking for or proving his or her own self-worth.

Your job in such a situation is *to direct the interview yourself.* Now, quickly, before you go running off to your next interview like a drill sergeant, let us explain what we mean: We don't mean that you should dominate the interview, or bully the interviewer into listening to what you say. We do mean *that you will take full responsibility to ensure that the employer hears what you want him or her to know about you.*

You do this by remaining attentive throughout the meeting, by knowing in advance the specific things about yourself that you want the recruiter to know, and by being able to lightly steer the conversation in the directions you want it to go. This can be done by mastering a few simple communications techniques:

- Keep your eyes and attention on the interviewer. This will tend to keep the interviewer on course and minimize wanderings.
- When the interviewer is wandering, use direct questions to bring the conversation back on course, e.g., "Yes, that's interesting. By the way, could you tell me how many orders a week are processed through this department?"
- Ask for the opportunity to communicate about yourself, e.g., "Would you be interested in hearing about my responsibilities regarding our HMO relationships?"
- Ask for feedback with questions such as, "Do you think that what I've told you about myself fits what you are looking for? What other areas would you like to explore?" This ability to get feedback along the way will give you a leading edge.

By using these techniques, and others that occur to you in practice, you will be able to direct the interview along the paths you feel support your best presentation.

Planning the Interview

No professional pilot would think of taking off on an important flight without investing time in preflight planning. The more thorough this planning is, the more comfortable and precise the trip will be.

The better you plan in advance for your interview, the more comfortable you will be in it, and the more able you will be to communicate your value for the employer.

Good preparation for the interview provides you with several very real advantages:

- You will not have to waste valuable interview time finding out general information about the organization, allowing you extra time to present yourself.
- You will know in advance what aspects of yourself to emphasize to suit the employer's needs or objectives.
- You can prepare notes to consult during the interview to ensure against forgetting anything important.
- With good preparation, you will be more comfortable and therefore better able to listen and observe.
- By anticipating possible negative aspects of your background that might come up, you can prepare appropriate responses and avoid possible embarrassment.
- With advance preparation, you can focus the interview in directions that satisfy your personal job targets.
- By knowing in advance what salary range is contemplated, you can probably negotiate for more money than you could if you were unprepared.
- With even a modest amount of advance planning, you will make a substantially better impression than most other job seekers.

It is clear that you have a lot at stake: the research, the phone calls, the turndowns and turnoffs. Many hours of effort and activity can be spent obtaining each interview, so it makes sense to protect your investment with an additional hour or two of research and planning.

Here are some important things you can prepare before the interview:

- What products or services does the employer produce or perform? Find out about all of them, not just the area of your interest.
- How are their products or services looked upon in their industry? What is their reputation?
- Who are their competitors? What are they doing in the same field? What new advances are being made?
- What are some common industry problems: government regulations, international price competition, etc.?
- What are the most important tasks or challenges facing

the particular department or division in which you would work?

- What are all the tasks you can think of that are probably associated with the job in one way or another? List, and then match each task with a related skill or ability of your own.
- What major organizational changes have taken place in the past few years? How have these effects been felt in the department you are targeting?
- What have been some of the major news items in business publications over the past year or six months?

Note: Depending on the level of your target job and other factors of completion, you may wish to research some of the items on the above list and skip others. Don't make the mistake of thinking that because you are after an entry-level or clerical or secretarial job, the items above are irrelevant to you; nothing could be further from the truth. More than a few secretaries have gotten better, higher-paying jobs because they were able to demonstrate a knowledge of the organization to an employer.

Q: **Enough is enough. You can't expect me to do all of this stuff for every interview.**

A: Why not?

Q: Well, it's too much work; there just isn't enough time.

A: How many interviews do you have scheduled?

Q: Well, there's one with Advanced Micro-Pro next week, and probably a couple after that.

A: When?

Q: I don't know.

A: So what's the big problem with time?

Q: Well, it's not just time. It's also that I don't believe it's necessary to do all this stuff. Why not just go in for the job like everybody else?

A: You can do that if you want your job campaign to look like everyone else's. On the other hand, you might want to go in with a competitive edge so you can have a better-than-average chance to get what you want.

Q: It just looks phony and pretentious. Besides, they're

going to decide whether to hire me or not based on whether I can do the job, not because I know how many offices they have or what the company president eats for breakfast.

A: Funny. Do you agree that presenting yourself for a job is a sales situation?

Q: Yes, although I don't like it. They should hire me based on how good I am, not how well I can sell myself.

A: How will they know how good you are if you don't tell them?

Q: You win. It is a sales situation.

A: Good. Now if it's a sales situation, don't you think you could do a better job of selling if you know what they are looking to buy?

Q: Yes, it seems to make sense, but why have people been able to get along so long without doing all this?

A: The people with the best jobs *have* been doing this. The people who have just taken the next job that comes along haven't. Are you willing to get the kind of job that would actually be what you want and give you pleasure as well as a paycheck?

Q: Yes, but it looks like work to do it, and I don't want to put in the time.

A: I know. That's what the problem really is, you don't want to put in the time.

Q: You're right. That's where I'm stuck.

Personal Probe and Prep

The outside research we've just outlined is an essential first step in your preplanning. Once that's done, you need to look inside and polish up those things about yourself that will make the best impression and make your interview go most

TACTIC #64

Pick five employers you wish to interview, or have scheduled for interviews. Call or write each employer (or stop by if you are rushed for time) and obtain a copy of their annual report (if public), service brochure, product information, and issues of the employee newsletter, if any. You can contact their advertising, public information, and sales departments. Continue this before each interview.

smoothly. Good preparation leads directly to good interviews. Poor preparation is a waste of opportunity.

Some tips for your best personal prep:

- List specific problem-solving skills or experiences you have demonstrated elsewhere that would assist the organization in meeting its needs.
- Get the names of two or three well-respected people who will vouch for your abilities.
- Anticipate any parts of your background or experience that may be seen as negative by the employer, and construct and write down assertions and qualities that can combat this negativism.
- Determine and list the key personal goals you expect to satisfy in the job. This is to clearly evaluate whether or not *you* want *them*.
- Select some examples of your work that might be appropriate to bring with you to the interview.
- Research and target a realistic and attractive salary target, and estimate the dollar minimums you will consider.

Dressing for Success

The way you dress is the single most important nonverbal communication you make about yourself.

Let that sink in. A surprising number of applicants, especially those just entering or reentering the job market, under-

TACTIC #65

List a number of questions you feel would be hardest for you to answer. Include things such as "Why have you been unemployed for five months?" or "Why were you terminated from your last job?" Consider the things you hope won't be asked. Get a tape recorder, ask yourself each question, and answer it on the tape. Then play back the answers and critique them. Continue this until you are satisfied with how you have answered these questions. Get outside coaching if you can.

mine their job campaign by the way they dress. A frequent attitude is: "If they don't like me the way I am, that's too bad," or "I'll be able to dress better *after* I get the job."

Please understand that to most people meeting you for the first time, the way you look is the way you are. That is where the interview *starts*. You may move up or down from that place, but probably not very far.

It is interesting to observe how people allow (or cause) their clothes to reflect the way they see themselves. A successful executive *looks* different from a person who is worried about his job. People who are experiencing a low self-image frequently dramatize that picture of themselves by dressing in sloppy, ill-fitting garments, inappropriate styles, frayed collars, poorly matched colors, run-down shoes, and so forth.

Part of your planning for the interview should be to put together clothes that will support you in making a good impression. Your clothes have only one purpose, to support you in getting what you want in life. In other words, decide what you *want* and dress for that, rather than just put on what you happen to own.

The best way to approach dressing is to identify people you feel have already become successful in the same or a related field, notice how they are dressed, and do likewise. Remember that Silicon Valley dresses differently from Route 28 or Wall Street.

Some basics:

- For most organizations you should dress on the conservative side. People in business don't like surprises. Set aside particular clothes you will wear for work. These will differ from your dress-up clothes and from the garments you wear to knock about the house.
- Pick fabrics that will not show wrinkles—especially in sweaty months. High-quality synthetics and blends can do admirably.
- Make sure your clothes fit you. Spend the extra money to have garments tailored after or when you buy them, or if you have expanded—or reduced—since you bought them.
- Don't try to be too individualistic in your approach. You should not stand out dramatically from the people you will be working with, particularly at the interview stage. On the other hand, don't totally adopt a uniform. Add a bit of individual flair to good basics.
- Women moving from secretarial or household duties into management training should specifically reappraise their outfits and move toward conservative suits, well-made skirts and blouses, and simple jewelry. No need anymore—we hope—for women to look or dress up like men. Wear good footwear, never sandals or open-toed shoes except if you know that others in the firm do.
- Candidates or students wishing to move into management training and similar responsibilities from lesser positions may have to invest $300 to $500 for a good-looking business outfit. This should be done *before* the interviews. No, we don't know how you can afford it. We do know you can't afford not to.
- Avoid wearing clanking jewelry, heavy fragrances, or too much makeup.
- Male or female, for most office or professional jobs bring an attache case or briefcase. This is the premier business accessory.
- Leave rain gear in an outer office. Be organized, buttoned, and early.

TACTIC #66

Use the buddy system to help organize your clothes
before starting interviews. Have someone qualified
by employment and experience be a friendly critic
of how you look, giving you feedback on how your
present wardrobe works for the level of interviews
you want. Encourage him or her to be as frank as
possible. Write down the things you need. Take
your most "pulled-together" buddies shopping with
you.

Lasting First Impressions

For years we have been convinced that your first impression
is an important determinant of the success or failure of your
interview. Testing this out recently by analyzing videotaped
employment interviews, we were surprised to find out that
not only was the initial impression important, in many cases
it virtually controlled the results of the interview.

We saw employer representatives appear to make up their
minds within the first five or ten minutes and then, throughout the balance of the interview, ask questions that would
produce answers to justify decisions already reached. Applicants would go right along with it. If the employer was
positively inclined, the applicant would relax, smile, and play
out the interview with energy. If the employer had decided
"no" in the opening minutes, and communicated it nonver-
bally, the applicant would appear to accept the inevitable,
literally slump in his chair, and lose interest.

This is not to say that a poor first impression will necessarily doom the interview. Using good techniques, it is
possible for you to turn the whole thing around. However,
just as in a master chess game or the Super Bowl, once you
get behind, it is very hard to catch up.

Besides making an impression with your personal appearance, there are things you should accomplish within the first
five or ten minutes of the interview that will get the process
off the ground.

1. Establish rapport. Greet the interviewer with a real smile, immediate eye contact, and high energy. A firm hand-shake.

2. Acknowledge or compliment the interviewer for something about his organization that you have learned or observed, such as a new product or the appearance of the offices. Keep it genuine; don't flatter.

3. Establish communication. Show that you are attentive and interested, that you hear what the interviewer is saying. If the meeting is getting off to a slow start, ask a question or make a comment that shows your interest in communicating about the job.

An important question to ask at the beginning of the interview is: "Could you tell me what you are looking for in the person who does this job?" Pay attention as the employer lays out what he or she is looking for, and feed it back during the interview.

1. Demonstrate by your comments and questions that you are most interested in finding out how you can assist the employer in accomplishing the job results. Answer questions from this point of view.

After ten minutes, take stock of how your opening moves have worked. Is the employer interested in what you are saying? See if you have been able to communicate your accomplishments, or if it has been appropriate for you to ask questions. Observe your own speech patterns and check for posture and breathing. If you notice that you are tense, RELAX. Make whatever correction is called for, and continue.

Intercom

As we've said earlier, most people don't communicate very well. Generally when you are telling the interviewer what you want her to know, she is figuring out the next question to ask, and while the other party is talking to you, your attention goes to the thoughts circling in your head: how am I doing, did I say the right thing, etc.

Regardless of the situation there is very little listening or communicating going on in most conversations—and, of course, in most interviews.

Communication tips and reviews:

TACTIC #67

Before each interview, write down on one side of a 3 x 5 index card five accomplishments or things you are proud of that you want the employer to learn about during the interview. On the other side of the card, list five intelligent questions to ask the employer that show the penetrating depth of your knowledge of the situation, and that will assist you in determining whether you wish to work there. (Save questions about vacation, benefits, salary, etc., until you have received an offer.)

- Remember, real communication requires you to be 100% responsible that a message is received, either by you or by the other party.
- If a question is asked that you don't understand, don't jump in with an answer, say so. There is no quicker way to disqualify yourself than by making up answers to things you don't understand. A good interviewer will check for consistency.
- Keep observing the interviewer to see if what you are saying is getting through. If not, rephrase your messages.
- Avoid superfluous information. Answer the question with the required information, add anything you feel is necessary or promotive of your abilities, and then either stop talking or ask a relevant question.
- Look for nonverbal signals. Don't try to figure them out exactly, but if you see the employer's attention wandering (finger tapping, eyes glazed over), change the subject or ask a question.
- Answer questions, not statements. If the employer comments about your background or experience, acknowledge the statement and avoid adding information unless it is clearly called for or is in your best interest.
- Keep coming back to the main subject. This will support the purpose of the organization and/or position. Communicate value clearly at every moment.

- Get feedback. Don't allow the interview to play itself out without knowing how you are coming across. Stop and ask: "Do you feel this is the kind of experience that could be valuable to your firm?" Or ask a similar question whose answer will show you what you have accomplished.
- Lighten up. Don't be so serious that the interview is without humor. Remember, people want to hire someone who will be pleasant to work with. Smile, laugh, be amused as frequently as you can while acting appropriately.
- Make course corrections. If you are midway into the interview and sense that you are not doing as well as you could, don't write off the balance of the meeting. Correct the situation immediately by getting your energy up, moving into other areas, or getting back on track.

TACTIC #68

Prepare to *demonstrate* to the employer what you can do for them. Bring some samples of your work, or anything else you can leave behind after the meeting. Remember, "a picture is worth a thousand words."

Decision Factors

There are three sectors in which the employer looks for information on which to base a hiring decision:

Education and training
Work experience
Personality factors

An interviewer is primarily guided by his own idea of what the job entails. This is usually rather inexact. If the interviewer is from the personnel department and interviewing in response to an advertised position, you will probably find that he is interpreting some very specific criteria for type and duration of experience, education level attained, and other qualifications. Since he has received this information from someone else, and it may not be an area in which he has experience, he will probably not be very flexible.

When you have an interview with someone who is responsible for the work itself, you will find much more flexibility in deciding your possible value to the organization. This is particularly relevant when you have approached the employer through your own creative job market research. The closer the person is to the actual problem being discussed, the easier it is to talk in terms of various solutions and values rather than in strict definitions of education and experience.

A typical interview may start with an open-ended question such as, "Tell me about your work experience," which allows you the flexibility of presenting yourself in more or less your own terms. The interview may then narrow down to closed-ended questions such as, "Have you operated a Macintosh CXR?" Next, there might be a probe question challenging something you said: "How sure are you that you could supervise that many programmers?" This cycle is repeated to cover the three major information categories listed above.

The Telegraph

Very often interviewers will often reveal what they are looking for by the way they ask questions. "You wouldn't mind doing some traveling, would you?" is a sample of a question that "telegraphs" the answer being looked for. There are many such questions, and if you keep your listening apparatus tuned in you will pick up many clues to what is actually being looked for.

Of course, the best interviewers give the least information, leaving the responsibility more in your hands. Keep looking for ways to communicate that demonstrate your ability to produce results. Use picture words (enlarge, shape up, accelerate) rather than jargon ("modify the interface," "calculate the modem ratios").

Here is what the personnel director of one of the nation's largest firms looks for:

The key word for what we are looking for is mastery. We learned a long time ago that past experience is not a guarantee of future performance. The fact that a person has five years experience doing one thing doesn't mean that they are going to be able to do what the new position calls for. It's that old question—did the person have five years experience, or one year of experience five times over? I look for the way a person has handled all the things they are involved in and whether they have mastered them.

For instance, take college students. Not much opportunity to gain experience in particular fields, but certainly they have enough everyday experience to demonstrate an ability to accomplish results.

TACTIC #69

At the beginning of your next interview, after the formalities are over, ask the recruiter this question: "Could you tell me in your own words what qualities you are looking for in this position?" Then listen. Most recruiters will give you a description of what they are looking for. Pay attention, take mental notes. Then for the balance of the interview, feed back to the recruiter the things he has said he is looking for.

Handling Negatives

Frequently what distracts applicants in an interview are the things about themselves they see as negative. This preoccupation with past failures or shortcomings often plays itself out with the candidate ashamedly blurting out the horrible truth: He or she got fired from his or her past job, or took off six months and went to Europe, or has only secretarial experience and now wishes to move to supervisory or management work. Here are a few principles for dealing with the things you feel are negative:

PRINCIPLE 1: *Things are generally only negative in context*—that is, in the way you frame them. It is your thoughts about activities that communicate the negative energy. If you apologize and look guilty about your six-month vacation from work, the interviewer will be convinced that you did something you shouldn't have. If on the other hand you are proud of that vacation and the life experience it gave you, the recruiter will look upon it as an asset. Even having been fired can be communicated as a positive learning experience.

PRINCIPLE 2: *Don't dwell on negatives.* Simply admit them and move on. Don't apologize or overexplain. Everyone has some shortcomings or has made some mistakes.

PRINCIPLE 3: *Balance negatives with positives.* If it is noted that you have been out of work for six months, acknowledge this and move on to describe how able you now are to solve the employer's problems. A strong positive can erase the experience of a preceding negative. Whatever you do, never say anything self-damaging.

TACTIC #70

List three things about yourself that you feel will appear as negatives. Underneath each one, list an offsetting positive characteristic.

Power Questions

Shown below are five powerful questions that summarize most of what you will be asked in interviews. If you can handle these five questions clearly, and communicate accomplishment at the same time, you are well on your way to effective interviewing.

TACTIC #71

Get someone to role-play with you or use a tape recorder and answer the five power questions above out loud, following your answers with an honest critique. Keep at it until the results are ideal.

1. What are your strongest abilities?
2. How do your skills relate to our needs?
3. What are you looking for in a job?
4. What would you like to know about us?
5. Why should we hire you?

Make More Money

It is important to make a conscious effort to keep your earnings high and rising, and to follow a specific personal development strategy designed to maintain and expand your earnings through promotions, raises, and job changes.

You already know that the primary theme of this book is for you to use your working years as an opportunity to create satisfaction for yourself and value for others. We do not encourage people to take jobs that offer little personal reward beyond the paycheck. On the other hand, we know that it is definitely possible to combine good earnings with fulfilling, rewarding work. It is important to note that even though greater earnings might not ultimately produce greater satisfaction, since satisfaction comes mostly from the work itself, when you make more money, you get bigger games to play . . . thus even more satisfaction from the work you love.

Don't use the fact that you love the work as an excuse to shortchange your paycheck. By assuming a passive role about salary, many highly skilled and productive workers end up making thousands of dollars less each year than others with similar abilities and interests.

Outside of union-protected work and highly bureaucratic jobs, *salary advancement does not happen automatically.* Like other areas of your career growth, it will flourish and expand if you take responsibility for it, and it won't if you don't. Without an assertive salary program you can find yourself down several thousand dollars a year, with very little chance of catching up. One of the dynamics at work in the job game is that after you have been working for a few years, people tend to evaluate your abilities based upon how much money you are making in relation to others in the same field. In other words, although you may be excellent in your chosen field, if you don't keep your earnings on the high side of the range you will be seen as less capable than others who make more.

The cardinal rule in all salary negotiations is that *money follows value.* If you want more money you must create more value, even if you don't immediately get paid for it. By continuing to feed value into the system, you will build up your worth both to the organization and to yourself. After you have established your valuable contribution, you can go for an increase to bring your compensation up to your value. Don't make the mistake of going after an increase on the grounds that you "need more money" and then, if you don't get it, lessening the quality of your performance. If you are not able to increase your compensation as you increase your value to the employer, and if you have communicated this responsibly, start looking for another game. Do this not out of a sense of disloyalty to your employer, but out of loyalty to yourself.

Salary Negotiating Strategies

Here are some of the basic salary negotiation techniques to use both in job changing and on the job itself:

- Always have a target figure in mind for right now and for one year from now. Stay in touch with the earnings of others in the field, watch employment ads in several cities, and get salary information from a trade or professional organization.

- As a candidate for a new job, try to find out what the salary is *before* you go in for an interview. Do what you can to have the employer name a salary figure first. If you are in effect creating a new job, you can pose a question such as, "What do you feel a position like this is worth?"

- If the employer states a satisfactory salary range, name the top of the range. He says: "The range for the job is eighteen to twenty thousand per year." You say: "Twenty thousand would be fine."

- Never answer the question "What is the minimum salary you would accept?" with an amount. You aren't looking for the minimum . . . are you? Respond with: "I don't have a figure in mind, but I am looking at several possible situations, and will undoubtedly accept the offer that offers the best combination of opportunity and salary . . . by the way, what is the range you have in mind?"

- Never accept an offer at the time it is given. Instead, respond with something like: "Thank you for the offer. I appreciate your confidence and know that I could make a contribution. Let me think about it and get back to you (week after next . . . in ten days, etc.). It's important to make sure I make the right choice."

- Once the offer is made, and you have negotiated a time period in which to decide, go for a ten percent increase over what you are offered. This is a tough one, particularly if you are anxious to get an attractive position, but if properly followed it can be worth many thousands of dollars over your career.

Simply call back a day or two after the offer was made, communicate again how you strongly feel you can make a contribution, and then suggest that the salary offered is less than what you were looking for by an amount double the increase you seek. Ask the employer to increase his offer and to split the difference. Don't capitulate immediately if the employer doesn't come up with the extra money. The most successful negotiations are those in which a party is willing to stick with a fair demand.

TACTIC #72

Write down the salary you would like to be making three years from now. Working backward, list target figures for each year from the target year to now. Do whatever research is necessary to confirm the validity of the figures in your particular job target area. If the prevailing salaries within this field do not meet your expectations, see how you can adjust your job target within your range of satisfaction and aliveness.

Role-Practicing

Going into an interview without some form of rehearsal or role-playing is like giving a speech without practicing. The speech may be good, but it won't be the best you can do. The purpose of role-playing is to give you an opportunity to put theory into practice and get valuable feedback in a simulated interviewing situation. The difficulty is that it takes time and organization to set it up and a willingness to encourage criticism.

You can role-play interviews at several levels, from practicing answers to only the difficult questions, or to the five sample questions suggested above, or by doing a complete interview.

The most effective role-playing situations involve four people, at least one of whom has had experience as an interviewer or personnel consultant.

Here is how to practice role-playing interviews:

1. Set up a time and place for you to meet with two or three others. Allow the others to prepare so they can also participate as candidates if they wish (good practice even if they are not in the job market).

2. If you haven't done so, prepare a resume and have at least four copies of it.

3. Write out a brief description of a job opening on top of a sheet of paper. At the bottom, list some questions that you feel are difficult to answer. Make three copies.

4. When you assemble the group, arrange the chairs in a small square so that the applicant (you) is *directly* across from the person playing the employer, and the observer(s) are on either side of the grouping.

5. Give each of the others a copy of the resume and job listing, and allow five minutes for them to read it. Suggest that the person taking the first turn as the employer start to think of questions he wishes to ask in addition to the ones you have provided.

6. Have the observers put their papers down and instruct them that their job is to observe closely, remaining silent, so they can make suggestions on how to improve your interviewing technique.

7. When everyone is clear about the instructions, begin the interview. Plan for a ten-minute interview (one of the observers should be timekeeper).

8. During the practice interview, stay in your role. Resist the temptation to make comments. Present yourself as you would if it were a real interview.

9. At the end of the interview, the observers and the person who played the employer representative should feed back to you all the ways you could have improved your presentation. While this critique is going on, you should be careful *not* to explain or apologize or even comment on the criticism, except to acknowledge and encourage it. This is very important, because people generally resist what appears as criticism. In this process it is a must.

10. After you have completed one cycle, you may change employers and redo the same interview, or change players or job targets as you wish.

The Wrap-up

Don't leave any interview without knowing clearly where you stand with the employer. As you near the end of the meeting you should get some feedback on how you have come across, and what, if any, additional information may be required.

TACTIC #73

Select two or three other people to spend an hour with you role-playing. Set up a time and place, and carry out the preceding instructions.

Do this by directly asking a question such as, "Do you feel that you have enough information?" or, "Is there any area where you need more information?" or even more directly, "Do you feel that I have the basic qualifications you are looking for?"

Try to discern, from the answers you get to these questions, whether or not the prospective employer clearly understands what you have to offer and how that will be of benefit to him or her. At this time, make your closing statements as positive as possible to leave a lasting impression.

If you end up with an offer you don't think you can accept, don't immediately reject it. Ask for a few days to consider it. You will need to develop your negotiating skills to determine whether the employer is willing to go higher, or that the stated salary figure is all they are prepared to offer you. In either case, it makes good sense to get as many offers (high or low) as possible, as it builds confidence and lets you know how well you're doing in your job search campaign.

If things are proceeding on a positive note, your next move is to ask, "What's the next step? Is there someone else in the organization I should see?" or a similar question designed to keep things moving along. Make it clear that you would like to do whatever you can to move the decision process along. Not that you *need* the job, simply that you are a person who needs to know where you stand. Ask for the directness and honesty you'd expect from any professional organization. Communicate to the employer that you know how to conduct business. This will tell them something about your value as a professional in the field.

In the next chapter we'll show you how to capitalize on some of the seeds you've just planted.

Reminders and References

REMINDERS

- The way you dress is your most important nonverbal communication. A wrinkled suit/skirt implies a wrinkled mind.
- Remember: communicate value and benefits to an employer, *not need*. The essential question in every interview is, "Why should I hire you?"
- The way to make more money is to produce more value.

REFERENCES

Winning the Job Interview Game. Jo Dana. Palamino Press, Jamaica, NY, 1985.

Salary Strategies. Marilyn M. Kennedy. Rawson, Wade, New York, 1982.

Robert Half on Hiring. Robert Half. Crown, New York, 1985.

Ready, Aim, You're Hired!: How to Job-Interview Successfully Anytime, Anywhere, with Anyone. Paul Hellman. Amacom, New York, 1986.

The American Almanac of Jobs & Salaries 1987–88. John W. Wright. Avon, New York, 1987.

11

End Game

Out of Sight, Out of Mind

Don't stop now. The game goes on, and it is possible to score valuable points in the last moments of play. It is also possible to lose the game.

Many people get to the interview stage of their job campaign, do a pretty good job of communicating to the potential employers, and then sit back and wait for the job offers to start coming in. They are frequently disappointed. "The interview went so well. Why didn't I get the job?"

RICHARD BLUE—Pushing Through Resistance

It's the job jitters again for Richard Blue, who has had six interviews and is still waiting for a response. As he waits, he slowly builds up resentment and frustration. "Mr. Nelson said he would get back to me soon. It's been three weeks. What do I do?"

Meanwhile, in his hectic Fresno office, John Nelson, city manager, is buried in six weeks' worth of paperwork. A 600-page evaluation of last year's shortage sits on his desk like a monument to his frustration. The budget of the City College is half done, correspondence is unanswered, and a dozen phone calls are unreturned.

Despite 12-hour days and working Saturdays, the backlog appears to be expanding rather than diminishing. Nelson replays in his head one more time the decision to terminate Alex Bosch. Perhaps if he had known how difficult it would be to get a replacement . . . but, no, it was the right move. Alex was clearly creating more problems than he was solving. He'd been wrong for the job in the first place, but how can you tell in a short interview? With a weary sigh, Nelson recalls the folder of resumes on his desk. He desperately needs an assistant but doesn't want to rush into hiring the wrong person again.

"I've seen six interesting candidates," he muses, "out of the 50 resumes I've received. How many more people should I see? Twelve? I can't even remember much about the six I've already seen. There was one woman that stood out—Tricia I think it was. I can remember her clearly. She seemed too shy. I don't know if she could handle the public appearances. And the other good one, what was his name? Blau? Blue. That's it, Richard Blue. It's already been a couple of weeks. I liked him, but there was something unclear about the interview. What was it? If only I had taken better notes. I remember that I was going to get back to him but there was something missing. I think I was concerned because he hadn't had enough government experience. I guess I'd better get some more interviews set up soon. Maybe one of them will have the perfect combination."

Just at that moment the phone rings and Nelson's secretary informs him Mr. Rich Blue is calling from Modesto. "He probably wants to find out what I've decided. What do I say? I did promise to get back to him. I'll pretend I'm in a meeting. Oh, hell, I'll talk to him."

"Hello, Mr. Blue. Thanks for calling back. Look, I'm sorry that I haven't gotten back to you sooner. It's just that I . . ."

Blue responds cool-headedly. "Oh, listen, don't worry about that. I could tell how busy you were just by looking at your desk. How are you coming with your budget?"

"Don't remind me! I think maybe I've reviewed six pages of it since I last saw you."

"Seems to me that you could use that new assistant

pretty soon." Richard laughs. "By the way, Mr. Nelson, do you remember telling me how you felt your budgeting procedures were significantly different from those we use in industry?"

"Yes. Frankly, I've got to tell you, that still bothers me. I don't know if we could take the time to train someone new in the system we've been thinking about." Nelson feels relieved that he can talk about the problem so easily.

Richard replies, "Yes, I knew you were concerned, so I decided to look into it. I spent a day at the Modesto City Hall looking through their budgeting procedures and the actual budgets for the last two years."

Nelson is tuning in now. Blue goes on with his planned follow-up: "I can tell you that you don't have to worry about a thing in that area. The procedures are almost identical to the approach we used to follow in the army six years ago when I was the finance officer at Travis. Give me a couple of days and I could have the whole thing handled."

Nelson's eyes stray to the budget folder on his desk. He thinks to himself, "Maybe I ought to decide on someone now and get this office back in shape. I'll never find the perfect person."

Richard Blue continues his approach: "One more thing, Mr. Nelson. As I went through that budget, I had some ideas about how we could make graphic displays of the key variables. You know, that's one of the things I did in my last job."

Nelson feels a wave of relief move over him. This one has what he is looking for. "That might be more costly than we could handle right now. It's a good idea, and we've talked about it before, but until this water situation clears up we've got to hold back on the costs."

"Yes, I know. But I have an idea that we could use some existing programs that are available at very low cost, that I could modify. I've written up some of these ideas in a short outline, and I wonder if you would like me to bring it over for you to review."

A smile crosses Nelson's face. He feels a growing

excitement about what he could do with a person like Richard. The resistance is opening up.

"That's a good suggestion, Rich. Why don't you plan to come over on Friday. I'll clear my schedule in the afternoon, and we can go over this in more detail."

"Okay, I'll be there at 2:00 P.M."

"Great. And, Richard . . . ?"

"Yes."

"Maybe afterwards we'll go out for dinner together."

Richard Blue played his end game masterfully. He proved to the potential employer that he was the best one for the job. Was he really? Perhaps another candidate would have worked out even better. No one will ever know. Or care. Richard made the move that got the job offer. His follow-up was not the typical "Have you decided who you are going to hire yet?" approach, it was an action based upon a communication of value in answer to a possible negative.

Sometimes success can be assured by a well-timed, well-planned follow-up presentation. A good follow-up insures that the investment of time, money, and energy you placed in getting the interview will not be forgotten by the prospective employer. It reminds them that you are still very much in the running, and sets up the possibility of sharing your mutual concerns so that you can both meet again and work them out.

Good follow-up strategies are not just for assistant city managers. Good follow-up works for desktop designers, telecommunicators, nurses, ranch foremen, consultants, and anyone else in the job game.

A good follow-up strategy will probably increase the odds of getting the offer you want by 30% or more.

Please remember that interviewers are human. After they talk to six or seven candidates for a position, the process starts to get a bit hazy. When you recontact the employer in a positive manner, you consciously reinforce the favorable image you wish to project. You move yourself ahead of the other candidates in the interviewer's consciousness by associating yourself directly with the solution to the employer's needs.

Blasting Out of the File Drawer

There is a twofold purpose to your follow-up activities:

- To increase the likelihood of your receiving a job offer
- To accelerate the employer's decision

Good follow-up is an art; it starts with your new personal acquaintance with the interviewer. Much of the initial "coldness" of the relationship is probably gone, and you have had the chance to learn more about what the employer does, how the interviewer has responded to your personal presentation, and what the job opportunity is about.

The most effective follow-up is initiated by telephone or, in the case of some of the more basic entry-level positions, in person. Follow-up by mail is generally less effective. The next step after the follow-up phone call might very well be another meeting, or a meeting with the next level of decision maker in the employment process. Or it could be a job offer.

The follow-up begins immediately after you have completed an interview. Before the experience fades, within 30 minutes if possible, sit down with a notepad and answer the following questions in writing:

- Do you want to receive an offer from this employer? (Even if you don't, answer the balance of the questions.)
- What valuable comments about yourself did you fail to communicate clearly?
- What questions would you like to have asked and didn't?
- What questions were asked of you that you feel you didn't answer clearly enough?
- What do you feel are the most positive impressions the employer got about you?
- What do you feel are the most negative impressions the employer got about you?
- Knowing what you now know about the job, what do you feel would be your strongest possible contribution?
- What information or attributes would you like to reinforce with the employer?
- How could you improve your personal presentation, either verbally or physically?

- What would be the next step to take with this employer (second interview, offer, etc.)?

TACTIC #74

List all the points for post-interview follow-up on one sheet or card, with blank spaces to write in answers and responses. Make a number of photocopies of this for use after each interview.

Some of the specific things you can accomplish with your follow-ups are:

To remind the employer who you are

To provide the employer with specific information that you did not have available at the time of the interview

To clear up any confusion you might have left with the employer

To discover what the employer thinks of your ability to do the job

To change any mistaken impressions

To repeat and reinforce the positive information you conveyed

To ask the employer if he is considering you for the job, or planning to make you an offer

To arrange for the next step to occur

TACTIC #75

If you have had prior interviews, even if you are not sure of the value for following up, fill out one of the forms from tactic #74 above. Try some follow-ups based on this information.

Reiterate the Benefit

You know by now that the way to get hired is to communicate a clear value to the prospective employer so that he is left with no question that you are the best person for the job.

The purpose of your follow-up is to reinforce or expand the employer's experience of your value.

The best way to accomplish this is to look for a new way to express or demonstrate value. You can refer back to something that was discussed or implied during the interview and highlight how you would handle it:

> "Miss Cox, this is Helen Starkes. We met last Thursday about Mrs. Popenoe's position. I'm the person who was working part-time for the Estuary Club, remember me?
>
> "Well, I've been thinking about what you told me about wanting to reorganize the organization's E-mail conferencing system, and the more I think about it, the more confident I am of my ability to help you. You know, we had to do that twice at our club, and I supervised both reorganizations. I know that my experience would be relevant. Do you think we could meet again so I could show you the approach I designed?"

Another way is to provide some additional information about a problem discussed. In other words, to start to contribute to the solution even before you get the job:

> "Mr. Wade, this is Carole Bell. We met for a few moments last Friday afternoon while I was in your building. You mentioned to me that you were thinking about having your training materials put on video disks. I took the liberty of contacting two people I know who have done that, and they have recommended several studios and techniques to do it in a way that is very cost-effective. I can stop by and give the contacts to you if it would be helpful. Will you be in this afternoon around 4:00 P.M.?"

You can correct negative information not by apologizing, but by adding advantages:

"Mr. Andrew, this is Peter Stiles. We had the pleasure of a brief interview last week on campus. You may not remember me, since I know you had a very full schedule that day. I was the person who talked about a fight with my art teacher. I wanted to call you to expand on that since I know it could have left an unfavorable impression. After our interview, as a result of what you said, I met with that teacher and apologized for my behavior. He and I spent over an hour together, and now I am back in the class on very friendly terms. So thank you for that suggestion. Since we didn't get around to discussing my design work, I've put together a collection of some of the things I've done that I'd like to show you next week. I think you'll find them relevant to your business. Thanks for your suggestions. Now we can move on."

You don't have to cook up a highly elaborate presentation to demonstrate the value you can contribute. Nor are the details of what you can do what make the biggest difference. What is important is the *position* you communicate, and the way in which you do it. The very fact that you are interested in making a contribution and that you communicate that enthusiastically will often be as important as anything else.

Remedial Action

One of the major benefits of a well-thought-out follow-up campaign is that you can use it as an opportunity to correct any mistaken impressions, to patch up any holes in your presentation, and even to change an employer's mind about you.

Most candidates coming away from an interview, particularly one at which they don't feel they made their best impression, are reluctant to take action. They have the tendency to simply write off the experience and move on to the next interview. Don't. A good follow-up call, properly timed, can do quite a lot to change a faulty first impression, to supply missing information, even to elevate a person's position from the inactive file to possible employment.

As we suggested in the previous tactic, after each interview review your performance and look for things that could have been communicated better or more clearly. Think of relevant accomplishments you could have described, or examples you could have given. Are there any questions that you wanted to ask and didn't? Even if you are not sure you want the position, go after it anyway. You can always turn down an offer if you are not interested in it. It will be good practice in testing your limits—showing you how far you can go in turning a situation to your advantage.

TACTIC #76

Use this if you need a big push for a position you really want, but didn't do the most convincing job in the interview, and you haven't heard from the employer yet.

Have someone whose name you gave as a reference call the employer a week later. Announce that she or he was one of the references given, and that, having been out for part of the week, your reference wanted to be sure the employer hadn't tried to reach her or him and missed. The reference now wants to give an opinion of you as a worker.

The New You

Frequently people come to our workshops, get to the part about resumes, and, as they slash out major areas of confusion and unconsciousness, complain about the fact that their old resume is already in the hands of a dozen or so employers—some of them interviewed, some not.

This problem is quickly turned to an advantage when we explain to people that when they redo their resume, it is a very natural time for them to revisit or recontact old prospects in order to exchange the brand-new resume for the out-dated one. In the process, of course, they remind the employer amply of the contribution they can make.

If you use the mails or fax to send your new resume, be sure to include a cover letter describing the relevance of your abilities and asking for another personal meeting.

In the above tactic it is possible to prepare a brand-new resume focused on a particular set of skills or targeted for a specific employer. You can use one of the computer-based resume kits for this customization to good effect.

Try Me

One of the more successful ways to break out of a hiring impasse is to get the employer to use you on a trial basis. This can work wonders if the decision-maker has difficulty making up his mind or is faced with external restraints. Simply approach the employer with the following strategy:

> "I know you are having a difficult time deciding whom to hire for this position. Why don't we get together for 90 days, and you can try me on the job. If you aren't totally satisfied with the contribution I am making, then we can part company amicably. If you are pleased, as I am convinced you will be, we can continue on a more long-term relationship."

With today's emphasis on versatile work agreements, people will more readily hire on a short-term or consulting basis than if they feel they are committing to a more permanent relationship.

When the Answer Is "No"

Keep at the follow-up until you are sure that there will be no forward movement, or until you decide to move away from this opportunity. In any case don't ever restrict your campaign to one employer. Even as you follow up on old attractions, you are developing new relationships. Even if you don't turn a negative situation around, there are important secondary benefits you can obtain from any follow-ups you do.

- You may find out about new openings in other divisions.
- You can get the names of other employers or agencies in the field.

One of the most important things to watch out for is not trying to apologize for or explain the negatives. Don't add weight to negative information. Add additional advantages, rather than explain or justify the disadvantages. So much of the hiring process is subjective chemistry. Accentuate the positive. Stay confident, upbeat, enthusiastic.

When the Answer Is "Yes"

The underlying principle in this book is that *you can make a difference in the quality of your worklife*. This is the single unquestioned observation we have made from our exposure to thousands of individual job seekers, and their use of the self-directed job search techniques we have shared with you. By following these techniques, you will be able to come up with interviews and offers in career fields of the 1990s that will prove satisfying and expanding. Don't jump at the first offer as though your life depended upon it. Know that by following the techniques we have shared with you, you can reactivate your job campaign at any level.

If the jobs you targeted are not what you thought they would be, step back and reevaluate. If you are running out of employers to contact, dig in with some new sources of job market research information and get back on the phone. At every level in the job search, you will find there are additional steps for you to follow that will produce positive results for you.

What you will discover is that *the final secret of the job search is your willingness to get what you want in life—now, and into the future.* If you are unwilling, then each tactic will look like an obstacle rather than a way to gain control of a valuable life process. As the 1990s unfold, the variety of opportunity and challenge is stimulating and real. When you feel old, burned out or bored, or simply underpaid and under-appreciated, you will know that your job game board needs turning.

In the final analysis, your worklife is measured by your own personal index of satisfaction and aliveness in the here and now. You are the only one who can judge whether or not your work is providing fulfillment in the day-to-day routine and variety of your activities.

By the same token, you are the one who can take the responsible actions to make things happen; to open the world of possibilities, break out of old boxes, and make your greatest visions real.

TACTIC #77

Do not accept the first offer you receive, unless you are certain it is what you want. Set up a scale of five criteria that an ideal job would have for you. Measure each offer against this scale, and after you have scored the offers, rank them in order of personal worth to you. You should have at least three possible offers before shutting off the flow of new potential and accepting the one that gets you what you are looking for.

Lest You Forget

One autumn day ten or so years ago, when I was on the lecture trail somewhere out in the Pacific Northwest, I turned to the rag-edged notebook that had served as lecture outline, idea log and program guide for so many years, and noticed that, somehow, during the past few months or perhaps longer, someone unknown to me had penned ten very wise reminders behind the index page of the book. These ten imperatives have served me well, and now it is time to share their powerful and simple wisdom with you:

1. Consider yourself a success
2. Make decisions
3. Love yourself
4. Love others
5. See the possible
6. Regard everything as good
7. Complete what you start
8. Live abundantly

9. Don't compromise
10. Be patient

Goodbye

This is the end of the book for us, and the inauguration of a process for you. If you haven't done the tactics yet, please go back to Tactic #1 and start doing them, or go forward a few pages and do the abbreviated 25 Fast Track Tactics. It is only through intended action that you will dependably manifest your fullest potential.

Look back over your progress from time to time and see what tactics you have skipped. Address them before moving on.

As you accomplish each tactic and step, please know that we are behind you, and that what you are doing will have a valuable lifetime payoff. As you go along, acknowledge the contribution your own life is making to you, and the personal satisfaction and aliveness that it inherently brings. Keep on keeping on; the process of life is endless and the rewards can be priceless. Thank you for having us participate with you in this process.

Q: Is this the end?
A: No. It's the beginning.

12

The Fast Track

(A selection of the most important tactics from the book.)

Exploring: Who Am I?

TACTIC #6

Start a fresh page in your notebook, and list at least 25 things you like to do whether at work or not. List anything that occurs to you, even if you consider it very basic, such as driving, cooking, writing reports, or just listening to music! List everything.

TACTIC #9

Now, list 25 things that you can do, problems that you can solve, results that you can produce. Don't stop short. Keep pushing until you get 25. Don't be surprised if you get some that are also on the list you created of things you like to do. That's the way it should be.

TACTIC #10

Now go back to your "I like" list from Tactic #6. Select the five items on the list that you now identify as your top interests or likes. Write them in your notebook. Next, select the top five things you can do to produce results from the list prepared in response to Tactic #9. Write these on the same sheet.

Targeting: Work/Career Possibilities

TACTIC #11

This is the synthesis of your top five "I likes" and "I cans" as uncovered in Tactic #10. List them in the form of a grid—with five skills down the left-hand side and your five interests across the top. Then draw horizontal and vertical intersecting lines. This will create 25 intersections of a skill and interest. Select 10 of these intersections, and for each, invent or recall two or three possible jobs utilizing the intersecting skill and interest. The result is a list of 20 to 30 job titles created from your own skills and interests. Important to do this one.

```
                                  INTERESTS
                          ┌──┬──┬──┬──┬──┐
          SKILLS          │  │  │  │  │  │
                          ├──┼──┼──┼──┼──┤
  •  _____       │  │  │  │  │  │
  •  _____       ├──┼──┼──┼──┼──┤
  •  _____       │  │  │  │  │  │
  •  _____       ├──┼──┼──┼──┼──┤
  •  _____       │  │  │  │  │  │
                          ├──┼──┼──┼──┼──┤
                          │  │  │  │  │  │
                          └──┴──┴──┴──┴──┘
```

TACTIC #12

Look over the results of previous tactics, particularly the list of possible jobs uncovered in Tactic #11. Select one of these or another ideal job target that you would be happy to see yourself in five years from now. Write it down. Under this, list a job you would need to be in three years from now, to be on target for your five-year ideal target. Under this, list the entry point for you to start the ball rolling toward your three-year goal.

TACTIC #16

A job family is a common interest grouping of jobs described under a single category. Each job family category includes dozens to hundreds of specific work descriptions, job titles, and opportunities for problem solving. For example, the automotive job family would include jobs in designing, selling, repairing, and transporting cars, writing safety brochures, and making safety inspections, to name a few.

Shown below are 72 job families. Go through the list three times. First, draw a line through each job family that holds no interest at all for you. Then go back and circle each family that interests you somewhat.

Then select the top four families that are most interesting and relevant to you. If you opt for a family we haven't listed, so much the better.

Accounting
Advertising
Aerospace
Agriculture
Animals
Architecture
Automotive
Banking
Boating
Bookkeeping
Building services
Children's
  services
Commercial art
Communications
Computers
Construction
Consulting
Counseling
Crafts
Criminology
Ecology
Economics
Education
  training
Electronics

Engineering
Entertainment
Family services
Finance
Fine arts
Food
Geriatrics
Government
Health care
Human resources
Industrial design
Information
  services
Insurance
Interior design
Journalism
Law
Leisure
Management
  services
Manufacturing
Marketing
Mathematics
Medicine
Mental health
Museum work

Music
Oceanography
Office services
Paper
Performing arts
Personal services
Photography
Politics
Public speaking
Publishing
Real estate
Religion
Repair services
Retailing
Sciences
Selling
Sports
Systems design
Television and
  video
Textiles
Toys
Transportation
Travel
Wellness

TACTIC #17

List each of the four job families you selected (in Tactic #16) on a separate sheet in your notebook. Under each job family list as many specific job titles, positions, opportunities, or descriptions of possible jobs as you can think of, regardless of whether they are jobs you feel you would like to do. List menial as well as senior jobs. Invent new ones. Keep at it until you have been able to list at least 20 different possibilities under each.

The object at this stage is for you to continue to expand the number of possible job situations that you are aware of in a given field. If you have difficulty in coming up with a full list, brainstorm with your family, call someone in the field, read trade journals or books about the subject, or call the relevant professional association.

TACTIC #18

You now have a list of 20 job possibilities in each of the job family areas you selected. Go over each list and cross out all those you *know* you would not find personally satisfying.

Then go back over the lists and cross out each job you feel would be highly impractical for you to identify or obtain. (Be careful here. Don't cross anything out unless you are certain there is a very real prerequisite that you don't have.)

Then list all of the remaining possibilities from all lists, in rank order of maximum satisfaction. Read down the list one by one and ask yourself the following question: "Am I willing to do what's necessary to get this job?" If the answer is yes, allow it to remain. If not, cross it out.

Blocks and Barriers:
How Do I Stop Myself?

TACTIC #20

You will find it helpful to know in advance what personal barriers or obstacles will get in the way of your job search. At this time, list all the things that you suspect might inhibit you or slow you down this time. List everything.

TACTIC #24

Go back to the list of potential job targets you were left with when you completed Tactic #18. Rank them in order of interest to you. Then select the top four as your job targets—with the understanding that you are willing to do what's necessary to get one of these positions.

Write each of the top four on a separate sheet in your notebook, then list all the things you can think of that could get in the way of your achieving these targets. After you have listed all the obstacles, go back and write down the things you would have to do to overcome the obstacles.

Researching: Job Targets

TACTIC #22

Visit your local library. Ask the librarian to put you in touch with some reference books or articles that discuss the development of industry and business (or other fields that appeal to you). Look through an index of articles in *Business Week*, *Industry Week*, *Fortune*, or *The Wall Street Journal*. Alternatively, call a trade association and ask what articles they recommend in your field.

TACTIC #26

List your most recent job or jobs, or your entry-level job targets *at* the entry level. Below, list an expanded position you would like to be in three years from now, and below that a five-year goal.

To the right of these listings, write down some of the specific skills you feel you need to make your three- or five-year jumps. Then, on the far right-hand side, list where you think you can obtain the training or develop the necessary skills.

TACTIC #30

Locate a copy of *Standard Rate & Data, Business Publications*, in the library or borrow an old one from an advertising agency media department.

Look up the topic area of your four job targets, and for each list three or four related publications as sources of information.

Contacting

TACTIC #34

Write down the names of anyone and everyone you know whom you consider to have professional standing, or to be good contacts.

Include all names regardless of whether or not you think they would help you. List as many as you can. Then go back over your list and underline those you would be willing to contact.

Get their phone numbers and contact them at the rate of 3–5 per day. As part of the contact, ask them for people they know whom you might not know, and get permission to contact them using this person as a reference. Get all names spelled right at the start.

TACTIC #36

Set aside ten hours, in three different sessions, for the sole purpose of contacting or using the various sources you have come up with to uncover the employer prospect names you seek. Keep going until you have listed at least 50 employer names in one of your job targets. Enter the name of each employer prospect on a separate 3 x 5 card.

TACTIC #38

Start your developmental interviews at the same time as, or before, your pitch for job interviews.

Select five or six of your prospective employers, or others to whom you have a personal referral. Start scheduling meetings for the purpose of gathering information, expanding your contacts, and planting seeds for future harvesting.

Preparing: Interviews and Resumes

TACTIC #46

List three activities that you will have to assume in the targeted job position that you don't feel qualified to handle at this time.

Analyze the work that these activities entail. Do they require technical expertise or basic work skills? Separate the technical requirements from what you know you can probably learn within a short amount of time.

TACTIC #49

With a tape recorder at hand, identify a real or imagined employer prospect in your job target field. Get a good mental picture of what he or she is looking for, and then turn on the tape.

Ask yourself the question, "Why should I hire you?" and then answer it into the tape. Repeat the process three times, giving different answers, and then play the tape back and listen to it as an employer. See how you, the candidate, communicated to you, the employer. What benefits did you communicate, and how well did you communicate them? Develop your skills to communicate confidence regarding your benefits. Keep repeating your description of your abilities until you hear authority and confidence in the tone of your voice.

TACTIC #54

List three objections you feel will be raised during the course of your job campaign. Then write down two answers to each objection. When you are satisfied with these answers, role-play them with someone.

TACTIC #55

Establish a definite written schedule for your interview "set up" campaign.

Allocate specific dates and times in advance,
and the number of calls you plan to complete on
each date. Keep to your schedule. Acknowledge
yourself when you meet your targets and note
when you don't. If you are consistently missing your
schedule, adjust it downward to a level where you
can experience success.

TACTIC #59

Set aside two three-hour periods to produce an
effective one-page, professional-looking resume.
Assemble any earlier resumes you have produced,
and any other work references or resources that can
help you.

Be willing to stay with an all-out concentrated
effort that will result in a well-written, effective resume. Use your support system to critique and assist
you.

TACTIC #60

Write a few actual or practice cover letters to
different prospective employers. Follow the steps
(p. 241) carefully and remember to include
some relevant piece of research that reflects
your understanding of the needs of the potential
employers.

Interviewing

TACTIC #67

Before each interview, write down on one side of a 3 x 5 index card five accomplishments or things you are proud of that you want the employer to learn about during the interview. On the other side of the card, list five intelligent questions to ask the employer that show the penetrating depth of your knowledge of the situation, and that will assist you in determining whether you wish to work here. (Save questions about vacation, benefits, salary, etc., until you have received an offer.)

TACTIC #72

Write down the salary you would like to be making three years from now. Working backward, list target figures for each year from the target year to now. Do whatever research is necessary to confirm the validity of the figures in your particular job target area. If the prevailing salaries within this field do not meet your expectations, see how you can adjust your job target within your range of satisfaction and aliveness.

Following Up

TACTIC #74

List all the points for post-interview follow-up on one sheet or card, with blank spaces to write in answers and responses. Make a number of photocopies of this for use after each interview.

About the Author

TOM JACKSON, chairman of Equinox Corporation and founder of The Career Development Team, has emerged as one of the nation's leading authorities and commentators on the nature and quality of human resourcefulness and high performance. Working at the cutting edge of a revolutionary new approach to the ways people deal with their worklives and careers, he is a graduate of the Wharton School of Economics, and has studied at Georgetown Law School.

The author of four popular books on career development and transition, and creator of more than two dozen programs, articles, and materials for professional counseling, Tom Jackson has lectured at more than 350 companies, universities, associations, and agencies.

For the past decade and a half, Jackson and his associates have created and implemented innovative programs for many of the nation's leading corporations, with more than 100,000 participants across the U.S.A., Canada, Europe, and the Mideast.